The South's
NEW POLITICS

The South's
NEW POLITICS

Realignment and Dealignment

EDITED BY
ROBERT H. SWANSBROUGH AND
DAVID M. BRODSKY

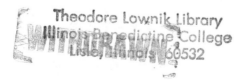
University of South Carolina Press

Copyright © University of South Carolina 1988

Published in Columbia, South Carolina, by the
University of South Carolina Press

First Edition

Manufactured in the United States of America

LIBRARY OF CONGRESS
Library of Congress Cataloging-in-Publication Data

The South's new politics: realignment and dealignment / edited by
Robert H. Swansbrough and David M. Brodsky. — 1st ed.
    p.   cm.
  Bibliography: p.
  ISBN 0-87249-566-3
  1. Southern States—Politics and government—1951–
I. Swansbrough, Robert H. II. Brodsky, David M. (David Michael)
JK2683.S68 1988
320.975—dc19   88–19784
                                                          CIP

Contents

INTRODUCTION

The Dynamics of Recent Southern Politics

David M. Brodsky

In the aftermath of each presidential election since 1948, political commentators have speculated on the future of America's two major political parties. The immediate postwar elections, marked by the 1948 Dixiecrat rebellion and the 1952 and 1956 Eisenhower landslides, raised questions about the Democratic party's ability to regain control of the White House and heightened anticipation of a major party realignment. The Goldwater debacle in 1964 led some commentators to conclude that the Republican party no longer represented a serious threat to Democratic dominance. In contrast, George Wallace's American Independent challenge in 1968 and Richard Nixon's victories in that year and in 1972 suggested a newly dominant Republican majority based on the West and in the previously Democratic South. Former Georgia Governor Jimmy Carter's election in 1976, based largely on southern electoral votes, prompted yet another round of conjecture, this time focused on whether the Democrats had halted the Republican tide and had regained their position as the party favored by most southern voters.

Ronald Reagan's back-to-back victories in 1980 and 1984, built in large measure upon his ability to attract votes from "traditional" Democrats, coupled with survey data showing roughly equal proportions of the electorate calling themselves Democrats and Republicans, intensified speculation by some political analysts that a long-awaited political transformation had at last occurred. Others rejected such a conclusion. Instead, they argued that, despite a decline in Democratic support, such conditions as public dissatisfaction with continuing budget deficits or the absence of Ronald Reagan from the ticket may allow the Democrats to maintain and, perhaps, expand their remaining edge in voter support.

The results of the 1986 elections, especially the Democrats' success in recapturing southern U.S. Senate seats won by the Republicans in conjunction with the Reagan victory of 1980, again muted talk of a new Republican majority. Some observers called attention to the Republican successes in gubernatorial contests and suggested these victories might provide the opportunity for future party building, especially in the drawing of legislative districts that will occur after the 1990 census. Others saw evidence of a Democratic resurgence while some pointed to the record levels of split-ticket voting and to the substantial number of voters who characterized themselves as independents as evidence that a bleak future lay ahead for both parties.

PARTISAN CHANGE IN THE SOUTH

Although most accounts of politics in the postwar South acknowledge the region's political life has undergone profound changes, these same accounts offer often competing accounts of what changes have actually taken place and what changes will likely occur in the future. First, while some analysts note the Republican party's largely uninterrupted string of successes in winning southern votes for their presidential candidates, they see little prospect for the GOP to develop the political clout essential to effectively compete with the Democrats in other election contests. Continued Democratic dominance of southern state legislatures and most local offices seem to support this line of reasoning.

Second, we find those commentators who conclude that party coalitions in the South have undergone a realignment with many southern voters abandoning their ties to the Democratic party in favor of the Republican party and its candidates. The continued success of Republican presidential nominees, GOP victories in congressional, senatorial, and gubernatorial elections, and apparent growth in the proportion of southern voters calling themselves Republican frequently constitute the evidence offered to justify claims of realignment.

And finally, some observers report evidence of a continuing dealignment or decline in the importance of political parties in the South, especially as guides to choosing among competing candidates. Analysts who see dealignment cite increases in split-ticket voting and in the proportion of self-identified independents among southerners as clues indicating the decay in the importance of party identification in determining election results.

ACCOUNTING FOR PARTISAN CHANGE IN THE SOUTH

Although few commentators would question that the political preferences of southern voters have changed, observers of southern politics have not yet reached agreement as to why these changes have occurred. Instead, they have offered a number of alternative explanations. For example, some analysts argue that white southerners have gradually *converted* to the GOP, because of anger over the national Democratic party's stand on civil rights and such other social issues as prayer in the schools, because improvements in their standard of living made the programs of the Republican party seem more in line with their own interests, or because of continued dissatisfaction with the candidates offered by the Democrats.

Other explanations focus on the *mobilization* of new voters, *demographic trends* that have changed the makeup of the southern electorate or a *decline in the importance of political parties* in electoral politics. Successful efforts by the Democrats to register and gain the active support of black voters and by the Republicans to attract younger, previously inactive whites provide evidence of mobilization while the steady out-migration of black Democrats and the in-migration of white professionals willing to support the GOP seem consistent with a demographic approach. Increases in the frequency of split-ticket voting and a continuing trend toward candidate rather than part-centered election campaigns suggest the utility of a decline in political parties explanation.

ASSESSING PARTISAN CHANGE IN THE SOUTH

Although most studies of partisan change strive to explain nationwide trends in party identification, Wattenberg and Miller (1981) and Miller (1986a; 1987) argue against relying solely on national survey data to reach conclusions about changes in support for the nation's political parties. The chapters in this volume heed Wattenberg and Miller's injunction and look at Southwide and state-by-state data to determine what sorts of partisan change have occurred in the region and what factors help to explain these changes.

Chapter 2 provides a review of the theoretical issues involved in the study of partisan change. Most studies of partisan change rely on national survey data. Consequently, the samples drawn from individual states frequently do not permit an analysis of changes at the state level. Here, each of the state chapters (chapters 3–14) examines aggregate state electoral data and previously unreported state-by-state survey data to assess the extent and sources of behavioral and attitudinal change. The use of these state data sources makes it possible to more fully assess partisan change in each state. Therefore, a more detailed and previously unavailable picture of party change emerges, a picture that shows wide variations in the pattern of change experienced in each state.

The state chapters, grouped into three categories—the *Sunbelt South* (Florida and Texas), the *Rim South* (Virginia, Tennessee, North Carolina, Kentucky, and Arkansas), and the *Deep South* (Alabama, South Carolina, Georgia, Mississippi, and Louisiana)—examine the partisan coalitions within each state. These chapters also consider the relative impact of such factors as demographic shifts, economic conditions, and political issues in altering (or maintaining) the balance of power between Democrats and Republicans.

Chapters 15 through 18 focus on changes across the South. Charles Bullock considers the question of realignment and dealignment by examining the Republican party's successes in presidential, congressional, gubernatorial, and state legislative elections and by comparing trends in the South with those in the remainder of the country. Harold Stanley and David Castle review the existing literature on southern partisan change, identify the factors that contribute to the often conflicting pictures painted, and offer an assessment of the changes that have transpired and an agenda for future research. Lee Sigelman and Thomas Konda examine national and southern trends in public evaluations of the Democratic and Republican parties from 1952 to 1984. In contrast to the "negativity" and "neutrality" hypotheses that seem to predict further party decline, especially in the South, their analysis suggests increased support for both parties nationally and the possibility of a southern realignment toward the Republicans. Laurence Moreland, Robert Steed, and Todd Baker use data drawn from surveys of delegates to the 1984 state party conventions in six southern states to focus on the role of ideology and issues in promoting realignment among party elites rather than the mass electorate.

In chapter 19, Robert Swansbrough offers a summary view, supplementing state data with data collected from ABC News Exit Polls conducted in 1986. The final chapter presents data tracking the Democratic party's showing in presidential, U.S. Senate, and gubernatorial elections from 1976 to 1986. It also examines partisan changes in each of the twelve southern states studied and identifies patterns among the states comprising the Sunbelt South, the Rim South, and the Deep South.

The discussions herein indicate the dangers of relying solely on national data to reach conclusions about partisan change in the South. Indeed, the state chapters make clear that, while some states have experienced the changes in the party coalitions and in the balance of political power associated with realignment, other states have experienced dealignment, a combination of realignment and dealignment, or little, if any, change. This diversity also extends to the sources of partisan change. Different combinations of factors account for the changes experienced in each state. Moreover, the state chapters also suggest a high level of volatility in the partisan preferences of southern voters. Consequently, continued change rather than the emergence of a new southern party system seems likely.

2

Partisan Change:

An Overview of a Continuing Debate

David M. Brodsky

This chapter addresses the theoretical issues underlying the existing literature on partisan change in the South. The chapter first considers the definitions of realignment and dealignment that guide most contemporary research. It then examines the measures used to assess partisan change. And finally, the chapter considers the factors thought to explain the shifts observed in southern partisan identification and southern voting behavior since the 1948 presidential election.

THEORIES OF PARTISAN CHANGE

Elections giving the mass of voters a direct voice in selecting their representatives and, at least, an indirect voice in the public policy-making process distinguish democratic polities from other political systems. Elections also serve a symbolic function, reaffirming the polity as the legitimate source of political power. While many factors influence the electoral decisions made by individual voters, students of mass voting behavior and partisan change accord special importance to the electorate's psychological identification with political parties and to the impact of this sense of partisan attachment upon election outcomes.

Realignment

Although Lamis contends "that the term realignment has been so loosely used for so many purposes that it no longer has any serious value, if it ever had any" (1986: 54), most academic observers of partisan change have quite specific, although divergent, notions of what constitutes a realignment. First, the concept of realignment represents a durable change in patterns of political behavior, specifically voting over several elections. For example, Key defines critical elections as those "in which there occurs a sharp and durable electoral realignment between parties" (1955: 16). Second, a realignment requires more than a change in voting behavior; realignment also requires a shift in the partisan attachments held by the voters (Sundquist, 1973; Campbell, 1966). Indeed, Maggiotto and Haggar argue "a realignment occurs only when the social bases of partisanship changes with respect to *both* voting behavior and party identification" (1985: 15).

Despite this common understanding of the need for durable attitudinal and behavioral transformations as preconditions for a realignment, scholars disagree as to the extent of the changes necessary before an electorate becomes realigned. Norpoth and Farah (1986) distinguish between two versions of realignment. One version defines realignment in terms of the overall balance of party support within the electorate. In this version, realignment occurs when the distribution of partisan identification among the voters shifts to create a new majority party, either through the creation of a new party or through the conversion of an existing minority party to majority status. According to the second version, realignment occurs even though the overall balance between the parties remains essentially constant. Instead, the social groups making up each party's electoral coalition change, perhaps leading to a transformation in the policy prescriptions of the dominant party as it seeks to align its policy agenda with the preferences of its new clienteles (Petrocik, 1987).

These alternative pictures of a completed realignment contribute to the current controversy over whether or not a fundamental restructuring of the nation's party system has occurred. Analysts looking for the first type of realignment might survey the contemporary scene and conclude no realignment has taken place because the Democrats remain the dominant party, albeit with a much-reduced margin over the Republicans. In contrast, investigators looking for the second type of realignment might see the changes in the groups making up the Democratic and Republican coalitions and determine that a realignment had indeed occurred, as groups formerly central to the Democratic coalition (e.g., white southerners) now identify with the Republican party and support its candidates, especially at the presidential level.

The conceptual definitions of realignment also differ in the treatment accorded to the pace at which changes in voting and partisan identification proceed. *Critical realignments* occur in elections marked by unusually high levels of voter concern and involvement and by very intense but short-lived disruptions in previously observed patterns of voting behavior (Key, 1955; Burnham, 1970). In contrast, *secular realignments* involve gradual, long-term movements from party to party by members of a population group, movements largely independent of the forces influencing the vote in any one election (Key, 1959). Consequently, those looking for a *critical realignment,* either nationally or in the South, might examine the available survey and electoral data, observe the absence of a rapid shift in partisan identification, and conclude that no realignment had occurred. However, those looking for a *secular realignment* might examine the same data, observe a gradual decline in the proportion of various population groups in the electorate identifying with the Democratic party and voting for Democratic candidates, especially presidential candidates, and conclude that a gradual realignment has been under way since the forging of the New Deal alignment.

Dealignment

Although the 1960s and 1970s failed to produce the expected realignment transforming the Republican party from minority to majority status, political scientists found ample evidence of far-reaching change in the electorate. As Sundquist (1973: 340) describes it, "Voters have been deserting the major parties by the millions in favor of independent political attitudes and behavior. A far greater number call themselves independents than ever before in the thirty-five years of polling. On election day, they split their tickets with far greater abandon than at any time in the country's history." In other words, rather than maintain existing partisan attachments or realign in accordance with new ones, a growing proportion of the electorate no longer identifies with either major party. Consequently, the proportion of independent identifiers in the electorate grew from roughly 25 percent during the 1952 to 1964 period (Norpoth and Rusk, 1982) to between 32 percent and 40 percent during the 1974 to 1984 period (Miller, 1986a). More importantly, for many voters partisan loyalties appeared to no longer exert a major influence on their choices among candidates (Sundquist, 1973; Wattenberg, 1986; and Miller, 1986a), a development indicated by a substantial increase in the proportion of the electorate reporting they split their ballots among candidates of the two parties, from roughly 33 percent in 1952 (Campbell and Miller, 1957) to more than 60 percent in 1986 (ABC News, 1986). Beck (1977), Campbell and Trilling (1980), and others characterize this process, where voters abandon their old party ties but fail to develop a psychological attachment to another party or where party identification becomes less central to political decision making, as *dealignment.*

While most studies of dealignment share similar conceptual and operational definitions and generally agree that dealignment has occurred throughout the electorate (Norpoth and Rusk, 1982; Nie, Verba, and Petrocik, 1976), the research reported to date reaches divergent conclusions about the consequences of the decline in party as a guide to voting. For example, Burnham (1970) and Ladd and Hadley (1978) speculate that dealignment, in conjunction with changes in the composition of the electorate and changes in political campaigning, has proceeded to such an extent as to make a partisan realignment highly unlikely. Similarly, Wattenberg (1986: 168) concludes that conditions in the future seem likely to "foster further party decline." Abramson, Aldrich, and Rohde (1986), however, interpret the 1984 election returns as evidence of the reemergence of party loyalties as important forces in the electoral process. And, Miller (1986a) notes that recent trends in partisan identification and vote choice favor the Republican party, which, if combined with effective performance in the second Reagan administration, could stimulate future movement toward a new party system dominated by a Republican majority.

MEASURING PARTISAN CHANGE

Realignment and dealignment involve changes in voting behavior *and* alterations in the distribution of partisan identification within the electorate. Consequently, studies of partisan change have operationally defined these concepts in terms of either *electoral data,* measuring changes in voting behavior, or *survey data,* measuring changes in party identification, evaluations of the parties, and reported voting behavior. Unfortunately, electoral and survey data each have inherent flaws as measures of partisan change.

Electoral data, on the one hand, suffer from two primary flaws. First, the demonstrated volatility of voting in presidential elections raises serious questions about the suitability of electoral data as a measure of long-term changes in partisan affiliation (Lipset, 1985; Miller, 1986a). And second, although electoral data frequently serve as the evidence used to support claims of increased ticket-splitting and, by implication, of independent voting and of dealignment, these aggregate data may tell us little about individual voting behavior (Feigert, 1979; Wattenberg, 1986).

On the other hand, survey data, especially data reflecting party identification, appear to have their own weaknesses as indicators of partisan change. At the most basic level lie concerns about the conceptual definition of party identification undergirding its use as an indicator of partisan change.

Fiorina (1981) questions what he describes as an essentially uncritical acceptance of the picture of partisan identification painted in *The American Voter* (Campbell, Converse, Miller, and Stokes, 1964). This picture includes three basic elements: an image of partisan identification as an exceptionally stable, enduring psychological attachment to a political party; an image of party ties forming early in life, prior to other political attitudes, strengthening the longer one holds them and becoming more resistant to change over time; and an image of partisan identity functioning as a "filter" that shapes perceptions of such short-term political forces as candidates and issues. Taken together, Fiorina (1981: 86) argues, these three elements provide a picture of party identification as "stable, affectively based, and relatively impervious to change except under extremely stressful conditions such as major depressions." Given this image of durability and stability, it comes as no surprise to find research focusing on realignment and dealignment making use of attitudinal data to survey the extent of partisan change. Miller (1987: 67, 68) typifies the impact of this picture when he writes, "Since party identification is a relatively enduring predisposition that helps define the alignment of the party system, trends in party attachment can help provide an interpretation of . . . change in election outcomes."

Recent research, however, has directly called into question the stability of party identification and indirectly raised questions about its suitability as an indicator of long-term change in the partisan affiliations of the electorate. For example, Fiorina (1981), while conceding an element of continuity in party identification, suggests that party preferences vary in response to how citizens evaluate the recent performance of the party in power, a short-term force. Page and Jones (1979) and Franklin (1986) also conclude that such short-term political factors as issue positions and candidate evaluations may influence party identification, and Lipset (1985) reports that roughly 20 percent of the 1984 presidential electorate changed their party preference to match their vote.

In addition to the concerns expressed about the long-term stability of party identification, political scientists trying to understand changes in partisanship have raised questions about the validity of the survey items used to assess the electorate's party preferences—the conceptual definitions underlying these measures and the criteria used for classifying respondents initially identifying themselves as either independents or

having no preference. Weisberg (1980) questions the traditional treatment of party identification as one dimension with strong Republican
identification at one end, political independence in the middle, and
strong Democratic identification at the other end. Instead, he suggests
treating Republican identification, Democratic identification, and political independence as separate objects, yielding a three-dimensional
model of party identification incorporating positive and negative attitudes toward each party and toward political independence. Hadley
(1985: 266), in a study of dual partisan identification, finds evidence to
support Weisberg's multidimensional explanation and speculates "that
the psychological attachment to the local party is so strong for a significant number of partisans that it produces inconsistent or dual rather
than changed partisan identifications." Miller and Wattenberg (1983)
and Wattenberg (1986) reanalyzed the 1964–1980 SRC/CPS (Survey
Research Center/Center for Political Studies) independent partisan
identification items and found two distinct groups of respondents, true
Independents and those with no preference between the parties. More
importantly, they also found that, beginning in 1968, much of the observed increase in Independents on the party identification scale as
traditionally derived consists of respondents in the "no preference"
group. This finding, in turn, led Wattenberg (1986: 48) to conclude
that "The proportion of the population labeling themselves as Independents has not risen nearly as much as has previously been thought,
while the proportion with no preference has increased steadily over the
last several elections."

Despite the shortcomings of electoral and survey data as the only
indicators of realignment and dealignment, much of the research reported to date has relied on either electoral data or survey data to the
virtual exclusion of the other (Miller [1986a] represents a notable exception). Thus, while such early students of partisan change as Key
(1955, 1959), Burnham (1970) and Sundquist (1973) primarily examined voting data, the more recent work in this area, including Beck
(1977, 1984a, 1984b), Norpoth and Rusk (1982), Stanley (1985) and
Wattenberg (1986), has primarily utilized survey data to assess changes
in the distribution of party identification, the composition of the party
coalitions, and the extent to which attitudes toward the parties affect
how people vote.

This reliance on either voting or survey data provides us, at best,
with an incomplete picture of partisan change. An analysis based on
electoral data precludes a full understanding of the attitudinal shifts
underlying changes in voting behavior, while an analysis based on sur-

vey data ignores the practical consequences of attitudinal change. Used together, however, behavioral and attitudinal data can provide a more accurate and complete picture of alterations in the distribution of party identification, the composition of the groups the party coalitions comprise, and the balance of political power between the parties.

EXPLAINING PARTISAN CHANGE

The discussion to this point has focused on different interpretations of partisan change and on the way in which conceptual and operational definitions contribute to the confusion over what sort of change, realignment, or dealignment, has taken place, and the extent of that change. Here the focus shifts to a consideration of the explanations political analysts offer to account for the observed changes in party identification and voting behavior.

Realignment

The literature concerned with partisan change suggests three theoretical explanations for realignment: (1) *conversion*, where members of the electorate alter their party identification in response to the ways in which the parties handle events, issues, or social changes; (2) *mobilization*, where significant numbers of voters previously outside the party system enter and become partisans; and (3) *demographic change*, where such forces as generational replacement and migration lead to alterations in the partisan preference of the electorate.

Conversion.

Critical and secular realignments take place as consequences of other major changes in the society (Key, 1959; Burnham, 1970; Ladd and Hadley, 1978). As Carmines, Renten, and Stimson (1984: 545) so forcefully put it, "Stripped of all its rich variation, realignment theory comes down to the notion that something happens and the public responds." In the case of conversion, significant segments of the public respond to a change in conditions by abandoning their existing party ties in favor of a new identification with another party. For example, Sundquist (1973) and Ladd and Hadley (1978), in explaining the New Deal realignment, argue that many voters who had previously cast their ballots for Republican candidates and who had identified with the Republican party voted for Franklin Roosevelt and other Democratic candidates. More importantly, these voters became converts; they transferred their partisan loyalty to the Democratic party and maintained their new party identification over future elections.

But, what factors might lead to such conversions as those that occurred during the New Deal realignment? Political analysts frequently assign changing economic and social conditions a critical role in their efforts to explain partisan realignments. Burnham (1970) and Sundquist (1973) conclude that economic conditions played a major role in fueling the New Deal realignment. Ladd and Hadley (1978: 139) find the South's postwar shift away from the Democratic party "has occurred as a result of developments associated with socioeconomic change, and the attendant replacement of old agrarian radicalism with new industrial conservatism." In this view, social and economic changes may "place persons in situations that make them susceptible to management by political leadership" (Key, 1959: 205). According to this reasoning, such trends as increasing industrialization or rising levels of unemployment create issues that provide party leaders with opportunities to win converts by articulating policies that appear to respond to the problems at hand. Perhaps the "southern strategy" pursued by Richard Nixon best illustrates a contemporary effort by a political leader to take advantage of social conditions, in this case changes in race relations, to alter the balance of partisan affiliation through the conversion process.

A second view of the impact of social and economic changes suggests conversions occur as individuals adjust their partisan preferences to match alterations in their socioeconomic status. From this perspective, newly affluent southerners may have switched their partisan loyalties to the GOP, the party more closely identified with their new-found status (Petrocik, 1987).

The public's perceptions of the policy positions taken by the parties, their evaluations of past and potential party performance, and their assessments of party leaders, especially the president, can also spark partisan conversions. Carmines, Renten, and Stimson (1984) and Ginsburg and Shefter (1985) report data that suggest that the increases in Republican identification observed throughout the South during the 1960s and 1970s represent, to a significant degree, conversions among white southerners displeased with the Democratic party's positions on issues related to race. Miller (1987: 77) credits shifts in the welfare policy preferences of the electorate as "a major explanation for the political realignment taking place in the United States," while Wirthlin and White (1987) see Ronald Reagan's popularity with the electorate as an important resource for the Republican party, especially since a majority of voters seem to link the two.

Partisan Mobilization.

Of the many functions ascribed to political parties, the mobilization of voters ranks among the most important. It comes as no surprise, then, that partisan mobilization offers a second possible explanation for realignment and involves the entry of previously inactive individuals into the partisan or electoral systems. Andersen (1979) attributes the New Deal realignment to the introduction to the party system of such groups as women and young adults who previously had relatively low levels of partisan awareness and participation. Burnham (1970) also cites the role played by the mobilization of previously inactive ethnic groups in reshaping the Republican and Democratic electoral coalitions of the 1930s. Converse (1972), Beck (1977), and Franklin (1986) account for much of the partisan change in the South since 1960 largely in terms of the mobilization of previously inactive black southerners as Democrats. And Norpoth and Farah (1986) point to the Republican party's success in mobilizing previously nonpartisan younger voters as evidence of a forthcoming realignment.

Demographic Changes.

The third theoretical approach to explaining realignment focuses on assessing the impact of such demographic phenomena as migration and generational replacement. Converse (1966; 1972), Burnham (1970), and Ladd and Hadley (1978) attribute much of the change in the pattern of partisan alignments to the flow of population groups between the North and the South. Specifically, the in-migration from the North to the South carried with it a disproportionate number of Republican partisans while the out-migration from the South to the North involved substantially more Democratic identifiers. These trends help account for the gradual increase in Democratic strength in the North and the parallel development of a substantial population of Republican identifiers and voters in the South.

Generational replacement explanations of realignment assume that electoral changes result from alterations in the distribution of partisan loyalties within the electorate as voters from younger generations replace older cohorts (Beck, 1984). New voters enter the electorate with a unique political imprint that distinguishes them from the rest of society. Then, according to Norpoth and Farah (1986: 5), "So long as this new generation maintains that imprint as it ages and manages to impress it on its own offspring, the whole society gradually takes on the outlook of that generation." From this perspective, party realignment proceeds at a gradual pace as generations replace each other in the electorate.

Dealignment

Efforts to understand the partisan changes characterized as dealignment explain the recent turning away from parties as a consequence of three related forces: a *decline in political parties* attributed to such factors as the rise of issue voting and candidate-centered political campaigns; a pattern of gradual *generational replacement* where younger and less partisan cohorts have slowly replaced the highly partisan cohorts of the New Deal realignment in the electorate; and a change in the balance between *cognitive mobilization*, participation fueled by initiatives taken by citizens with the skills and resources necessary to seek out and act upon political information, and partisan mobilization, political participation largely driven by external party cues, as sources of political activism.

Party Decline.

The party decline explanation of dealignment attributes increases in the proportion of Independent identifiers and split-ticket voting to the interaction of several forces. First, although the parties continue to play a major role in the electoral process, their importance as sources of political information and as vehicles for electoral mobilization has declined as the media and candidate-centered campaign organizations have come to play increasingly important roles in recent elections (Burnham, 1970; Ladd and Hadley, 1978). Second, the diminished roles played by the parties have affected, in turn, the public's perceptions of them. Nie, Verba, and Petrocik (1976) see evidence of increases in the proportion of respondents offering negative evaluations of the parties. Wattenberg (1986), however, finds increasing proportions of the public have neither positive nor negative images of the parties (cf. Konda and Sigelman in chapter 17) and concludes that the decline in partisanship experienced over the past thirty years results largely from this increased neutrality. And finally, according to Miller (1986b: 225), "party identification declined during the 1960s and 1970s because an increasingly large proportion of citizens had no consistent expectations or schema of which party would handle the problems confronting society more effectively."

Cognitive Mobilization.

The party decline model attributes dealignment to the assumption of such party functions as communication and mobilization by other institutions and to an increase in the proportion of the electorate lacking a clear image of the parties and what they stand for. In contrast, theories of cognitive mobilization view changes in the educational and skill levels of the electorate, changes that accompany postindustrial socioeconomic development, as major factors contributing to the demise of party identification and party voting. Specifically, as the levels of education and the number of sources that make available political information rise in a society, many voters no longer need depend on party identification as a cue in making their voting decisions. Instead, a growing number of well-educated, politically sophisticated citizens analyze political information and use their own understandings of issues and of candidates in deciding how to vote (Dalton, 1984). As a consequence of this reduced need for party attachments, whatever affective ties these individuals had to a political party weaken (Dalton, Beck, and Flanagan, 1984).

The gradual expansion of the proportion of the electorate comprising these cognitively mobilized, nonpartisan voters, with their interest in issues and candidates rather than in parties, has contributed to the electoral dealignment experienced not only in the United States (Ladd and Hadley, 1978; Craig and Martinez, 1986) but also in other industrialized democracies (Dalton, 1984; Dalton, Beck, and Flanagan, 1984). Whether the continued growth of this cognitively mobilized proportion of the electorate means further dealignment remains an open question. Dalton, Beck, and Flanagan suggest two rival scenarios—one characterized by continued dealignment and one characterized by the political parties using such modern electoral techniques as targeted direct mail to lead these voters to develop partisan ties.

Generational Replacement.

Although theories of generational replacement figure prominently in efforts to explain realignment, Beck (1984a) accounts for dealignment in similar terms. As Beck sees it, the American electoral system moves through a more or less regular cycle of *realigning periods,* marked by elections where substantial alterations in the party coalitions occur, periods of *stable alignment,* characterized by little variation in the partisan division of the electorate and by minimal change in the distribution of party identification, and *dealigning periods,* in which the party coalitions decay and political independence increases.

For Beck, generational replacement and the process of political so-
cialization provide the keys to understanding the regularity of this electoral cycle. The "realignment generation," those who directly
experienced the forces spurring realignment, acquire strong party ties
that they pass on to their children. This generation, the "children of
realignment," lacking the firsthand experiences of their parents, develop weaker party loyalties, largely as the result of parental socializa-
tion. They, in turn, transmit to the next generation, the "children of
normal politics," little in the way of partisan ties. This lack, when
coupled with the muted conflicts characteristic of a period of stable
alignment, provides the basis for the rise in political independence that
marks dealigning periods.

CONCLUSION

The extensive and still growing literature concerned with partisan
change in the United States supports three conclusions about the American political system. There is strong evidence that electoral politics in
the United States follows a more or less regular cycle of realignment,
stability, and dealignment. Furthermore, changes in the partisan preferences of the citizens influence "government policies and practice"
(Beck, 1984b: 542). And finally, studies of partisan change unquestionably confirm that profound transformations have taken place in the
national and southern party systems since World War II.

Despite these areas of agreement, a lively debate still thrives about
whether the observed changes represent partisan realignment or
dealignment and what developments will likely occur in the future.
This ongoing debate stems, in part, from disagreements in five critical
areas.

First, students of partisan change have not yet reached common understandings about the conceptual and operational definitions of such
key concepts as realignment and dealignment. Second, although current theories of realignment and dealignment seek to explain changes in
the distribution of party identification in the electorate, considerable
controversy now surrounds the theoretical and operational definitions
of this critical concept. Indeed, growing evidence suggests that the classic understanding of party loyalties as deeply held and relatively immu-
table may inaccurately portray reality, a reality where voters may
continuously adjust their partisan preferences in light of new information. Third, the realignment and dealignment literature abounds with

often competing explanations for the changes observed: the parties
have declined; generational replacement has prompted a realignment
or a dealignment; the parties have mobilized new voters; issues and
candidate images have become more important than party identification in determining the vote. Fourth, the data used to study partisan
change also contribute to the disagreement about what has occurred.
Studies relying on electoral data frequently reach conclusions that differ from those reached in studies relying on survey data. And finally,
the current literature offers divergent pictures of likely future developments. Some see continued Republican growth while others find evidence of a Democratic resurgence.

The chapters in this volume add to the substantial literature on
southern politics and seek to further clarify our understanding of partisan change by providing additional new data, much of it from previously unreported statewide surveys. Given the problems associated with
the volatility of electoral behavior and continuing questions about the
conceptual and operational definitions that inform much survey research, the state chapters rely, insofar as possible, on both behavioral
(electoral) and attitudinal (survey) data.

THE
SUNBELT SOUTH

3

Shifting Party Tides in Florida:

Where Have All the Democrats Gone?

Suzanne L. Parker

In Florida over the past twenty years, many who watch politics have predicted that the state is on the verge of developing a competitive party system. Certainly there have been indications that this was, in fact, the case. Prior to the 1950s, V. O. Key (1949) described Florida as a "political curiosity." It was a one-party state like most of its southern neighbors, but unlike other southern states its politics were characterized by a multitude of loosely organized factions that lacked permanence because they reflected the personal followings of individual politicians. As a result of this fragmentation in politics, Key noted that "Florida is not only unbossed, it is also unled. Anything can happen in elections, and does (1949: 82)." Three factors have been noted in explaining why Florida differs so dramatically from other southern states: (1) a rapidly growing nonnative population, (2) a highly diversified economy, and (3) a highly urbanized population (Dauer, 1972; Stern, 1984; Colburn and Sher, 1984; Lamis, 1984).

In the 1930s and 1940s, the Republican party in the state showed little interest in contesting elections in the state, and therefore the Democratic party dominated not only in presidential elections but in state elections as well. This began to change, however, in the 1950s when Republicans began organizing on the state and local levels, and Floridians began to show greater support for Republicans on the presidential level. Starting with Eisenhower's first run for the presidency in 1952, Floridians have supported Republican presidential candidates in seven of the last nine presidential elections (1952, 1956, 1960, 1968, 1972, 1980, 1984).

When Republicans Claude Kirk and Edward Gurney were elected in 1966 and 1968 (the first time since reconstruction that Florida had a Republican governor *and* senator) there was speculation that Florida was finally becoming a Republican state on all levels, not just on the presidential level. Reubin Askew's and Lawton Chiles' victories in the

1970s, Florida's support for Jimmy Carter over Gerald Ford in 1976, and Bob Graham's win in 1978 seemed to indicate that such expectations might have been somewhat premature (table 3.1).

Table 3.1

Democratic Share of the Vote for President, Senator, and Governor, 1977–1986

Year	President	Senator	Governor
1976	53%	63%	
1978			56%
1980	39	48	
1982		62	65
1984	35		
1986		55	46

Recently, however, there are new signs of a Republican resurgence in the state. Ronald Reagan's strong showing in Florida in 1980 and 1984, and the coattail victory of Paula Hawkins in 1980 have given renewed hope to those looking for signs of a shift in the partisan behavior of Floridians. In addition, there are signs that the Republican party has been gaining adherents. Paul Beck (1982) has written about the beginnings of a realignment in Florida based on shifts in party identification in the state between 1980 and 1982.

. . . we see the recent partisan changes as signifying the first stage of a critical realignment in Florida. The size of these changes, unprecedented in modern times, their disproportionate location in the youngest age group, and their consistency with ideological orientations all increase the probability that they will have lasting significance . . . Barring a complete reversal in the climate of the times, there is good reason to believe that a major and lasting transformation of Florida politics has taken place. (pp. 435–36)

Moreover, recently released figures indicate that the Republican party has been making gains in party registration. While the Democrats still maintain a large advantage over Republicans—in 1986 Democratic registration is 57% and Republican registration is 36% — Democratic registration has declined since 1984 at the same time that Republican registration has increased by about 2%. The Republicans also increased their proportion of the state delegation in the U.S. House of Representatives from 27% in 1980 to 32% in 1984.

On the surface, these changes seem to bear out Beck's speculation that a realignment is in progress in Florida. Caution should be used in accepting this proposition, however, given the ups and downs that the state's Republican party has experienced in the last two decades. It may be that such changes occurred in response to strong period forces (societal and political conditions peculiar to an era) that favored the Republicans over the Democrats. This analysis is designed to identify trends in party identification in Florida between 1980 and 1986, and to speculate about their causes.

PARTY LOYALTIES IN FLORIDA: 1980–1986

Data Collected by the Survey Research Center at Florida State University between 1980 and 1986 can be used to shed light on shifts in party loyalties. These data are collected annually from a statewide telephone survey of Floridians eighteen years old and older.[1] The surveys are designed to measure the policy attitudes of residents on issues facing the state of Florida. As noted by William Claggett (1981), party choice constitutes one of three dimensions of party identification—acquisition, choice and strength. In examining the party identification of Floridians, party choice is of primary concern; strength and acquisition are examined only insofar as they illuminate changes in party choice.

As indicated in table 3.2, the Democrats held a two to one edge over Republicans in party identifiers in 1980. The first substantial rise in Republican identifiers occurs between 1981 and 1984: the percentage of Republicans rises from 21% in 1980 to 30% in 1984. This increase is not monotonic; there is a 4-percentage-point drop in Republican identifiers in 1983, before the rise of 8 percentage points between 1984 and 1986. Over the entire period, the number of Republicans in the electorate increases by 17 percentage points. In 1986, Republican identifiers outnumbered Democrats by 6 percent.

The rise in Republican identifiers is matched by a decline of 13 percentage points in the number of Floridians identifying with the Democratic party. The sharpest declines in the number of Democrats occur between 1980 and 1981 (a 5-percentage point decline) and between 1984 and 1986 (an 8-percentage point decline). In contrast to the changes in party identifiers, the proportion of independents in the electorate holds fairly steady at about 30 percent.

These percentages suggest that the gains made by the Republicans came at the expense of the Democrats. Rather than a significant de-

Table 3.2
Party Identification of Adult Floridians

Party	1980	1981	1982	1983	1984	1985*	1986
			Party Choice				
Republican	21%	29%	33%	29%	30%	35%	38%
Independent	34	31	27	29	20	29	30
Democrat	45	40	40	42	40	36	32
N	848	1,018	1,086	923	911	1,018	929
			Strength of Party Attachments				
Strong Republican	9	13	14	14		18	15
Weak Republican	12	17	19	16		17	24
Leaning Republican	8	8	8	10		12	10
Independent	16	16	11	11		11	12
Leaning Democrat	11	7	8	9		6	8
Weak Democrat	28	25	22	22		21	18
Strong Democrat	16	15	18	19		15	14

cline in the number of independents, which would indicate that people are shifting from an absence of party loyalty to a party identification, the number of independents changes by only 4 percent over the entire period. Where, then, has the Republican conversion come from? That is, did strong Democratic identifiers become more Republican, or were the shifts limited to the weak identifiers, or did some combination of the two contribute to the increases?

The full 7-point party identification scale is available in six of the seven surveys (table 3.2). From the complete scale, it is apparent that the largest changes occur in the weak partisan categories for both the Republicans and the Democrats. The gain in the strong Republican category is less than in the weak category (a 6-percentage-point gain for the strong category and a 12-percentage-point gain in the weak category). The loss in strong Democrats is between 2 and 5 percentage points, while the loss in the weak category is 10 points.

RACIAL DIFFERENCES IN PARTY SHIFTS

Another question warranting further investigation is whether shifts are pervasive throughout the population or tend to be concentrated in certain subsets. According to earlier studies, shifts in party identification in the South are centered primarily in the white population. The data for Florida display racial differences similar to these earlier studies. The largest increases in Republican identifiers are displayed by the white population, whereas blacks tend to maintain their Democratic ties.

At no time during the time period has the Democratic edge over Republicans among blacks been less than ten to one. The Democratic lead in 1986 is considerably smaller, however, than the nineteen to one advantage held by the party in 1980. This shrinking margin results from a substantial drop in Democratic identifiers among blacks and an equally substantial rise in the percentage of independents. The proportion of blacks identifying with a party drops from 91% in 1985 to 71% in 1986. Excluding the 1986 decline, black attachments to the Democratic party actually increased between 1980 and 1985.

Shifts in the strength of party attachments among blacks reveal that the weak Democrat category registers the largest declines.[2] The Leaning Democrat category displays the largest increases in 1986. While there has been an increase in the percentage of Strong, Weak, and Leaning Republicans, on the whole the Republicans do not appear to have been the beneficiaries of black shifts out of the Democrat party.

Republican gains among white Floridians are marked over the six years and come at the expense of the Democrats. Among whites in 1980, Democrats hold a comfortable 19% advantage over Republicans, but by 1986, this advantage turns into a 12% disadvantage: Republicans outnumber Democrats 41% to 29%. The number of white independents fluctuates during the period between a low of 28% in 1982 and a high of 35% in 1980. In the most current time period the number of white independents stands at 30%. Hence, despite the shifts in identification the number of independents remains relatively steady throughout the period.

The strength of party attachments among whites indicates that the bulk of the Democratic supporters fall into the weak category. This category also shows the most substantial declines. Conversely, weak Republicans show the most substantial growth. In light of these findings, our examination of changes in party loyalties shifts to the white population.

EXPLAINING CHANGES IN PARTY IDENTIFICATION AMONG WHITES

Several factors have been suggested by previous studies as accounting for political changes in Florida. The first is a large influx of immigrants to Florida from nonsouthern parts of the United States; these immigrants are assumed to be substantially less Democratic than native Floridians. A second possible source of partisan changes is the shift of conservatives from the Democratic to the Republican party. That is, it is plausible to expect Floridians to bring their partisan attachments in line with their ideological leanings. Third, Beck (1982) suggests that 1980 marked the start of a partisan realignment in Florida in which the younger cohorts in the electorate are identifying in increasing numbers with the Republican party. This type of generational shifting has been associated with past realignments on the national level. A final explanation is that substantial shifts have occurred throughout the electorate (both conversion and replacement) in response to period forces, specifically the Reagan presidency.

Immigration

First, the shifts among white Floridians are examined to determine the impact of the influx of new residents. Natives and long-time residents (people who came to Florida prior to 1960) are more apt to be Democrats than newer residents. Even in 1986, when newer residents (those migrating to Florida between 1960 and 1980) are substantially more Republican than Democratic (26% Democratic versus 44% Republican), natives and long-time residents are more Democratic (40% Democratic versus 35% Republican). The Democratic lead over Republicans exists in every time period among native and long-time residents. On the other hand, among those migrating between 1960 and 1980, Republicans outnumber Democrats in every time period (except 1980) and among the newest residents (those migrating since 1980) the same Republican domination persists in every time period (except 1984).

At the same time that newer residents display less attachment to the Democratic party than natives and long-time residents, they are becoming a larger proportion of the total population. Whereas natives and long-time residents comprise 43% of the population in 1980, they are 33% of the population in 1986. Thus, Democratic strength is being diluted because new residents identify less with the party and this group is becoming a larger part of the population with each passing year.

Finally, one further feature of the party identification of natives and immigrants is noteworthy. The percentage of Republican identifiers increases in all groups regardless of the length of residence. It is unclear whether the 23-percentage-point increase among the natives is due to the conversion of former Democrats to the Republican party or due to the growth in the number of younger natives who identify with the Republican party. Among the long-time residents, however, there is clearly some conversion to the Republican party (a 10-percentage-point increase since 1980), and among the newest residents, the percentage of Republicans has increased by 12 percent. There is also a greater tendency for newer residents to classify themselves as independents than the native and long-time residents.

Ideology

A second factor suggested as a cause of the increase in Republican identifiers is ideology. Beck (1982) notes that older southerners have maintained ties to the Democratic party despite the fact that their issue and ideological positions are more akin to the Republicans. It may be that a conservative, Republican president in the White House has aided many Floridians in bringing their party affiliation in line with their ideological beliefs. Alternatively, it may be that conservatism is growing in Florida and this has produced a shift to the more conservative Republican party.

The second suggestion can be rapidly dismissed. There has been no sizeable growth in the percentage of conservatives in the total population. The percentage of conservatives stands at around 40% for the entire period, and the percentage of liberals (ranging from 17% to 22%) and moderates (ranging from 37% to 42%) remains fairly stable. Therefore, it is unlikely that a new surge in conservatism has led to increases in Republican identifiers.

The suggestion that the increase in Republicanism among white Floridians results from conservatives bringing their party identification in line with their ideology also fails to shed light on the shifts. Since 1982 there has been a greater tendency for conservatives to identify with the Republican party: The percentage of conservative Republicans increases by 10 points while the number of conservative Democrats decreases by 9. The shifts to the Republican party are not confined, however, to the conservatives. Liberals show a 15-point decline in Democratic identifiers and a 7-point increase in the number of Republican identifiers. The smallest shifts are registered for the moderates, who since 1982 have displayed a 2-percentage-point decline in Democratic identifiers and a 6-point increase in the percentage of Republicans.

In sum, there is no evidence of growing conservatism among the Florida electorate. Since 1980, the percentage of conservatives has consistently been larger than the proportion of liberals. Although there is

some indication that conservatives have been bringing their party identification into line with their ideological position, there is also evidence
that liberals as well as conservatives have been moving to the Republican party. This is contrary to what would be expected if an ideological
realignment were taking place in the electorate.

Issues

Since the surveys contain few national issue questions, it is difficult to
dismiss the idea that the rising Republicanism is the result of a realignment on national issues. However, there are at least two areas in which
Reagan and the Republicans have staked out policy positions in marked
contrast to the Democrats that might help to examine this question.
The first area is that of taxing and government spending; Reagan has
consistently attacked the Democrats as big taxers and big spenders.
Second, the Republicans have been opposed to the Equal Rights
Amendment. If Floridians have moved increasingly closer to the Republicans on the taxing and spending issue and on the ERA, then a
shift to greater Republicanism might be expected to occur.

On the issue of taxing and spending, respondents were asked if they
thought that state and local taxes should be reduced even if it meant
services had to be cut, or if they thought that services should be maintained even if taxes remained the same. The percentage of Floridians
opting for services over tax reduction increases across the time period
from 64% in 1980 to 82% in 1986. On the issue of the ERA, support
for the amendment increases by 18 percentage points between 1981
and 1986. While it might be preferable to use national issues, these
data indicate that on these two partisan issues, there is little evidence
that the opinions of adult Floridians are following the Republican lead.

Mobilization and Conversion

The final set of factors to be examined bear directly on the issue of
whether the increased Republicanism in Florida is an expression of a
realignment of party attachments. According to many political scientists, both the mobilization of new and unattached voters and the conversion of older voters occur during realignments; mobilization is
considered to the be strongest factor.

If the recent growth in Republican identifiers is an indication of a
realignment of the party ties of white Floridians, expectations for each
of the age cohorts are as follows: First, the youngest age cohorts should
show the greatest growth in Republican identifiers. Among the younger

cohorts this growth should result both from the conversion of former
Democrats to the Republican party and the movement from independence to Republican identification. Second, the older age cohorts are
expected to exhibit the smallest growth in Republican identifiers. Any
conversion taking place among these older groups should result primarily from the switch from independence to party identification and only
secondarily from changes from Democratic identification to Republican identification. The data on Florida fail to exhibit such clear
patterns.[3]

The most striking feature of table 3.3 is the sizeable growth in the
number of Republicans in *all* age cohorts. This growth ranges from a
low of 8 and 10 percentage points among the cohorts that entered the
electorate between 1936 and 1947, to a 36-percentage-point gain in the
cohort entering the electorate between 1948 and 1953. Between these
three extreme groups, the other cohorts display gains of about 20 per-

Table 3.3
Age-Related Differences in Party Choice among White Floridians

Age Cohort	Year of Birth	Year of Entry	1980	1983	1986	Change 1980–86
		Percent Republican				
1	1957–62	1978–83			42	
2	1951–56	1972–77	16	23	39	+ 23
3	1945–50	1966–71	19	26	40	+ 21
4	1939–44	1960–65	23	38	42	+ 19
5	1933–38	1954–59	15	34	33	+ 18
6	1927–32	1948–53	15	31	51	+ 36
7	1921–26	1942–47	25	32	33	+ 8
8	1915–20	1936–41	27	34	37	+ 10
9	1909–14	1930–35	25	32	48	+ 23
		Percent Independent				
1	1957–62	1978–83			40	
2	1951–56	1972–77	42	43	36	– 6
3	1945–50	1966–71	46	39	28	–18
4	1939–44	1960–65	39	25	35	– 4
5	1933–38	1954–59	46	30	23	–23
6	1927–32	1948–53	34	32	21	–13
7	1921–26	1942–47	30	25	30	0
8	1915–20	1936–41	24	24	30	+ 6
9	1909–14	1930–35	29	26	25	– 4

centage points. Contrary to what might be expected of a cohort entering the electorate during the New Deal realignment, those entering
between 1930 and 1935 show as large a gain as the youngest cohorts.

Moreover, in only three of the eight cohorts do these gains appear to
result from sizable shifts from independence to attachment to the Republican party (cohorts 3, 5, and 6). The people entering the electorate
between 1966 and 1971 and between 1948 and 1959 show the greatest
tendency to shift to a party attachment. For the rest of the cohorts the
changes in independent status are modest (ranging from a 6-
percentage-point gain in independents to a 6-percentage-point decline). Contrary to the dynamics of a mobilized realignment, the
youngest cohort shows no greater tendency to move from independence
to party affiliation than do the oldest two cohorts.

Finally, turning to movements from Democratic identification, the
bulk of the cohorts show sizable shifts out of Democratic status (five of
the eight cohorts), but contrary to a realignment explanation based on

Table 3.3 Continued

		Percent Democrat			
1	1957–62	1978–83			18	
2	1951–56	1972–77	41	35	25	–16
3	1945–50	1966–71	35	35	32	– 3
4	1939–44	1960–65	38	38	23	–15
5	1933–38	1954–59	40	36	44	+ 4
6	1927–32	1948–53	51	36	28	–23
7	1921–26	1942–47	46	43	37	– 9
8	1915–20	1936–41	49	42	32	–17
9	1909–14	1930–35	46	42	28	–18

			Cohort Ages		
Cohort	Age in 1980	N	Age in 1983	N	Age in 1986	N
1	18–23	62	21–26	91	24–29	103
2	24–29	73	27–32	75	30–35	83
3	30–35	85	33–38	97	36–41	80
4	36–41	66	39–44	77	42–47	74
5	42–47	48	45–50	47	48–53	52
6	48–53	47	51–56	80	54–59	61
7	54–59	61	57–62	76	60–65	91
8	60–65	75	63–68	74	66–71	83
9	66–71	83	69–74	78	72–77	61

mobilization, three of the four *oldest* cohorts show substantial movement out of the Democratic category (cohorts 6, 8, and 9). This movement among the older voters is matched by substantial declines in two
of the three youngest cohorts. Thus, there is no evidence of the differential rates of conversion among the youngest and oldest cohorts that
might be expected during a realignment period.

AN ALTERNATIVE EXPLANATION OF PARTY SHIFTS
IN FLORIDA

The trends in party choice suggest that some force operating in the
period between 1980 and 1986 drove most groups in the white population toward greater identification with the Republican party while
leaving the black population relatively unchanged. One variable that is
likely to have affected only the white population and that could have
moved all subgroups of that population in the same direction is Ronald
Reagan's popularity in Florida. Examining Reagan's performance ratings among all Floridians shows that they have increased in every time
period since 1983; by 1986, his performance ratings are actually higher
than during the early years of his first term. In 1986, 72% of the
sample rated his performance as excellent or good, whereas in 1982,
57% rate his performance as excellent or good, and 44% in 1983.

If Reagan's popularity helps to explain the growth in Republican
identifiers, there must be distinct differences between the ratings he
receives from blacks and whites. Ratings for both groups indicate that
blacks' ratings of Reagan's performance are distinctly more negative
than his ratings among whites. At the start of Reagan's first term, there
is a 40-percentage-point difference between black and white positive
ratings. This disparity is largest in 1985 when 68% of the whites rated
his performance as excellent or good, while only 18% of the blacks
gave him positive ratings.

To test the effect of Reagan's performance evaluations on party identification, these ratings are included in a regression equation with several other important predictors of party choice. Jimmy Carter's ratings
for 1980 are included in the regression equation for that year to serve as
a benchmark against which Reagan ratings can be compared. Included
in the equation for each year are two variables that have been found to
be significantly related to white party attachments in the cross-
sectional data—ideology and length of residence—as well as several
standard demographic variables (education or income, age, and race).

Cohort is included to determine if party identification varies by age within each cross-section as might be expected if a realignment had occurred in party identification. That is, if younger voters are more likely to be mobilized than older voters, increasing cross-sectional differences in party identification that are based on age should be evident. Finally, both income and education are used as alternate measures of socioeconomic status.[4] The regressions are performed on three groups— all respondents, white respondents and black respondents. Race is included in the equation when the regressions are run among all respondents. If Reagan's popularity can account for shifts to Republicanism in Florida, it should have a significant association with party identification even after the effects of other important predictors of party choice have been partialed out. Further, Reagan's popularity should overshadow the effects of these other variables in influencing party choice, and its effect should increase over time, corresponding to shifts in party choice.

In the regressions with all relevant variables included, presidential performance ratings have a significant effect on party identification in all time periods in the entire sample. They also have a significant effect among white Floridians. Among black Floridians, however, they are significant in only two time periods (1982 and 1984).

In the entire sample and among whites, both ideology and length of residence have a significant impact in most time periods. Age is not significant in any time period, indicating that there are no age-related differences present. Education is significant only in 1980 and 1983 among the entire sample and among whites. Using income in lieu of education to measure status still results in no significant relationship between party choice and socioeconomic status. Hence, there is no indication that higher status Floridians are bringing their partisan identification in line with their status.

Reducing the equation to only those variables that are significantly related to party identification (table 3.4) indicates that the strength of the effect of performance ratings on party identification increases with time as would be expected if they were driving the rise in Republicism among whites. The coefficients for Reagan's performance indicate that movement toward positive ratings of Reagan leads to movement toward the Republican end of the party scale.

While both ideology and length of residence have a significant effect on party identification, their effects do not increase over time. This suggests that they play a minor role in the increases in Republican identifiers that we have detected. Further, examination of the Betas

Table 3.4

The Influence of Presidential Ratings, Ideology, and Years of Residence on Party Choice among White Floridians

Year	President's Ratings		Ideology		Years of Residence		R^2
	b	Beta	b	Beta	b	Beta	
1980	−.20*	−.22	.20*	.18	.004*	.21	.13
1981	.28*	.26	.18*	.15	.003**	.12	.12
1982	.31*	.34	.17*	.15	.004*	.18	.19
1983	.33*	.37	.08	.07	.005*	.19	.19
1984	.36*	.39	.19*	.16	.005*	.19	.23
1985	.38*	.42	.21*	.18	.003*	.12	.26
1986	.35*	.39	.16*	.14	.004*	.16	.23

*p = .000
**p = .01

indicates that performance ratings have the strongest effect of the three variables on party identification in every time period.

These findings support the contention that Ronald Reagan's popularity provides the impetus for shifts in party identification between 1980 and 1986. They also cast doubt on the existence of a Republican realignment. The regression findings and the earlier findings suggest that a period effect is largely responsible for the change in identification among whites. Finally, the lack of a relationship between the performance evaluations and party identification among blacks would explain why the shifts are confined to the white population: Reagan has not been popular enough among blacks to lead them to shift to the Republican party.

DISCUSSION AND CONCLUSIONS

The contention that the growth of Republicanism among whites is the result of presidential popularity runs counter to the traditional view of the nature of this variable. It has generally been viewed as a short-term force that is insufficient in strength and durability to affect party identification, which is viewed as a long-term force. Under most circumstances this conceptualization is correct. As John Mueller (1973) points out, most presidents enjoy their highest popularity during the early part of their first term in office—"the honeymoon period." The longer the president serves, the more his popularity declines because of the coalition of minorities effect. That is, the longer a president remains in office, the more people he is likely to affect negatively because of the actions he takes while in office.

Mueller points to one notable exception to this generalization, Dwight D. Eisenhower. Instead of declining with time, Eisenhower's popularity remained high throughout his term. Mueller calls this the Eisenhower Phenomenon:

> The variable [coalition of minorities] fails for the Eisenhower Administration, however, especially for the General's first term. The analysis suggests then that if a president wants to leave office a popular man, he should either (1) be Dwight David Eisenhower or (2) resign the day after inauguration. (1972, p. 233)

To these two suggestions, it is now possible to add a third—become Ronald Reagan. Reagan's popularity has actually increased in Florida during his term in office.

That the president's high levels of popularity alone are not sufficient to guarantee a realignment in Florida is evident from the results of the November 1986 election. In that election, Paula Hawkins, the incumbent Republican senator, was defeated by Bob Graham, the outgoing Democratic governor. This defeat came despite campaign visits by the president, Hawkin's strong support for Reagan's policy agenda, and sizable campaign funds. In that same election, the Republican candidate for governor, Bob Martinez, defeated his Democratic opponent, becoming only the second Republican since Reconstruction to hold that post. Yet, even Martinez must face an elected cabinet composed of six Democrats and Democratic majorities in both houses of the state legislature.

The high level of split-ticket voting reflected in these results also belies the notion that a realignment has occurred in Florida. Instead, these election returns suggest that party affiliation played a secondary role to the individual characteristics and qualifications of the candidates seeking office, a contention that supports a continued dealignment interpretation of the events in Florida. Further, the 1986 results give no clear indication that Republicans will be advantaged in the 1988 elections by their numerical superiority in party identifiers. In fact, it appears that continued dealignment of the electorate gives both parties an equally good chance of success in these elections.

In sum, the conclusion of this research is that a period effect and not a realignment has caused the shifts in partisanship apparent in Florida.

This does not necessarily mean, however, that these shifts are only temporary. If Reagan's popularity continues unabated and he is followed by a series of equally popular Republican presidents, these shifts may become permanent. On the other hand, such shifts in response to presidential popularity may affect presidential voting behavior without having any lasting effect on congressional elections or on state politics. Just as it took time for this trend to develop, it will take time to evaluate the substantive impact of such shifts in identification.

One further trend warrants future investigation. Until the latest survey, blacks have displayed strong attachments to the Democratic party; in fact, they have presented an example of what a strong alignment would look like—a high percentage in the strong partisan identifier category, the bulk of the subgroup aligning with one of the two parties and only minimal shifts away from that party. While it is dangerous to speculate from the findings of one cross-sectional survey, especially when that survey appears to deviate from other trends, still the tendency of blacks to move away from the strong and weak Democratic categories to the leaning category bear further watching. If such a trend continues, it may indicate that Florida blacks are beginning to display the same tendency toward dealignment that whites have been displaying for years.

NOTES

1. The wording of the party identification question in each time period is: "Generally speaking, do you usually think of yourself as a Republican, a Democrat, an Independent, or what?" Respondents who mentioned some other party are excluded from the analysis as are respondents who said "don't know." In the 3-point scales, leaners are coded with independents. The 1985 data are weighted to provide a representation of blacks similar to previous years. The surveys were taken: March–April 1980; January–February 1981; January–February 1982; January–February 1983; February, 1984; February–March 1985; February–March 1986. The sampling error for these surveys is plus or minus 4%.

2. It should be noted as well that the 42% strong Democrats in 1980 and 43% in 1986 are substantially lower than the 61% registered in 1982 and the 50% in 1983. It is not possible to tell, however, which is more near the norm for blacks—40% to 43% strong Democrats, or 49% to 61%.

3. The best method for examining age-related effects is through the use of a long-term panel so that individual level changes can be identified. In lieu of such panel data, analysis of aggregate data arrayed by cohort has been used. Certain caveats about this method are necessary. Cohort analyses are plagued by an underidentification problem. That is, aging, generational, and period

effects cannot be separated in a cohort table because they are collinear; the value of any one effect is uniquely determined by the values of the other two. Only by assuming one effect is zero can a solution to the problem be derived. However, the results of the analysis will vary according to the effect that is assumed to be zero.

In the analysis of these data, there is little choice of which effect to set at zero. Because detection of aging effects requires a much longer time span of data than are available in the case of Florida, there is no choice but to set it at zero and assume either generational or period effects, or both. In one sense this selection is a logical one. Most recent analyses agree that party choice hardens as people pass through the life cycle. Therefore, any aging effect should lead to the strengthening of partisan ties in the Florida electorate rather than to the growth of Republicanism. Thus, in order to disentangle the three effects, it is necessary to assume one effect is zero. The logical candidate is the aging effect. Hence, conclusions drawn from the cohort analysis of these data must be tentative and speculative in nature. In determining whether the growth of Republicanism is the result of a realignment, total reliance on the results of the cohort analysis is avoided; other factors bearing on change are also examined. Using this side information in conjunction with the cohort analysis allows the evaluation of all the evidence bearing on the question of whether a realignment of the Florida electorate has taken place.

4. In the regression analysis, the variables are coded in the following manner:

Party Identification: (1) Republican, (2) Independent, (3) Democrat

Reagan Rating: (1) Excellent, (2) Good, (3) Fair, (4) Poor

Ideology: (1) Conservative, (2) Middle of road, (3) Liberal

Length of residence: Number of years of residence, (100) natives

Education: (1) Less than high school graduate, (2) High School graduate, (3) Some college, (4) College graduate and postgraduate degree

Income: (1) $5,000 or less, (2) $5,000–10,000, (3) $10,000–15,000, (4) $15,000–20,000, (5) $20,000–25,000, (6) $25,000–30,000, (7) Over $30,000

Cohort: Coded the same as in table 3.3

4

THE CHANGING TEXAS VOTER

Arnold Vedlitz, James A. Dyer, and David B. Hill

Texas is a state undergoing considerable change. Even the casual observer is aware of Texas's move from the status of a somewhat atypical and idiosyncratic "southern" state to its new position as a prominent member of the fast-developing Sunbelt. A driving force behind many of the social and political changes that mark this transition and that we will elaborate in this chapter, is the extremely rapid and profound population change that has taken place in Texas.

The population of Texas has increased tremendously for most of the past fifteen years. From 1970 to 1980, the Texas population increased 27%, over 3 million people, while the nation's population rose only 11% (Skrabanek, Murdock, and Guseman, 1985: 1–4). But what is particularly significant about this change, in addition to the numbers themselves, is the source of much of this population rise.

Whereas natural increase (the excess of births over deaths) has been the major source of Texas growth for several decades, net inmigration became the major source of population change during the 1970s. Thus, during the 1960s, only 214,000 of the State's 3.1 million increase in population was due to net inmigration while 1.4 million was due to natural increase. During the 1970s, over 1.7 million of the State's 3.1 million increase in population was due to net inmigration while 1.4 million was due to natural increase. Whereas migration accounted for roughly 12 percent of the State's growth during the 1960s, it accounted for nearly 55 percent in the 1970s. During the 1970s, Texas became a major destination for inmigrants from across the Nation (Murdock and Hwang, 1986: 1).

This trend continued through 1983, but recent economic problems have begun to significantly reduce the proportion of in-migrants. While it is difficult to predict how long Texas's oil-based recession will dampen in-migration, it is quite likely certain that the state, upon recovery, will return to its earlier position as an attractive destination for citizens from other states.

In addition to in-migration, the rapid growth of the Texas population has other features that have had an important impact on the political and social climate of the state. One such factor is the growing urbanization of the Texas citizenry. The 1920 census was the first time a majority of our nation's citizens lived in urban areas. For Texas, this change did not occur until 1950 (Skrabanek, Murdock, and Guseman, 1985: 1–4). Today, over 80% of Texans live in urban areas, and almost half of the state's population live in just six metropolitan statistical areas (Harris County-Houston, Dallas County-Dallas, Bexar County-San Antonio, Tarrant County-Fort Worth, El Paso County-El Paso, and Travis County-Austin) (Texas State Data Center, 1986: 9).

A second factor is the relative youth of the Texas population. As is the rest of America, Texas is aging, but the rate of increase is less than for the rest of the country. Between 1970 and 1980, Texas's 18–24-year-old and 25–34-year-old populations increased 43.9% and 72.4% respectively. And while "Lower rates of births and deaths have pushed up both the Texas and U.S. median age . . . migration of young families to Texas and the state's above-average birthrate have kept Texas younger than the rest of the country (Bullock, 1986: 6)."

Another major factor related to demographic change in Texas is the growing importance of minorities in the state, particularly the dramatic increase in the number of Hispanics. While the black population in Texas did increase between 1970 and 1980, its percent of the total population actually decreased from 12.5% to 12%. Hispanics, on the other hand, increased their proportion of the state's population from 18.4% in 1970 to 21% in 1980. While their combined strength grew only slightly from 1970 to 1980, by that date one-third of the Texas population was of black or Hispanic origins (Skrabanek, Murdock, and Guseman, 1985: 1–4). Between 1980 and 1985, the Hispanics in Texas increased another 27%, to over 24% of the state's population (while the percentage of blacks during this period was actually decreasing to 11.5%) (Bullock, 1986: 6). By 1985, then, the two minority groups made up more than 35% of the Texas population. The already important position of Hispanics in the state will likely be enhanced by the new immigration laws that now enable long-term illegal residents to become citizens.

The Texas population is in a transitional period where old alliances and ways of thinking and behaving are likely to give way to new political and social realities. In the analysis of the political and social attitudes and behaviors that follows, the importance in this transition of key demographic factors like ethnicity, length and place of residence, and age will become very apparent.

TEXANS' CHANGING POLITICAL AND SOCIAL ATTITUDES

Hollywood has helped foster a mystique about Texans as defiantly independent, conservative, rugged individualists. Like most myths, this one
has elements of truth and exaggeration. Early public opinion surveys of
Texans taken by Belden and Associates[1] indicate this ambiguity. Surveys
taken in the 1950s and 1960s show Texans feeling too much is being
spent on foreign aid (56% in 1956) but strongly supporting state government regulation of companies that make small loans (70% in 1970).
While Texans were fiercely religious and nonunion, a majority of citizens in 1958 would admit that state government was not spending
enough on public schools, teacher salaries, old age pensions, water con-
servation, or hospitals for the mentally ill. Texans, like citizens of other
states, exhibit significant variations in their social and political attitudes. We will look at past and present Texans' attitudes on two important attitudinal dimensions: social integration and the role of
government.

Integration

After the Supreme Court's landmark desegregation ruling in *Brown* in
1954, Texans did not rush to embrace integrated education or other
forms of social integration. In a survey taken in November of 1954, just
after the *Brown* decision was announced, 19% of Texans interviewed
felt schools should be kept separate even if laws had to be disobeyed.
Another 25% urged the search for ways to get around the law. Thirty-
five percent supported a gradual mixing, and only 14% said obey the
law and mix now. By 1970, not much had changed. In a 1970 poll,
52% of Texans felt school desegregation was moving too fast, and over
80% opposed busing for purposes of integration.

Similar negative racial attitudes were seen in other areas of social
interaction. Table 4.1 lists social distance measures of white Texans
toward blacks in 1968 and compares these to similar questions examined in 1986. There has clearly been a great deal of movement within
Texas toward more moderate racial attitudes. A number of social interaction items that received little support in 1968 were widely accepted
in 1986.

To demonstrate the effect of demographic changes on this movement, we present the breakdown of support, by our key demographic
indicators, for the most problematic item in 1986—having a black as a
close relative by marriage. Youth, newcomers, urban dwellers, and

Table 4.1

The Social Acceptance of Blacks by Whites in Texas in 1968 and 1986

	% Accepting	
Social Situation	1968[a]	1986[b]
Attend same school	69%	90%
Use same swimming pool	37	87
Work same job site	80	96
Have as boss	—	91
Have at gathering in home	36	86
Live next door	43	88
Have as child's college roommate	26	77
Teach your child in school	63	94
Have as close relative by marriage	—	45
Have as president	—	75

a. Belden and Associates, Texas Poll, 1968.
b. Harte-Hanks Communications/Texas A&M, Texas Poll, 1986.

Hispanics—all increasingly important categories of the Texas population—show the greatest support for racial interaction, while Anglos, older Texans, and natives don't seem to have changed much from the 1968 positions. Changes in racial attitudes, then, may be less due to individual or group conversions than to substantial shifts in the relative strength of supporting and nonsupporting elements of the Texas population.

Role of Government

While many Texans may admit that greater government spending is needed for a number of social programs, a majority of citizens have, in the past, been reluctant to endorse the taxes needed to support program expansion. In a survey of Texans taken in May of 1960, respondents were asked a series of questions about teacher salaries. Forty-seven percent of respondents felt teacher salaries were too low, 44% about right, and only 3% felt they were too high. When asked if they would vote for a teacher pay raise if they were a member of legislature, 50% said they would, 35% would not, and 15% were undecided. When asked if they would vote for a tax increase to raise teacher pay, only 44% said they would.

Texans don't like taxes, but if they have to have one, the sales tax is seen as the least offensive. In 1962, 57% of Texans admitted that sales taxes were a good way to raise revenue, and 56% felt they were very

Table 4.2

Racial Interaction Attitudes by Demographic Category

Category	Would Have Blacks as a Close Relative by Marriage				
	Completely Reject	Reject Somewhat	Accept Somewhat	Completely Accept	DK/NA
Race:					
Anglo	39%	15%	17%	24%	4%
Hispanic	22	12	19	44	3
Age:					
18–24	23	13	18	35	11
30–44	27	14	18	28	12
45–61	41	14	14	20	11
62 +	51	8	11	12	18
Place of Residence:					
Large metro	27	12	18	27	15
Metro	32	12	15	28	13
Towns/rural	44	14	13	17	12
Length of Residence;					
Lt 10 years*	22	14	21	34	10
Gt 10 years, not life	34	13	15	26	12
Entire life	37	13	14	21	15

*Not sum to 100% due to rounding
Source: Harte-Hanks Communications/Texas A&M, Texas Poll, 1986.

little burden. Still, in survey after survey, a vast majority of Texans showed little support for any action to raise the sales tax, even one-quarter of 1 percent. For example, a September 1969 survey asked Texans their opinion of a recent tax bill passed by the legislature. On one provision of that bill, a raise in the sales tax from 3% to 3 1/4%, 69% of the respondents rated the provision negatively, with over 50% giving it the most negative rating possible.

This sentiment appears to be changing, however. In surveys of Texans taken in the past few years, Texans show a much greater willingness to support higher taxes to continue and expand programs they think are important.

The spring 1986 Texas Poll asked Texans if they supported or opposed the 1/8th cent increase in the sales tax instituted to support teacher salary increases and school reforms. Seventy-eight percent of all respondents agreed with the legislature's action and, although the differences were not overwhelming, newcomers, youth, and urban dwellers were the most supportive citizens. And when asked if they preferred cuts in public services or increased taxes, spring 1986 Texas Poll respondents answered overwhelmingly (73%) in favor of keeping public services even if taxes had to be raised. Clearly, Texans have become more willing to tax themselves to support needed public services, and while the differences are not as pronounced as in the area of racial attitudes, Texas's emerging demographic categories seem to be more supportive of this trend than do their fellow citizens, although support is relatively widespread throughout the citizenry.

PARTISAN CHANGE

One of the most significant political changes in Texas has been the change in the partisan division of the electorate. Although Texas may have been politically different from the rest of the South in some ways, it was no less Democratic in party identification. As can be seen in figure 4.1 in the 1950s, only 6% to 10% of Texans said they were Republicans, while 61% to 67% said they were Democrats. The percentage of Republicans increased very slowly throughout the 1960s, and by the early 1970s, only about 10% to 12% of Texans identified as Republicans while Democratic strength ranged from 55% to 59%. For

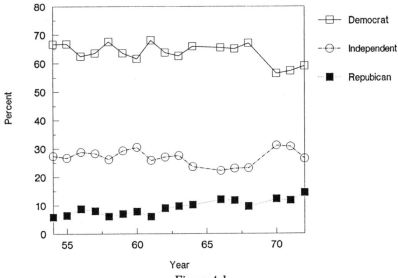

Figure 4.1
Party identification in Texas, 1954–1972.

the 1970s we do not have systematically collected data on partisanship, but the Public Policy Resources Laboratory at Texas A&M began conducting the Texas Poll in December of 1983 and has conducted a poll quarterly ever since then. The Texas Poll data from the 1980s are displayed in figure 4.2.

By 1983, 25% to 30% of the Texas electorate was identifying with the Republican party. There was an increase in Republican partisan identification around the 1984 election and a corresponding decline in Democratic identification that brought each party close to parity in early 1985. The new Republican strength was fairly stable throughout 1985, but slipped in 1986. What both the long-term trend from the 1950s and the short-term change in the 1980s suggest is that any partisan realignment in Texas should be thought of as a process that is occurring over several years or decades. Republican strengthening and Democratic weakening have occurred as a series of shifts. The data suggest that Republican identification grows, probably spurred by presidential contests, then slips back, although still ahead of the position from which it started. This ratcheting effect is most likely due to an increased willingness on the part of many new voters to stay with the Republicans after the excitement of the presidential election has subsided. Voting and party identification are habits, and additional presi-

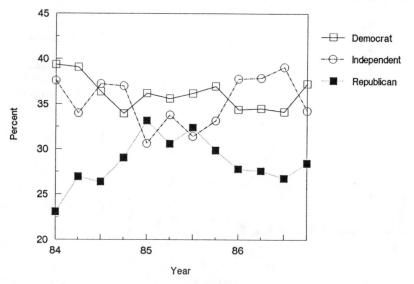

Figure 4.2
Party identification in Texas, 1984–1986.

dential election experiences among new voters probably help cement the pro-Republican feelings engendered in these major electoral contests.

The increasing proportion of Republicans and declining proportion of Democrats can be explained, in part, by new voters entering the electorate. Texas has had a great deal of in-migration and it also has a relatively young population. We find that migrants to the state and younger voters are contributing to the increased numbers of Republicans. Table 4.3 displays party identification by age and amount of time in Texas. The data are aggregated across the four Texas polls conducted in 1986. Partisanship was quite stable during this period and by combining the surveys, the size of the sample is increased.

The fact that the younger voters in Texas are more likely to be Republican is clear from the data presented. The percentage of Republicans increases and the percentage of Democrats decrease as we move from older to younger categories. The oldest group (62 and over) has 21% Republicans and 48% Democrats compared to the youngest group (18 to 29) with 37% Republicans and 27% Democrats, and it is only the youngest group where the Republican identifiers outnumber the Democratic identifiers. It is also interesting to note that although younger voters are usually the most likely to say they are independents, the 19- to 29-year-olds in Texas are less likely to say they are independents than are the 30- to 44-year-olds. For whatever reason, the youngest cohort of Texans have found the Republican party very attractive.

The youthfulness of the Republican party has further implications. First, the most Democratic group, those over sixty-one, will be leaving the electorate and will be replaced by age categories that are significantly more Republican. This could result in an acceleration of the move toward partisan balance in Texas. However, young voters are typically less reliable partisans than are older voters. The partisanship of the young is less well-established and more likely to change and more likely to be ignored in the electoral decision. Further, the younger voters are less likely to participate. Thus, a major problem for the Republican party in Texas will be in retaining its advantage among younger voters as they age and in mobilizing its young partisans.

The impact of migration on partisanship in Texas is also clear. As can be seen in table 4.3, for those who were not born in Texas, Republican identification exceeds Democratic identification. Among lifelong Texans, 41% are Democratic compared to only 23% who are Republicans. Republicans outnumber Democrats 35% to 28% among those nonnatives here more than ten years and 35% to 24% among those here ten years or less. Although some of this difference can be explained by newcomers to the state being younger, the differences are found in all age groups.

The migration into Texas was tied to factors that have now changed. Not only is the number of migrants declining, but the kinds of migrants

Table 4.3

Party Identification in Texas by Age and Length of Residency

Category	Republican	Independent	Democrat	N
Party Identification*				
Age:				
18–29 years	37%	37%	27%	(962)
30–44 years	27	42	31	(1285)
45–61 years	23	36	41	(777)
62 + years	21	31	48	(678)
Lived in Texas:				
10 or fewer years	35	42	24	(600)
Over 10, but not life	35	37	28	(825)
Entire life	23	36	41	(2264)
Party I.D. by Length of Residency, Controlling for Age				
Age = 18–29				
Lived in Texas:				
10 or less	40%	40%	20%	(214)
Over 10, but not life	45	32	22	(121)
Entire life	35	36	30	(600)
Age = 30–44				
Lived in Texas:				
10 or less	32	45	23	(279)
Over 19, but not life	33	45	22	(246)
Entire life	22	40	37	(743)
Age = 45–61				
Lived in Texas:				
10 or less	27	37	36	(64)
Over 10, but not life	33	36	31	(245)
Entire life	17	36	46	(459)
Age = 62 +				
Lived in Texas:				
10 or less	33	39	27	(33)
Over 10, but not life	31	34	36	(202)
Entire life	15	30	55	(437)

*Don't Knows and Undecideds omitted. Rows may not sum to 100% due to rounding.
Source: Harte-Hanks Communications/Texas A&M, Texas Poll, 1986.

are changing as well. Using the aggregated 1986 surveys, we can compare those who have arrived during the last two years with those who arrived during the preceding eight years. The group arriving in 1985 and 1986 is less educated (21% college compared to 43%), less likely to be earning more than $30,000 a year (27% compared to 43%), and less Republican (22% to 33%) and more Democratic (31% to 21%) than those who arrived earlier in the decade. This suggests that migration may not only play less of a role in future partisan change, but the impact of the migration that does occur may no longer be to the advantage of the Republican party.

Transformation of voters is another source of partisan change. The major explanation for partisan shifts is that, as partisan identifications no longer represent the important political divisions in society, shifting will occur to align the party with these political divisions (Converse, 1966). The Democratic party in Texas has been a coalition of groups that have great potential for conflict. Although predominantly conservative, the party has always had a liberal wing. As urbanization and inmigration changed the distribution of political attitudes and as the national politics of the Democratic party identified it more strongly with liberal issues, the strain between the conservatives and the liberals in the Democratic party increased. Further, although racial politics may have played a less important role in Texas than in other southern states, it was still a factor. The effective expansion of voting rights and the increase in the proportion of minority citizens and their mobilization into the electorate, largely as Democratic partisans, produced additional strains on the Texas Democratic party.

Have conservative Democrats left their party to seek ideological solace with their fellow Anglo conservatives in the Republican party? Without a panel study we are limited in the ways we can observe this transformation. One possible method is to use reported previous partisanship as an indicator. In the November 1986 Texas Poll, we asked respondents if their party identification had ever changed, and, if so, what had they been previously. Using this information we can determine the number who perceive themselves as having changed and the direction of the change.

When we look at changes among different subgroups, we get some idea of the nature of the changing that has been going on. Among self-identified conservatives, 37% of those who said they were once Democrats have left the party, 23% presently identifying as Republicans. Only 14% of conservatives who said they were once Republicans do not now identify with that party. The differences across ethnic groups are even more pronounced. Among Anglos who report having been Democrats, 43% say they no longer are. Anglos leaving the Democratic party are about evenly split between Republican (23%) and Independent (20%) identification. Blacks and Hispanics tended to be Democrats and to have stayed that way.

The continuing problem for the Democratic party is apparent from figure 4.3, which shows the ethnic and ideological composition of the two parties. The Republicans are relatively homogeneous, dominated by conservatives (54%) and moderates (34%), with few liberals (12%), while the Democrats are nearly evenly split between liberals (27%) and conservatives (29%), with 44% moderates. The lack of ideological consensus in the Democratic party is a potential cause of future partisan shift toward the Republican party. The greater number of moderates in the Democratic party, and the need to try to bridge the differences among its members could predispose the party leadership toward moderate positions and compromises that could make it more attractive than the Republicans if that party is dominated by uncompromising conservatives. On the other hand, experience suggests that Democratic candidates identified with the liberal wing of the party often drive conservative Democratic partisans to vote for the Republicans or stay at home. A recent example is the loss of liberal Democrat Lloyd Doggett for United States Senator to conservative Republican Phil Gramm in 1984.

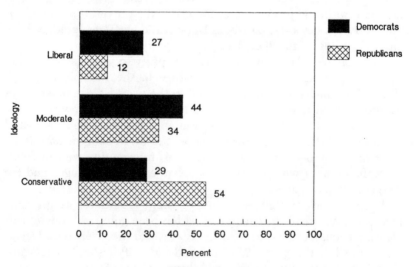

Figure 4.3
Ideological composition of parties in Texas.

The ethnic divisions of the Democratic party reported in figure 4.4 also indicate a problem for maintaining party unity. The Republican party is 90% Anglo and only 2% black and 8% Hispanic. The Democratic party is only 61% Anglo, 18% black and 21% Hispanic. Texans' acceptance of minorities has probably increased; however, there are still major problems with minority-majority interaction. To the extent that the Anglo Democrats, especially conservative ones, perceive the party to be dominated increasingly by minorities, they may more be likely to leave the party.

VOTING BEHAVIOR

As we might expect, given the shifting nature of Texas's political demography and attitudes, the voting behavior of Texans has changed significantly in recent decades. No longer do Texans routinely cast straight-ticket votes for Anglo Democrats. Since the Eisenhower era, Texans have supported the Republican nominee in every presidential election except for native son Lyndon Johnson in 1964 and Jimmy Carter in 1976. Republican Bill Clements was elected governor in 1978 and again in 1986. Table 4.4 presents the Democratic vote for president, senator, and governor in Texas from 1976 to 1986. The strength of

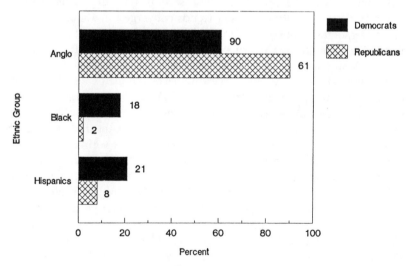

Figure 4.4
Ethnic composition of parties in Texas.

Table 4.4

Democratic Support for President, Senator, and Governor, 1976–1986*

Year	% President	% Senator	% Governor
1976	51.6	57.3	—
1978	—	49.7	49.6
1980	42.8	—	—
1982	—	59.1	53.6
1984	36.2	41.4	—
1986	—	—	46.6

*Percentage of total Democratic and Republican votes cast, independents and third parties not included.
Source: Compiled by the authors from electoral data.

the Republicans in statewide contests in Texas has been significant in this past decade. In addition, Republicans currently hold ten of Texas's twenty-seven seats in Congress, up from none as recently as 1964. Republicans are increasingly competitive for state and local offices, virtually dominating countrywide offices in areas like Dallas and parts of West Texas.

Texas is also electing a more diverse group of office holders racially and ethnically. There are currently 1,466 Hispanic office holders and 281 black office holders, including several minority congressmen. These partisan and ethnic voting trends converged in 1986 when Hispanic Democrat Raul Gonzalez was elected Supreme Court justice, and Republican Roy Barrera captured 45% of the statewide vote in a bid to unseat Democratic incumbent Attorney General Jim Mattox.

Although there are no reliable estimates of the incidence of straight-ticket voting for prior decades, it must have been quite high judging from even a casual perusal of election results. Few Republicans even sought public office, and those who did seldom captured more than one-third of the votes cast. Currently straight-ticket voting is relatively low, and even that which occurs is no longer Democratic only. Two separate postelection studies conducted in 1986 estimated straight-ticket voting to be practiced by only 29% to 36% of the electorate.[2]

Both surveys showed straight-ticket voting down from 1984 when a Reagan landslide substantially bolstered GOP straight-ticket voting. The Tarrance organization also saw straight-ticket voting down from 1982 levels. Their post-election polls showed straight-ticket voting to be 41% in 1982, 47% in 1984, and 29% in 1986.

Both the 1986 postelection surveys show a convergence between ideology and partisan voting patterns. Conservatives overwhelmingly supported Republican Clements, while liberals voted for Democrat White. In both cases, ideologues supported their partisan alter ego by two-to-one margins. According to NBC News exit polls, 71% of conservatives voted for Republican Clements, while 69% of self-described liberals voted for White. This is particularly noteworthy for conservatives, many of whom were conservative Democrats who had to vote against their party's nominee to achieve ideological balance. According to the Tarrance survey, 44% of conservative Democrats voted for Clements, the Republican.

The vote for Roy Barrera also emphasized these trends in Texans' voting behavior. Texas Republicans remained loyal partisans and supported their party's nominee, despite the fact that Hispanic candidates have traditionally been associated with liberalism and the Democratic party in Texas. Sixty-two percent of Republicans voted for Barrera. Also, more than one-fourth of the conservative Democrats crossed over party lines to support Barrera, perhaps because of widespread impressions that he was more conservative than his Democratic opponent. Hispanics, however, remained mostly Democratic. Only 33 percent supported Barrera.

Despite the significant geopolitical and attitudinal shifts already cited, perhaps not all of the effects of those trends have yet been demonstrated in Texas elections because of comparatively low voting registration and turnout rates among several growing groups in Texas. Hispanics, younger Texans, and new residents of the state lag behind others in exercising their franchise rights. As some or all of these groups begin to participate in Texas elections, the results of Texas elections could deviate even further from those held prior to the 1980s.

CONCLUSION

The trends we have identified here will have continued importance in shaping the future of Texas politics. Republicans have been making steady gains in the state for the past several years. The election of Governor Bill Clements in 1986 should not, however, be viewed as a signal of new Republican ascendancy in Texas politics. Clements won in 1986, but the Republican party did not experience a surge of new identifiers after his election. Republicans in 1986, however, continued to hold their own vis-à-vis the Democrats. As the demographic and political forces shaping Texas politics move the Republican party into a more competitive position with their Democratic rivals, both parties will begin to undergo significant changes.

Because Republicans will now have a real chance to capture most statewide offices, Republican primaries that were once only anointing rituals for the party organization-selected-candidates will become more competitive affairs. Republican candidates can expect more divisive and more costly primaries in the future, and the party can no longer expect to control the entry of Republican candidates or office holders. What has been a relatively elite-controlled, homogeneous party (in comparison to the Democrats) will become more open, more heterogeneous, and probably more moderate.

Democrats too can expect major changes as they enter this more competitive political environment. As conservatives leave the Democratic ranks, liberals will begin to control the outcomes of Democratic primary contests. Candidates who represent this faction will be able more easily to win Democratic primary contests. It will be tempting for the liberal wing of the party to press its advantage by presenting liberal slates before the public in general elections. If this occurs, the Democratic party can expect to accelerate a movement to minority party status as it cuts itself off from the more moderate, centrist elements within the electorate it will need to be successful in general election contests.

The Republican party is composed disproportionately of those who are college educated, newcomers, Anglos, large metropolitan area residents, have higher income, and are under thirty. Democrats are strongest among minorities, older residents, natives, those with lower levels of income and those with less education. The influx of newcomers to the state, which has for most of this decade been beneficial to Republican party interests, may be changing in degree of importance due to the state's economic downturn. The growth in minority populations, which is projected to continue, will benefit the Democrats.

The current preference of young Texans for the Republican party is certainly not the last word on this subject. Young, new voters are also likely to be more peripheral voters whose allegiances to parties are less strong. This group may not, then, be lost to the Democratic party.

The stage is set for a long struggle between Republicans and Democrats for the control of Texas politics. Both parties will have to deal with the demographic situation and form political strategies and policy programs that address the needs of these groups in order to create and maintain coalitions that can win elections in Texas.

NOTES

1. Texas is fortunate to have an archive of survey data that dates back to the 1950s. Belden and Associates conducted the Texas poll from the 1950s through the mid 1970s. Beginning at the end of 1983, Harte-Hanks Communication has sponsored a quarterly survey of 1,000 Texans conducted by the Public Policy Resources Laboratory at Texas A&M University. This survey is also called the Texas Poll. Unless otherwise specified, data referred to in this chapter from surveys taken before 1983 are from the earlier Belden polls; surveys reporting findings from 1983 to the present refer to the Harte-Hanks/Texas A&M polls.

2. The two, independent, postelection studies were a Texas Poll of 1,000 respondents conducted November 8–23, 1986, and a Tarrance, Hill, Newport, and Ryan survey of 600 voters conducted on November 11, 1986.

THE
RIM SOUTH

5

Virginia's Changing Party Politics, 1976–1986

John C. McGlennon

Understanding party identification in Virginia over the past few decades requires an observer to recognize one fact about the Commonwealth and its political leaders. If Virginia's voters can be said to have had an inconsistent history of party identification and support, they are simply following in the tradition of the state's political elite. Harry Byrd, Sr., head of the state's dominant Democratic organization for forty years, refused to endorse Democratic presidential nominees for a quarter-century; Virginia's only recent two-term governor, Mills Godwin, served one term as a representative of each major party; his challenger in one election, Henry Howell, had to actively dissuade the Democratic party from endorsing him; and recently retired Senator Harry Byrd, Jr., spent twelve years in the United States Senate as a Democrat who won election as an Independent against Democratic candidates. No wonder the voters sometimes seem unsure of their party affiliation and attachment.

State politics has been characterized by three distinct trends during the same era. First was the close of the "Byrd Machine" period of Democratic hegemony over state politics. The disarray in Democratic politics that accompanied the decline of the Byrd organization led to a decade-long ascendancy of the Republican party during which the GOP won the governorship and a majority of the state's congressional delegation. Finally, the 1980s has seen a resurgence of Democratic success and the emergence of a highly competitive two-party system.

PARTY POLITICS IN VIRGINIA, 1949–86

Ever since V. O. Key labeled Virginia a "political museum piece" in 1949 (Key, 19), the politics of the Old Dominion has undergone a succession of radical changes. The most serious internal challenge to the dominance of Virginia by the rural-based Byrd organization in the

1949 Democratic primary was followed by a competitive Republican campaign for the governorship in 1953.

In the mid-1950s, the three-decade-old organization was energized by popular support for its defense of segregation. However, that support came with a price—the expansion of the state's electorate by tens of thousands of new voters helping to "send a message" to the federal government that, on the issue of civil rights, the Byrd organization spoke for white Virginians.

For a political machine that had depended on low voter turnout (Key, 2), the temporary successes of the 1950s would prove costly. Combined with the enfranchisement of blacks through the Civil Rights Act of 1964 and the Voting Rights Act of 1965, the result was an electorate that almost doubled between the presidential elections of 1956 and 1968, and the gubernatorial elections of 1957–69.

These new voters caused a major reshuffling of Virginia's political order. Byrd organization forces seemed torn between the desire to remain fiscally conservative and resistant to integration, and the need to recognize the growing importance of more liberal Democratic voters such as blacks and urban whites who were, by 1965, almost a majority of the primary electorate. After 1969, as table 5.1 shows, the rate of growth in gubernatorial elections slowed and finally reflected a slight decline in 1985. Presidential election turnout continued to show steady but slower growth.

During the late 1960s and early 1970s, Virginia became a state of "no-party" politics, as conservative Senator Harry Byrd, Jr., won a three-way election as an independent. Liberal Democrat Henry Howell did likewise to take the lieutenant governor's office in 1971, and in the 1973 gubernatorial election, the Democratic party actually failed to nominate a candidate, settling instead for a "commendation" of independent Howell to the voters.

Republicans grew ever more aggressive as they extended their string of presidential victories in the Old Dominion, winning in 1952, 1956, 1960, and 1968. Only Lyndon Johnson's 1964 candidacy attracted a majority of Virginia's voters to a Democratic presidential ballot. The GOP won its first statewide nonpresidential election in 1969. After three straight defeats in which GOP candidates for governor failed to attract 40% of the vote, Linwood Holton, a moderate-progressive who ran unsuccessfully four years earlier, became the state's first post-Reconstruction Republican chief executive.

Republican success arrived despite growing tensions between moderate and conservative factions over the future direction of the party. Moderates, led by Governor Holton, argued that GOP successes could

Table 5.1
Turnout in Virginia Elections, 1956–85

Year	Vote	% Increase
	Presidential Elections	
1956	697,000	—
1960	771,000	10.6%
1964	1,042,000	35.2
1968	1,361,000	30.6
1972	1,457,000	7.1
1976	1,697,000	16.5
1980	1,866,000	10.0
1984	2,133,000	14.3
	Gubernatorial Elections	
1957	517,000	—
1961	394,000	(23.8)
1965	562,000	42.6
1969	915,000	62.8
1973	1,035,000	13.1
1977	1,258,000	21.6
1981	1,420,000	12.9
1985	1,338,000	(5.8)

be built on his base of traditional Republicans and anti-Byrd Democrats. Holton had been endorsed by teachers and labor organizations, and received substantial support from black voters. More conservative Republicans argued that the conversion of Byrd Democrats to the GOP would ideologically polarize the Virginia electorate to the advantage of the Republicans.

The conservatives won the debate and, through the 1980 election, they seemed to have proven their case. Conservative Republicans won a United States Senate seat in 1972, effectively blocked a Republican candidacy in opposition to Senator Byrd in 1976, and guided the election of former Byrd Democratic Governor Mills Godwin to a second term in 1973, this time as a Republican. John Dalton's election as governor in 1977 assured Republican control of the office for the entire decade, and in 1980 the GOP won an astonishing nine of the ten Virginia seats in the House of Representatives. The only Virginia Democrat left in the U.S. Congress was a Byrd organization Democrat first elected in 1968.

During this decade, the Virginia Republican party became a model for state parties across the nation, with a strong financial base, a clear ideological posture, and impressive organizational abilities. Only at the state legislative and local levels were Republicans frustrated, and most party leaders expected rapid erosion of Democratic strength here by virtue of electoral defeats or party switching.

The problems besetting the Democrats in the 1970s were also the result of ongoing factional disputes over party control. Party liberals and conservatives fought bitterly in primaries and conventions, with the better-organized liberals normally winning contests with low participation rates by the electorate at large. Voting in the Democratic primary, which had exceeded general election turnouts in the not too distant past, dwindled to a fraction of the November vote in the 1970 and 1977 nomination contests.

More importantly, Democratic primary voters no longer bore a close resemblance to the electorate at large, but were more likely to be liberal, black, and/or urban (Abramowitz et al., 1980:90; Sabato, 1979:31). Candidates who won Democratic nominations or who swept Virginia's presidential convention delegates (e.g., George McGovern in 1972) were rejected at the polls in November. Even a candidate with demonstrated appeal to southern voters, Jimmy Carter, was unable to convince Virginia to join every other state of the Confederacy in support of his successful 1976 presidential campaign (see tables 5.2 and 5.3).

When the Democrats lost the governorship for the third straight time in 1977 behind their repatriated nominee, Henry Howell, they were in deep depression. The party had last won a statewide election for president in 1964, for governor in 1965, and for U.S. Senate in 1966. In 1978, driven by their frustration with electoral failure, the Democratic party moved decisively toward more moderate candidates by effectively eliminating the statewide primary.

Virginia law permits the political parties to determine their method of nomination. They may choose either open primaries (Virginia has no party registration) or a caucus/convention system. The GOP has used the convention system almost without exception in modern times. The Democrats just as frequently used the primary—until 1978. That year, the Democrats met in convention to choose a U.S. Senate candidate and nominated a moderate who had lost the 1977 gubernatorial primary to Howell. Though he ultimately lost the election, former Attorney General Andrew Miller drew support from all party factions and came within 5,000 votes of victory. His nomination demonstrated that

Table 5.2

Virginia Election Results, 1976–85

Year	Office	Republican	Vote	Democrat	Vote	Other	Vote
1976	President	Ford	836,554	Carter	813,896		
1976	Senator			Zumwalt	596,009	Byrd	890,778
1977	Governor	Dalton	702,334	Howell	545,621		
1978	Senator	Warner	613,232	Miller	608,511		
1980	President	Reagan	989,609	Carter	752,174	Anderson	95,418
1981	Governor	Coleman	659,398	Robb	760,357		
1982	Senator	Trible	724,571	Davis	690,839		
1984	President	Reagan	1,337,078	Mondale	796,250		
1984	Senator	Warner	1,406,194	Harrison	601,142		
1985	Governor	Durrette	590,597	Baliles	732,094		

Table 5.3
Democratic Vote by Office, 1976–85

Year	President	Governor	Senator
1976	48.0		38.3[a]
1977		43.4	
1978			49.8
1980	40.3[b]		
1981		53.5	
1982			48.8
1984	37.3		29.9
1985		55.3	
Average D %	41.9	50.1	41.7

a. Sen. Harry Byrd, Jr., won reelection this year with 57.2% of the vote. There was no Republican candidate.
b. John Anderson received 5.1% of the vote as an independent candidate.

liberal party activists were willing to back a candidate of moderate philosophy and apparently greater electoral appeal (Abramowitz, et al., 1981).

Since 1978, the Democrats have successfully used the convention system to nominate electable statewide candidates. Miller's narrow loss and the election of Ronald Reagan to the presidency over Carter in 1980, as the GOP Picked up nine of Virginia's ten seats in the House of Representatives, delayed Democratic hopes of resuscitation. But in 1981, Democrats nominated Lt. Governor Charles Robb for governor, and he and his two moderate running mates for lieutenant governor and attorney general scored the first one-party sweep of the three top state offices since 1965. In 1982, Democrats were eventually forced to draft Lieutenant Governor Richard Davis for the U.S. Senate seat being vacated by Harry Byrd, Jr., and despite a late start and being outspent two to one, Davis received 49% of the vote against the successful Republican nominee, Paul Trible. Democrats gained three new seats in the House of Representatives in 1982, defeating two incumbents and gaining an open Roanoke Valley seat held by the GOP since 1952.

Democratic victory has not been complete in the 1980s. Ronald Reagan carried the state comfortably in both presidential elections. Republicans gained an open U.S. Senate seat with Trible's election, and Senator John Warner won a second term in 1984 by a record-setting margin. But a second straight sweep of the top three state offices in 1985 indicated a basic resurgence of Democratic strength.

Gerald Baliles, who had been elected attorney general on Robb's ticket in 1981, won the right to replace Robb (who was not constitutionally permitted to succeed himself). Virginians made history by electing Baliles' running mates, black State Senator L. Douglas Wilder and woman Delegate Mary Sue Terry as lieutenant governor and attorney general, respectively. In 1986, the U.S. House delegation was split evenly between the parties for the first time since the Watergate Congress elected in 1974, as Democrats won another open-seat contest created by a Republican retirement in the Norfolk-Virginia Beach Second District.

In ten years, the Virginia Democratic party had gone from a fragmented, disorganized, bankrupt shell to a highly efficient, unified apparatus with a million-dollar annual budget and high morale. It had become the model for state Democratic parties in the 1980s.

PARTY IDENTIFICATION AND PARTY STRENGTH

This brief history of party organizations and successes raises questions about the relationship of these developments to the attitudes and affiliations of the Virginia voters. Studies of partisanship in the South have generally noted a sharp decline in Democratic identification, and corresponding increases among Independents and Republicans.

One might expect these dramatic changes in partisan affiliation to be even greater in Virginia. The Old Dominion, along with Florida and Texas, has experienced greater than average increases in population due to migration in every decade since the 1940s. The areas of northern Virginia and the Tidewater especially have seen dramatic population growth, much of it the result of transplanted northerners attracted by federal government- and defense-related jobs.

No other state of the Confederacy has elected three successive Republican governors. None has been without a Democrat in the U.S. Senate since 1973. Not one has seen a nearly complete sweep of its congressional delegation by the GOP. Few have experienced the dramatic resurgence of the Democratic party witnessed by Virginia in the 1980s. During a period of rapidly changing party fortunes, voter identification might provide some clues as to the long-term prospects of realignment.

Party Identification in Virginia, 1976–86
Two factors hamper the examination of partisan identification in Virginia. First, public opinion polling has not been systematically con-

ducted by any academic institution in the Commonwealth. A private, commercial polling operation has conducted regular surveys of voter opinions, but the available data, welcome as they are, will never allow full treatment of this issue. Changes in questionnaire wording and treatment of independent "leaners" make it difficult to probe beneath the surface of party identification. Second, Virginia voters are not asked to declare a party affiliation when they register to vote or when they vote in a primary.

Nonetheless, this chapter will examine available data from statewide surveys conducted by Media General, Inc., for the *Richmond Times-Dispatch* and *Richmond News Leader*. These 13 statewide samples, ranging in size from 505 to 993 respondents, were conducted in September and October of statewide election years between 1976 and 1986 (see table 5.4). All were telephone surveys, and consistently appeared to reflect the characteristics of the Virginia electorate. While the polls were generally conducted to analyze the "horse-race" question of who was leading in the upcoming general election, party identification also concerned the polling organization.

During the first five years of the Media General surveys, no effort was made to determine the party preferences of those who declared themselves independents. The standard polling practice of probing independents to determine whether they leaned toward either of the two parties did become a part of the survey instrument in 1981, and continued through 1985. Even without this refinement of polling practices, these two time periods show obvious trends in voter identification.

The surveys conducted between 1976 and 1980 show two continuing results—independents constituted a majority of the Virginia electorate, and those who did choose a party favored the Democrats. The Democratic margin among party identifiers declined throughout this period, from a two to one advantage in 1976, the year that Southern Democrat Jimmy Carter won the presidency, (though narrowly losing Virginia) to three to two in 1980, when Ronald Reagan won Virginia and forty-three other states for the GOP in ousting Carter from the White House. All the while, more than half of the voters maintained their nominal independence of either party.

The impact of Reagan's victory on party identification was felt almost immediately in the Media General surveys. In September 1981, the number of independents dropped below 50% for the first time, and virtually all of the change came in increased Republican identification.

Each survey conducted during the second five years of polling (1981–85) shows an absolute majority of partisan identifiers and, with one conspicuous exception, higher support for the GOP. Republican identi-

Table 5.4

Party Identification in Virginia, 1976–1985

Date	Election	Sample	Democrats	Republicans	Independents
September 1976	Presidential	505	31%	17%	52%
October 1976	Presidential	635	29	16	55
October 1977	Gubernatorial	800	30	15	55
September 1978	Senatorial	677	32	16	52
October 1978	Senatorial	683	30	16	54
September 1980	Presidential	519	29	20	51
October 1980	Presidential	708	27	18	55
September 1981	Gubernatorial	665	28	26	46
October 1981	Gubernatorial	909	—	—	—
September 1982	Senatorial	834	29	22	49
October 1984	Presidential	892	24	28	48
September 1985	Gubernatorial	947	29	33	38
October 1985	Gubernatorial	993	28	31	41

fication, which never exceeded 20 percent prior to 1981, climbed to the mid-20s in the year following the presidential election, despite Democrat Charles Robb's election as governor that fall. By 1984, when Ronald Reagan was sweeping Virginia along with forty-eight other states in his triumphal reelection campaign, pure Republican identifiers outnumbered self-professed Democrats for the first time. They retained that advantage in 1985 polling, as nearly one-third of all Virginians declared their identification with the Republicans.

Between 1976 and 1985, the number of Virginians declining to declare themselves members of one of the two major parties dropped from 53% to 39%. All of that decline, and more, was reflected in growth of the GOP, from 17% to 32%. Democrats suffered a statistically insignificant 1% decline, but politically the relative change in party fortunes was anything but insignificant.

The Democratic decline was even more noticeable when independents were pushed to indicate which of the two parties they preferred (see table 5.5). Republican affinity among independents allowed virtual ties in 1981 and 1982 between the parties, and gave the GOP the single largest advantage enjoyed by either party throughout the ten-year period in October 1984 in anticipation of the Reagan landslide. In 1985, the Republican lead declined to 6 points as Democrats won all three statewide elections. But even with a sweep of the Commonwealth's top offices, the Democrats had failed to restore themselves to dominance in party identification.

Trends in Party Identification

The general pattern of static Democratic affiliation and dramatic Republican gains to a competitive level suggests fairly strongly that a long-term realignment of the Virginia electorate has occurred (see figure 5.1). Two surveys conducted during the Reagan era do present vastly different pictures of party support, probably best explained by the effects of short-term factors.

Polls conducted during 1982 suggest the trend of Democratic decline and Republican advance may have been arrested and reversed. For the only time during the Reagan presidency, Democrats had leads among both pure identifiers and identifiers plus leaners. The 1982 election occurred during an economic recession that reduced the president's approval rating to a mid-40 percent level.

Exactly the opposite phenomenon exhibited itself during the 1984 election. For the only time in the ten-year period, one party could claim the support of a majority of Virginia voters (allocating indepen-

Table 5.5

Party Identification with Independent "Leaners" Allocated to Preferred Party[a]

Date	Election	Sample	Democrats	Republicans	Independents
September 1981	Gubernatorial	665	39	41	20
October 1981	Gubernatorial	909	40	38	22
September 1982	Senatorial	834	39	36	25
October 1984	Presidential	892	35	52	13
September 1985	Gubernatorial	947	40	46	14
October 1985	Gubernatorial	993	39	45	16

Source: Media General Research Department, Richmond, Va.

a. Those who indicated that they were "independents" on the party identification question were asked to indicate which party, if either, they felt closer to.

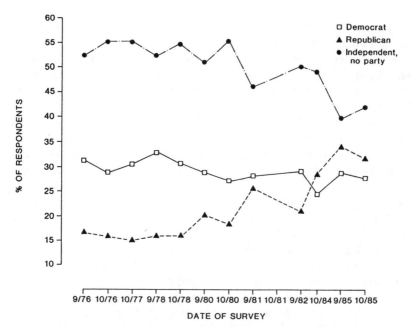

Figure 5.1
Party identification in Virginia, 1976–1985.

Source: Media General Research Department, Richmond, Va; October 1981 data
missing.

dent leaners to the parties). Fifty-two percent of the survey respondents
indicated their identification with or preference for the GOP. This temporary majority disappeared in the surveys of the next year, but left a
residue of increased Republican support.

COMPONENTS OF PARTY SUPPORT IN VIRGINIA

The competitive two-party system that has emerged at least in Virginians' party identifications is superficially simple. GOP strength has increased in three steps—from a growing minority prior to the Reagan
presidency to a statistical tie with the Democrats in Reagan's first term,
to a plurality of the electorate after his reelection landslide. All the
while, Democratic support remained static.

These surface trends resulted from what appears to have been some
rather dramatic movement within subgroups of the population, some
consistent with and others in opposition to these trends. Demographic

breakdowns of party support help to illustrate the shifting allegiances of Virginia's electorate.

Four surveys were selected to show the movement of subgroups in the electorate during a four-year period. The first survey, conducted in September 1981, reflected the Reagan-inspired gain in GOP support, but during a campaign in which Democratic gubernatorial nominee Robb was favored by the respondents. The second survey, conducted during September 1982, reflected disaffection with Republican economic policies during a recession—though GOP Senate candidate Paul Trible won a close November election. The third survey was conducted in October 1984, as the Reagan reelection landslide approached. Finally, the October 1985 survey was conducted at a time of strong presidential popularity for the Republican incumbent but within a month of the Democratic sweep of statewide offices.

Table 5.6 shows the fluctuations in support for the parties among demographic subgroups. While the four surveys together show virtually no change in Democratic affiliation, and an eventual net gain in GOP support at the expense of Independents, a great deal of movement appears to have taken place within various voter subgroups.

Between 1981 and 1985, the GOP registered its greatest gains among young voters (+ 14%), a trend that has been observed nationally and that must hearten Republican adherents. Support also grew at above average rates among blue-collar workers (+ 9) and whites, Protestants, middle-income earners, and those not in the work force (7% gains in each). Democrats gained most sharply among Catholics (+ 11), high school graduates (+ 8%), middle-income earners, and suburbanites (+ 5). These gains allowed the Democrats to offset losses among blacks (–7), those with less than a high school diploma and blue-collar workers (–6), for no net change.

Regionally, the GOP gained in all but one of the seven sections into which the state was divided by the survey (see table 5.7). Republican gains of 11% (Roanoke-Lower Piedmont), 10% (Central Virginia-Valley, Richmond Metro), 9% (Southwest), and 7% (Tidewater, Southside) surprisingly contrasted with a 7-point drop in Republican support in what had been the party's strongest base—Northern Virginia. Democrats advanced in Northern Virginia and Southwest (+ 6), Southside (+ 3) and Richmond Metro (+ 1), while dropping in Tidewater (–4) and Roanoke-Lower Piedmont (–3), and remaining stable in Central Virginia-Valley.

In the 1981 survey the well-publicized "gender gap" in party identification gave Democrats an advantage among women that offset a Re-

Table 5.6
Characteristics of Virginia Party Identifiers, 1981–85

Category	1981	1982	1984	1985	% Change 1981–85
Total					
R	26	22	28	31	+ 5
D	28	29	24	28	—
I	46	49	38	41	− 5
Race:					
White					
R	29	25	32	36	+ 7
D	21	26	19	23	+ 2
I	50	49	49	41	− 9
Black					
R	7	11	6	10	+ 3
D	68	63	62	61	− 7
I	25	26	32	29	+ 4
Residence:					
City					
R	x	x	26	27	+ 1
D	x	x	30	34	+ 4
I	x	x	44	39	− 5
Suburb					
R	x	x	33	35	+ 2
D	x	x	19	24	+ 5
I	x	x	48	41	− 7
Rural					
R	x	x	28	32	+ 4
D	x	x	26	30	+ 4
I	x	x	46	38	− 8
Age:					
18–34					
R	25	x	33	39	+ 14
D	25	x	25	24	− 1
I	50	x	42	37	− 13
35–54					
R	25	x	29	30	+ 5
D	26	x	21	29	+ 3
I	49	x	50	41	− 8
55 or older					
R	28	x	24	27	− 1
D	32	x	27	34	+ 2
I	40	x	49	39	− 1

Table 5.6 (*continued*)
Characteristics of Virginia Party Identifiers, 1981–85

Category	1981	1982	1984	1985	% Change 1981–85
Education:					
H.S. or less					
R	21	19	21	28	+ 7
D	43	46	40	37	– 6
I	36	35	39	35	– 1
H.S. Grad					
R	25	18	27	28	+ 3
D	24	35	25	32	+ 8
I	51	47	48	40	– 11
Some college					
R	23	27	31	32	+ 9
D	27	28	21	26	– 1
I	50	45	48	42	– 8
College grad					
R	34	29	32	36	+ 2
D	23	20	20	25	+ 2
I	43	51	48	39	– 4
Income:					
Under $20,000					
R	24	21	22	24	—
D	35	39	30	39	+ 4
I	41	40	48	37	– 4
$20,000–49,999					
R	25	24	32	32	+ 7
D	23	26	23	28	+ 5
I	52	50	45	40	– 12
$50,000 +					
R	35	28	32	40	+ 5
D	19	23	14	20	+ 1
I	46	49	54	40	– 6
Occupation:					
White collar					
R	28	26	32	33	+ 5
D	22	25	21	26	+ 4
I	50	49	47	41	– 9
Blue collar					
R	22	14	27	31	+ 9
D	35	38	22	29	– 6
I	43	48	51	40	– 3

Table 5.6 *(continued)*
Characteristics of Virginia Party Identifiers, 1981–85

Category	1981	1982	1984	1985	% Change 1981–85
Other workers					
R	22	25	34	26	+ 4
D	38	32	30	32	− 6
I	40	43	36	42	+ 2
Not in workforce					
R	26	24	25	33	+ 7
D	31	35	28	32	+ 1
I	43	41	47	35	− 8
Religion:					
Protestant					
R	28	25	28	35	+ 7
D	28	30	24	28	—
I	44	45	48	37	− 7
Catholic					
R	19	23	41	22	+ 3
D	27	30	24	38	+ 11
I	54	47	35	40	− 14
Sex:					
Male					
R	30	29	28	36	+ 6
D	21	27	22	25	+ 4
I	49	44	50	39	− 10
Female					
R	23	19	29	29	+ 6
D	33	34	27	32	− 1
I	44	47	44	39	− 5

Source: Media General Research Department, Richmond, Va.

publican edge among men. By 1985, however, while the male gap had grown, GOP gains among women had almost eliminated the Democrats' advantage.

Most significantly, close examination of the four surveys shows just how unstable party identification is in Virginia in the 1980s. The level of support for the Republican party fluctuated by more than ten percentage points during the four-year period among whites, 18–34-year olds, high school graduates, those earning $50,000 or more, Catholics, blue-collar and other nonwhite-collar workers, and women. In fact, this period showed a 9-point swing in Republican support overall, from 22 percent in 1982 to 33 percent in 1985.

Table 5.7
Virginia Party Identification by Region

Party	1981	1982	1984	1985	% Change 1981–85
Republicans:					
Tidewater	22	15	28	29	+ 7
Northern Virginia	37	26	30	30	– 7
Central Virginia	27	30	30	37	+ 10
Richmond	26	30	32	36	+ 10
Southside	25	21	23	32	+ 7
Roanoke	23	25	30	34	+ 11
Southwest	24	22	27	33	+ 9
Democrats:					
Tidewater	33	33	27	29	– 4
Northern Virginia	22	28	23	28	+ 6
Central Virginia	24	23	15	24	—
Richmond	24	24	16	25	+ 1
Southside	27	40	37	30	+ 3
Roanoke	32	30	21	29	– 3
Southwest	29	39	29	35	+ 6
Independents:					
Tidewater	45	52	45	42	– 3
Northern Virginia	41	46	47	42	+ 1
Central Virginia	49	47	55	39	– 10
Richmond	50	46	52	39	– 11
Southside	48	39	40	38	– 10
Roanoke	45	45	49	37	– 8
Southwest	47	39	44	32	– 15

Source: Media General Research Department, Richmond, Va.

The regions are as follows: Tidewater and Eastern Virginia; Northern Virginia; Central Virginia and the Valley; Richmond Metropolitan area; Southside; Roanoke and the Lower Piedmont; and Southwest Virginia.

Finally, it is instructive to examine the most recent composition of the two parties (table 5.8). How important are the various components to the overall strength of the parties? For the GOP, the picture is not too surprising. The party is predominantly white (94%), middle- (56%) and upper-income (24%), young (38% under 35), white-collar (51%), college graduates (40%), suburban (42%), Protestant (81%) and male (55%). Democrats have a larger black constituency (31%), more low- (35%) and middle-income (52%) adherents, older (only 26% under 35), less educated (45% without college), rural (38%), more reli-

Table 5.8
Composition of Virginia Parties, 1985

Characteristic	Republicans	Democrats	Independents
Race:			
White	94	69	90
Black	5	31	10
Other	1	—	—
Sex:			
Male	55	44	49
Female	45	56	49
Religion:			
Protestant	81	70	71
Catholic	7	14	11
Other	9	10	9
None	3	6	9
Age:			
18–34	38	26	29
35–54	39	42	44
55 or older	23	32	27
Education:			
College grad	40	31	33
Some college	27	24	29
H.S. grad	23	30	27
Some H.S. or less	10	15	11
Income:			
$20,000 or less	20	35	25
$20,000–$49,999	56	52	56
$50,000 or more	24	13	19
Occupation:			
White collar	51	45	52
Blue collar	13	14	14
Other workers	6	8	6
Not in workforce	30	33	26
Neighborhood:			
City	21	30	24
Suburb	42	32	40
Rural	37	38	36

Source: Media General Research Department, Richmond, Va.

giously diversified but still largely Protestant (70%), and female (56%).

PARTY IDENTIFICATION AND ELECTION OUTCOMES

A superficial comparison of party identification figures and election outcomes during the decade under study would suggest a counterintuitive finding: Republican gains in identification accompanied renewed Democratic success at the polls. In fact, a more plausible explanation would suggest that Virginia has become a highly competitive state with relatively close levels of partisan affiliation among the voters, a certain fluidity to their affiliation based on current candidates and issues, and that the parties may have found it possible to adapt to electoral preferences better in Virginia than in states that rely on the primary to nominate statewide candidates.

Surveys of nominating convention delegates in Virginia and other states that use the caucus/convention system for selecting their presidential convention delegates have demonstrated that electability is an important factor in candidate choice among this level of party activists (Rapoport, et al.) Such calculation is less common among primary electorates, who are more likely to select candidates based on issue and ideological proximity. The fact that Virginia parties use conventions exclusively to nominate statewide candidates may mean that Virginia's political parties are better able to respond to changes in voter partisan loyalty and, as Virginia's Democrats have in the 1980s, nominate candidates who have an appeal to members of the opposition party.

The more stable base of Democratic support may also help to explain the recent success of Democratic candidates for state and congressional offices. Democratic voters as well as activists may be more pragmatic in their willingness to support nominees who might have failed the ideological "litmus tests" of the right or left in the 1970s.

Certainly that pragmatism is suggested in the high degree of straight-ticket voting for Baliles, Wilder, and Terry in the 1985 election. Pre- and postelection polls found high party loyalty among Democrats and significant defection among Republican identifiers.

SUMMARY AND CONCLUSIONS

Party politics in Virginia appears to have undergone a basic realignment in the past decade. First, a decline in majority party identification is accompanied by a surge of nonaffiliated voters. A critical election essentially provides the impetus to move these unattached voters into the ranks of the opposition party, and the 1980 election seems to fit that description. Certainly the growth of Republican affiliation from a two-to-one deficit compared to Democrats in 1976, to a plurality of identifiers in 1985, reflects a dramatic change. However, the evident fluctuation in identification in the individual surveys suggests strongly that the possibility of instability in party identification will continue in the foreseeable future. Just what this portends for future party success is also unclear. The Virginia GOP, having attained the lead in identifiers, was by all accounts internally divided and floundering in the mid-1980s suffering defeats in both gubernatorial elections in the 1980s and the loss of four House seats.

Nationally (and in the South as well) the GOP began to suffer a decline in identifiers as the Reagan administration became increasingly involved in the Iran-Contra scandal, and as this presidency drew to a close. The ability of the GOP to retain its position in the face of such challenges remains to be seen. What is clear, however, is that the GOP during the early 1980s attained historic levels of party attachment in Virginia, and partisan competition has firmly established itself in at least this part of the South.

6

TENNESSEE:
Weakening Party Loyalties and Growing Independence

Robert H. Swansbrough and David M. Brodsky

Commentators often point to the rise of a competitive Republican party in Tennessee as a harbinger of party realignment in the South. The GOP manifested strength in Tennessee long before the Republican party became a viable challenger to Democratic dominance in many other southern states. The Civil War issue of slavery established a Republican bastion in East Tennessee; the state's eastern counties voted twice against secession from the Union in 1861. Nevertheless, this GOP enclave failed to prevent the Democratic party from dominating the Volunteer State's politics for over a century. Tennessee Republicans gained statewide influence only through coalitions with conflicting Democratic factions.

The Tennessee Republican party expanded from its eastern stronghold in the 1960s to win statewide elections with increasing frequency, suggesting to some observers a possible Tennessee voter realignment to the GOP banner. But lately a growing trend toward ticket-splitting also reveals a lessening of traditional partisan loyalties to both Republican and Democratic candidates.

This chapter examines Tennessee's statewide elections between 1970 and 1986 and analyzes attitudinal data drawn from 1981 and 1985 surveys of Tennessee voters to assess whether the Volunteer State is experiencing either the political phenomena of partisan realignment or dealignment. It also identifies some of the factors associated with changes in party affiliation and voting behavior in Tennessee.

HISTORICAL BACKGROUND

V. O. Key observed that two one-party systems coexisted in Tennessee; Republicans won local elections and congressional seats in East Tennessee, while Democrats dominated politics in the state's Grand Divisions of West and Middle Tennessee (Key, 1949:75). Between 1947 and 1952, two East Tennesseans were the only Republican Representatives in the South's 105-member congressional delegation (Bartley and Graham, 1975, p. 80–81).

In the 1930s and 1940s, Memphis political boss E. H. Crump marshaled his control over populous Shelby County in West Tennessee to play a key role in statewide politics. The conservative Democratic Crump organization, with its base of black Memphis voters, negotiated alliances with East Tennessee Republicans to select candidates, influence the state's policies, and wield patronage power. Middle Tennessee Democrats led the opposition to the Crump machine, with the 1948 victories of Senator Estes Kefauver and Governor Gordon Browning signaling the erosion of Crump's power.

The 1948 Dixiecrat revolt didn't prevent President Harry Truman from carrying Tennessee's electoral vote, although Strom Thurmond received some West Tennessee support. The state's major political conflicts occurred between competing Democratic party factions, rather than close statewide confrontations between Democratic and Republican candidates. The more liberal Democratic faction headed by Senator Kefauver and Senator Albert Gore challenged the conservative Democratic faction led by Governors Frank Clement and Buford Ellington. Although Dwight Eisenhower won Tennessee's presidential ballots in 1952 and 1956, his popularity failed to bolster the success of the state's GOP candidates (Green, Grubbs, and Hobday, 1975).

Democratic party fortunes began to ebb in 1966, with the election of Republican Howard Baker to the U.S. Senate. The Republican congressional delegation also rose that year from three to four House seats. In the 1968 presidential race, Hubert Humphrey finished behind both the winner Richard Nixon and American Independent candidate George Wallace. The Republicans also gained control over the General Assembly's House of Representatives when an independent legislator broke a 49 to 49 partisan tie, electing Representative William Jenkins as Speaker.

Republican Winfield Dunn won the governorship in the 1970 election, and Bill Brock defeated Albert Gore, putting both of Tennessee's U.S. Senate seats in Republican hands (figure 6.1). However, the Democrats managed to wrest back control of the General Assembly's lower house. In 1972 President Nixon won 68% of the Tennessee vote over George McGovern. At the same time, Senator Baker resoundingly defeated his Democratic challenger and the Republicans gained control of five of the state's eight congressional seats.

The Watergate scandal contributed to Democrat Ray Blanton's 1974 move into the governor's mansion and a five to three Democratic ma-

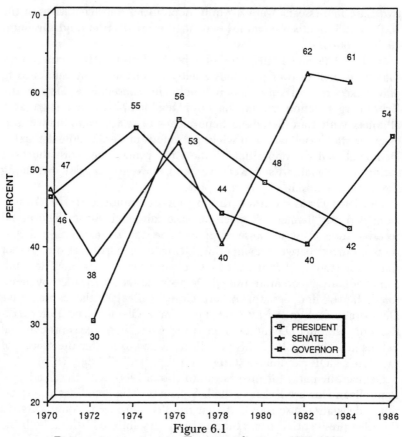

Figure 6.1
Democrat percent major Tennessee elections, 1970–1986.

Source: *Tennessee Blue Book*, 1971–72 to 1985–86 editions and certified election returns
    from November 4, 1986, general election.

jority in the congressional delegation. Fellow southerner, Jimmy
Carter, won Tennessee in 1975, his coattails helping Democrat Jim Sasser defeat Senator Bill Brock with a strong demonstration of straight-
ticket voting (Freeman, 1980:25).

A 1978 scandal in the Blanton administration, and a well-publicized
walk across the state in a red plaid shirt, boosted Republican Lamar
Alexander into the governor's chair. In 1980 Ronald Reagan defeated
President Carter by a slim 0.3% of the popular vote, with Independent
John Anderson draining critical Carter support (Swansbrough,
1985:34). Governor Alexander won a second term with 60% of the
1982 votes, while Tennesseans split their ballots to reelect Democratic

Senator Sasser. The Volunteer State's voters divided their ballots again in 1984 to return President Reagan to the White House with a 58% win, while 61% chose Democratic Congressman Albert Gore, Jr., to occupy the Senate seat vacated by retiring Howard Baker.

In 1986 Speaker Ned McWherter became governor, defeating former GOP Governor Winfield Dunn; Republican Alexander's personal gubernatorial popularity failed to overcome Dunn's campaign stumbling over his payment of minimal income taxes and membership in an exclusive country club. Thus, after the 1986 election the Democratic party held the Tennessee governorship, both U.S. Senate seats, a six to three majority of the congressional delegation, and solid majority control in the State Senate (23 to 10) and the General Assembly's House (61 to 38).[1] Nevertheless, as this chapter indicates, the decline in Democratic party self-identification and the rise of ticket-splitting challenge the Democratic party's recent dominance of Tennessee's politics.

WEAKENING REGIONAL PARTISAN TIES

West Tennessee Democrats increasingly stray from their traditional party allegiance. Although populous Shelby County, which includes Memphis and its large number of black voters, stays firmly in the Democratic camp, the predominantly white, rural West Tennessee counties in the old cotton belt often abandon statewide Democratic candidates. Between 1970 and 1986, the Republican candidates for president, U.S. senator, and governor received a plurality of the West Tennessee vote in seven out of fifteen electoral contests: 1970 (Governor Dunn, Senator Brock), 1972 (President Nixon, Senator Baker), 1978 (Governor Alexander, Senator Baker), and 1984 (President Reagan).

But historically Republican East Tennessee also manifests some erosion of rigid partisan support. In 1976 President Gerald Ford eked out a bare 50% to 49% plurality over his Georgia competitor, Jimmy Carter. East Tennesseans split their ballots in the 1982 election to cast 71% of their votes for Governor Alexander, then shifted parties to give 56% support to Democratic Senator Jim Sasser over GOP Congressman Robin Beard. In 1984 two-thirds of the Republican-oriented region voted to reelect President Reagan, while half of them cast ballots for Democratic Senate candidate Albert Gore, Jr., and only 43% voted for fellow East Tennessee Republican State Senator Victor Ashe. In both 1982 and 1984, the weakness of the candidates and the negative nature of their campaigns reduced traditional straight-ticket voting by many

GOP loyalists. Although Ned McWherter failed to carry East Tennessee in the 1986 governor's race, he captured the bedrock Republican 1st Congressional District (53%). This feat occurred largely as a result of former Governor Dunn's unwillingness to establish a medical school in this Tennessee Republican heartland during his 1970–1974 administration.

Middle Tennessee remains a Democratic base, although Democratic defections occur in this region as well. In six out of fifteen election matchups between 1970 and 1986, Republican candidates received a majority vote from Middle Tennesseans: 1972 (President Nixon, Senator Baker), 1978 (Governor Alexander, Senator Baker), 1982 (Governor Alexander), and 1984 (President Reagan). In 1986 Governor McWherter received 58% of the Middle Tennessee votes and 57% of the West Tennessee ballots. Clearly, both Democratic and Republican regional loyalties have eroded in the Volunteer state.

PARTY REALIGNMENT AND DEALIGNMENT

Methodology

Two statewide surveys of Tennessee voters provide the data for this chapter. Both surveys employed random digit dialing techniques to ensure that the sample included listed and unlisted telephone numbers. The March 1981 survey included 461 respondents, with a plus or minus 4.5% sampling error at the 95% confidence level. The March 1985 survey interviewed 620 Tennessee voters, with a plus or minus 4% sampling error.

An interesting aspect of this analysis consists of data generated from questions asking respondents to state their party identification when they first voted in an election and their present party identification. The respondents were asked to use a seven-point scale (Strong Democrat, Not So Strong Democrat, Independent-Leaning to the Democrats, Independent, Independent-Leaning to the Republicans, No So Strong Republican, and Strong Republican) to characterize their partisan identification at the time they first voted. The voters then referred to the same seven-point scale to describe their party preferences at the present time. The responses to these questions led to the construction of two new variables: a simple measure of partisan change or partisan stability; and a more complex measure of stability to assess realignment (change from one party to another or change from an independent identification to a partisan self-classification) and dealignment (change from a partisan identification to an independent status).

Political scientists usually define split-ticket voting in terms of a split result between the votes for candidates for president and the House of Representatives (DeVries and Tarrance, 1972). However, Feigert (1979) notes that most studies of ticket splitting suffer from two basic flaws: (1) their reliance on aggregate data, which cannot directly show if split outcomes actually result from individual voters splitting their tickets and (2) their inability to take into account the almost inevitable drop-off in the number of votes cast for president and for U.S. Representative.

The present study addresses both of these problems. First, although aggregate data are used to assess the magnitude of split-ticket voting in Tennessee, the respondents' own reports of how they voted in the 1984 election serve as the primary indicator of split-ticket voting. Second, to minimize the drop-off problem the analysis focuses on the contests for president and for United States senator. The survey instrument asked the respondents to identify the candidates they voted for in the 1984 presidential contest between Walter Mondale and Ronald Reagan and the senatorial contest between Republican Victor Ashe, Democrat Albert Gore, Jr., and independent Ed McAteer, a conservative Republican who failed to win his party's nomination. Votes for the following pairs of candidates were classified as split tickets: Reagan-Gore and Mondale-Ashe.

Overall Trends

Democratic party identifiers fell from 42% in 1981 to 32% in 1985. In contrast, Independent identifiers increased by 6% to 39% and self-identified Republicans rose from 25% to 29% (see table 6.1). In the March 1985 poll, Independents outnumbered Democrats, while Democrats comprised a plurality of all respondents in 1981. These findings fit with the results of other polls. For example, ABC's 1984 Election Day exit poll found 37% of Tennessee's voters called themselves Democrats, 30% Independents and 29% said they were Republicans; the remainder identified with some other party or refused to answer (ABC News Poll, 1984). Another study, based on an aggregation of 1,489 Tennessee respondents included in CBS News-*New York Times* polls conducted between 1974 and 1982, estimated that 38% of the Volunteer State's "active electorate" were Democrats, 34% called themselves independents, and 24% identified with the Republican party; the balance

Table 6.1
Tennessee Party Identification by Demographic Characteristics and Ideology, 1981 and 1985

Party Identification*

Demographic Characteristics	1981				1985			
	Democrat %	Independent %	Republican %	Total Responses % (n)	Democrat %	Independent %	Republican %	Total Responses % (n)
Total	42	33	25	100 (422)	32	39	29	100 (606)
Sex:								
Male	42	34	24	100 (202)	32	40	28	100 (291)
Female	42	31	27	100 (219)	32	39	28	100 (313)
	$\chi^2 = .65$ df = 2 p = ns				$\chi^2 = .02$ df = 2 p = ns			
Race:								
White	39	33	28	100 (373)	28	41	31	100 (532)
Black	65	26	9	100 (46)	68	23	9	100 (66)
	$\chi^2 = 12.80$ df = 2 p < .01				$\chi^2 = 44$ df = 2 p < .001			
Region:**								
East	30	34	36	100 (117)	26	42	32	100 (256)
Middle	56	31	13	100 (127)	34	40	26	100 (187)
West	45	32	23	100 (117)	40	33	27	100 (143)
	$\chi^2 = 27.32$ df = 4 p < .001				$\chi^2 = 10.25$ df = 4 p < .05			
Income:								
Under $10,000	57	24	19	100 (117)	35	38	27	100 (93)

$10,000 to $20,000	38	41	21	100 (152)	41	36	23	100 (163)
Over $20,000	34	32	34	100 (152)	27	41	32	100 (291)
		$\chi^2 = 21.86$	df = 4	p < .001		$\chi^2 = 10.6$	df = 4	sig < .05
Ideology:								
Liberal	60	32	8	100 (38)	46	39	15	100 (117)
Moderate	42	38	20	100 (151)	36	44	20	100 (220)
Conservative	34	32	34	100 (167)	23	34	43	100 (240)
		$\chi^2 = 18.9$	df = 4	p < .001		$\chi^2 = 47.34$	df = 4	p < .001
Age:								
18 to 29	28	44	28	100 (109)	31	31	38	100 (126)
30 to 54	38	35	27	100 (176)	30	48	22	100 (283)
55 or above	60	19	21	100 (133)	37	32	31	100 (186)
		$\chi^2 = 29.11$	df = 4	p < .001		$\chi^2 = 21.06$	df = 4	p < .001
Education:								
Less than HS grad	54	21	25	100 (130)	29	36	35	100 (119)
High school grad	45	34	21	100 (147)	43	38	20	100 (221)
Some college and above	29	41	30	100 (143)	25	42	3	100 (263)
		$\chi^2 = 20.80$	df = 4	p < .001		$\chi^2 = 22.5$	df = 4	p < .001
Union:								
Union household	48	31	20	100 (93)	48	37	15	100 (118)
Non-union household	39	33	28	100 (316)	28	40	32	100 (484)
		$\chi^2 = 2.94$	df = 2	p = ns		$\chi^2 = 20.27$	df = 2	p < .001

Data computed from March 1981 survey and March 1985 survey

*Democratic and Republican classifications exclude Independent leaners
**The three historic Grand Divisions of Tennessee

refused to answer or didn't know their party identification (Wright, Erikson, and McIver, 1985). While the three sets of statistics were collected at different times, all three survey sources recognize that the Democratic party led the Republican party in partisan support.

The decline in Democratic party identifiers from 1981 to 1985 and the increase in self-identified Republicans initially seem to indicate a trend toward partisan realignment in Tennessee. However, the accompanying increase in the percentage of independents appears to signal partisan dealignment, rather than a major shift to the Republican party. This appears congruent with Beck's (1977) findings of a southern dealignment to the independent identification. Independents now outnumber Democrats in Tennessee, a traditionally Democratic state.

The Reagan Factor

At first glance, the 1980 and 1984 election victories of the Republican party's presidential candidate, Ronald Reagan, appear to reflect an erosion of Tennessee's Democratic party loyalties. However, one must note that Reagan (49%) defeated President Jimmy Carter (48%) in 1980 by less than 0.3% of the state's popular vote, with John Anderson garnering 3% of the ballots. Likewise, Reagan's strong 1984 win over Walter Mondale fell short of the percentage of ballots Democratic Senate candidate Albert Gore, Jr. received from Tennessee's voters.

In 1985 Reagan increased his Tennessee support from all the groups that gave him majority support in 1981. In particular, almost two-thirds of the men in the March 1985 survey and in ABC's 1984 Exit Poll stated they cast ballots for President Reagan. While Reagan captured a majority of Tennessee's female vote in both years, women provided him with slightly less support in 1984 than men, demonstrating that Reagan's "gender gap" existed in Tennessee as well as nationally.

A significant proportion of Tennessee white voters rejected the Democratic presidential candidate, Walter Mondale. The percentage of whites voting for President Reagan rose from 59% in 1980 to 68% in 1984. The ABC Exit Poll found similar white backing for Reagan (69%), but more solid black support (95%) for Mondale than the present study. ABC's Election Day Polls found that southern whites cast 87% of their ballots for Reagan, while southern blacks gave Mondale 90% of their votes. Although the March 1985 survey and ABC's Exit Polls indicate Reagan polarized southern voters along racial lines, it must be noted that in 1984 Tennessee whites gave Walter Mondale a greater percentage of their support than the South overall.

Young Tennessee voters climbed aboard President Reagan's campaign express; the president jumped from 53% to 65% support from adults between the ages eighteen to twenty-nine. Reagan also bolstered his thirty to fifty-four-year-old voter backing from 56% to 67%. Reagan did least well among older voters (57% support), who remained the most loyal Democratic age cohort.

Party Identification

Walter Mondale's pollster, Peter Hart (Hart and Wirthlin, 1985:26), declared after the presidential election that the "single most dramatic factor of 1984 was the movement in party ID." The study reported here examined the shift in Tennessee party identification between 1981 and 1985 among demographic subgroups and also found substantial changes. Men appeared to increasingly abandon (42% to 32%) their identification with the Democratic party (table 6.1). However, Tennessee males tended to shift their allegiance more to an independent self-classification, with a narrow plurality still favoring the Democratic party (32%) over the GOP (28%). The movement of Tennessee women from the Democratic party to an independent identification was even more pronounced (an 8-percentage-point increase in female independents), although they also favored the Democratic party (32%) over the Republican party (28%).

The Tennessee data underscore the sizable drop in white support for the Democratic party. In 1981 a plurality of white respondents identified with the Democratic party (39%); however, by 1985 only 28% of white voters called themselves Democrats. Tennessee white voters then preferred the Republican party (31%) over the Democratic party, with independents achieving a clear plurality (41%) over both partisan groups. Table 6.2 reveals that when independent leaners are grouped with partisans, whites comprise 35% of the Democratic and 45% of the Republican identifiers in the state.

The erosion of white backing for the Democratic party in Tennessee follows a regional trend. A *Los Angeles Times* 1984 Election Day Exit Poll found 37% of white southerners calling themselves Republicans, with only 23% identifying with the Democrats. But although white Tennesseans may be loosening their historic partisan attachments, they appear reluctant to take the more dramatic step of calling themselves Republicans. Thus, the key question centers on whether this exodus of Tennessee and southern white voters from the Democratic camp truly represents a realignment to the Republican party, as some analysts and pundits suggest, or a dealignment from both parties.

Table 6.2

Party Identification of White and Black Tennesseans, 1985*

Affiliation	Total Sample	Whites	Blacks
Strong Democrats	20%	16%	52%
Weak Democrats	12	12	17
Independent–Leaning Democrat	7	7	8
Independent	20	20	14
Independent–Leaning Republican	12	14	1
Weak Republicans	11	12	4
Strong Republicans	18	19	4
	100%	100%	100%

$\chi^2 = 56.6$ df = 6 sig. at .000

*Data compiled from March 1985 survey of 620 Tennessee voters.

The proportion of young Tennessee voters identifying with the Republican party increased by 10 percentage points between 1981 and 1985. While the 1981 survey found young Tennesseans equally divided between the parties, with 44% calling themselves independents, by 1985 the Republicans achieved a plurality (38%) over both Democratic (31%) and independent (31%) identifiers. This shift occurred mostly at the expense of independents, as the percentage of young people describing themselves as Democrats also increased slightly.

A regression analysis sought to pinpoint the determinants of the Tennessee respondents' 1985 party identification. The final model, which consisted of seven variables, explained 50% of the variance in party identification.[2] The most important factor was a respondent's presidential vote in the 1984 general election. This finding conforms to several studies that highlight Reagan's personal popularity as an important catalyst for the possible 1984 realignment to the Republican party; this evidence also suggest that some people shift their party identification to match their presidential vote (Lipset, 1985). The Republican party's image among the 1984 Tennessee voters as the party most likely to help people like themselves and the perception of the GOP as the party of prosperity also helped explain the respondents' party identification.

Long-Term Partisan Shifts

The March 1985 survey asked the Tennessee respondents to state their partisan identification in the first election they voted and then declare their current party identification. A larger number of respondents indicated they dealigned their partisan identification to an independent self-classification (14%) or realigned to become Republicans (10%), than realigned to the Democratic party (4%). However, when one combines the percentage of realigners to both parties (14%), the proportion of total partisan realignment among Tennessee voters equaled dealignment to the independent classification. Almost three-fourths of those respondents dealigning to an independent identification formerly called themselves Democrats; half of the new Republican identifiers realigned from the Democratic party and half formerly considered themselves independents. On balance, the Democrats lost the most support through realignment and dealignment.

These data suggest that in Tennessee more partisan dealignment to the independent self-identification has occurred than realignment to either the Republican or Democratic party respectively. The change in partisanship has developed largely at the expense of the Volunteer State's historic Democratic loyalties. Dealigning converts comprised 36% of all independent identifiers. Of the 172 Republicans in the sample, one-third had realigned to the GOP. In contrast, the Democrats gained only 12% through realignment.

The findings also underscore the movement of Tennessee white voters out of the Democratic column; 16% of the whites declared they had dealigned to the independent category while 10% said they realigned to the Republican party. Considerable partisan change occurred among persons earning over $20,000 and those with some college education; they appeared quite mobile, with a tendency to gravitate to an independent or Republican identification, with independent preferred. Conservatives, not surprisingly, found the greatest attraction in migrating to the Republican standard.

Ticket Splitting

DeVries and Tarrance (1972), among others, have called attention to the problems associated with relying on self-proclaimed partisan identification as an indicator of actual behavior in the voting booth. To assess the construct validity of our measure of partisan identification, we developed a simple additive index of partisan loyalty based on the respondents' reported votes in four recent statewide elections: the 1980 presidential election, the 1982 gubernatorial election, the 1984 presidential election, and the 1984 election for United States senator. The behaviorally strongest partisans should have voted for the candidates of their party in all four of the elections considered, while behaviorally weaker partisans should have defected in one or more contest.

The data displayed in table 6.3 indicate a relatively close fit between professed partisan identification and voting behavior for the 384 respondents who voted in each of the four contests. More than four-fifths (84%) of the Strong Democrats and three-fifths (60%) of the Strong Republicans voted for their party's candidates in at least three out of the four last statewide elections. Weak partisans proved somewhat more likely to have crossed party lines with 51% of the Not So Strong Democrats and 70% of the Not So Strong Republicans voting for at least two candidates from the opposition party.

A total of 1,701,926 voters cast ballots for either Ronald Reagan or Walter Mondale, while 1,557,623 Tennessee residents voted for either Victor Ashe or Albert Gore, Jr. The fall-off of 144,303 votes between the election for president and the election for United States senator represented a decline of 9% in the two-party vote for president. Five hundred and eighty-four respondents in the sample delivered their presidential ballots to either Reagan or Mondale, while 525 voted for either Ashe or Gore. The resulting fall-off of 59 votes between the two elections represented a loss of 10%, a proportion very close to the actual decline for the electorate at large.

The Tennessee election results suggest widespread ticket-splitting. However, any judgment about the presence or absence of ticket-splitting requires an examination of the voting patterns reported by individual members of the electorate. Five hundred and twenty-five

Table 6.3

Behavioral Party Identification by Professed Party Identification

Behavioral Party Identification	Professed Identification				
	Strong Democrat (%)	Not So Strong Democrat (%)	Independent (%)	Not So Strong Republican (%)	Republican (%)
4 Democratic votes	56.6	12.2	3.4	—	—
3 Democratic votes	27.6	36.7	17.4	5.4	2.7
2 Democratic votes	15.8	51.0	60.4	70.3	37.0
1 Democratic vote	—	—	18.8	24.3	60.3
Total Responses					
%	100.0%	100.0%	100.0%	100.0%	100.0%
(N)	(76)	(49)	(149)	(37)	(73)

respondents (85%) of the total sample cast ballots for either of the major party candidates in the 1984 election contest for president and for United States senator. Swansbrough (1985) used aggregate electoral data to estimate that 19% of Tennessee voters crossed party lines to elect Reagan and Gore. However, almost two-fifths (39%) of the respondents who voted in both elections reported that they voted for presidential and senatorial candidates from different parties, while slightly more than three-fifths (61%) said they voted a straight ticket. This confirms Feigert's (1979) caveat that aggregate data may mask the true extent of ticket splitting.

White voters proved almost twice as likely as black voters to have reported casting a split ballot. Although 41% of whites said they voted a split ticket, only 21% of the black respondents indicated that they had voted for a Republican and a Democrat. The data reveal a consistent relationship between income levels and the incidence of split-ticket voting among the respondents. The proportion of Tennesseans who split their votes increased from 24% of those with incomes below $10,000 to 39% of those with incomes between $10,000 and $20,000 and to 46% of those with incomes above $20,000. Voters age eighteen to twenty-nine (36%) and voters age fifty-five and older (31%) also proved significantly less likely to have split their tickets than did respondents in the thirty- to fifty-four-year-old age group (46%).

The data in table 6.4 show that respondents who identified with the Democratic party (21%) proved least likely to have split their tickets, followed by Republican identifiers (47%) and independents (50%). Not surprisingly, strong partisans of each party demonstrated greater resistance to dividing their ballots than did their not so strong fellow identifiers. Only among dealigners (voters who now viewed themselves as independents although they had previously identified themselves with one of the two major parties) did a majority (59%) of the respondents split their tickets. Realigners (42%) and voters whose partisan identification remained unchanged (35%) proved less likely to have split their ballots. Ideology emerged as the only political characteristic not significantly correlated with split-ticket voting.

Campbell and Miller (1957) found that southern voters who chose Stevenson in 1952 and 1956 almost always voted a straight Democratic ticket, while only one-third of the voters who selected Eisenhower voted a straight Republican ticket. Tennessee voters in 1984 followed the same general pattern. Only 6% of Mondale supporters failed to complete a straight ticket by casting a vote for Albert Gore, Jr. In contrast, well over one-half (60%) of those who voted for President

Table 6.4

Split Ticket Voting by Political Characteristics and 1984 Votes

Political Characteristics	Straight Ticket (%)	Split Ticket (%)	Total Responses (N) (%)	
Ideology:				
Liberal	64.9	35.1	(97)	100
Moderate	60.6	39.4	(198)	100
Conservative	57.9	42.1	(214)	100
	$\chi^2 = 1.38$ df = 2 ns			
Party Identification:				
Democrat	79.5	20.5	(171)	100
Independent	49.7	50.3	(197)	100
Republican	53.3	46.7	(150)	100
	$\chi^2 = 38.71$ df = 2 sig. at .001			
Partisan change:				
Realigned	58.0	42.0	(69)	100
Unchanged	64.8	35.2	(369)	100
Dealigned	41.3	58.7	(75)	100
	$\chi^2 = 14.52$ df = 2 sig. at .001			
1984 Presidential vote:				
Reagan	40.5	59.5	(328)	100
Mondale	94.4	5.6	(197)	100
	$\chi^2 = 147.54$ df = 1 sig. at .001			
1984 Senate vote:				
Ashe	95.0	5.0	(140)	100
Gore	50.3	49.7	(370)	100
	$\chi^2 = 84.85$ df = 1 sig. at .001			

Reagan split their tickets and failed to vote for Victor Ashe, the Republican candidate for United States Senate. When the respondents' votes for senator were treated as the independent variable, this pattern reversed itself. Only 5% of the Ashe supporters voted for Mondale while one-half of Gore's supporters marked their ballots for Reagan.

An Explanatory Model of Split-Ticket Voting

The study developed a step-wise regression model that incorporated eight variables to explain 34% of the variance in the type of ballot voted by the respondents. The voters' image of President Reagan emerged as the most powerful contributory factor, accounting for slightly more than 16% of the total variance. Respondents with positive images of President Reagan proved more likely to split their tickets.

According to Ladd and Hadley (1978) split-ticket-voting serves as a behavior measure of a voter's independent status. Similarly, Key (1966) and Boyd (1985) suggest that vote switching, voting for candidates of different parties in successive elections for the same position, also represents a form of independent voting. Consequently, STANDPAT, a variable assessing whether the respondents voted for presidential candidates of the same party in 1980 and 1984, was added to the regression equation and resulted in a 7% gain in explanatory power. Voters who switched from either Carter to Reagan or from Reagan to Mondale also tended to have voted a split ballot in 1984. The voters' assessments of Albert Gore, Jr., also contributed to the regression equation's explanatory power, explaining an additional 3% of the total variance. The other variables entered into the equation included scores on the Democratic party Image Index, income, confidence in the Republican party, support for government efforts to assist blacks and other minorities, and the perception that the Republicans favored increased defense spending. Variables considered but not entered into the final equation included race, sex, age, education, party identification (with Democrats, independents, and Republicans coded as dummy variables), ideology (with liberals, moderates, and conservatives coded as dummy variables), and party change (with realigners, dealigners, and those remaining with their original party coded as dummy variables).

CONCLUSIONS

This study reinforces the findings of other scholars about an exodus of particular voter groups from the Democratic electoral coalition to a new identification with the Republican party, most notably whites and young people. For many realigners to the Republican party, feelings that the Democratic party has become too committed to the interests of blacks and other minorities contributed to their conversion to the GOP (Swansbrough and Brodsky, 1987). The most loyal Democrats remain Tennessee blacks, who have evolved into the backbone of today's Democratic party. Union households also comprise a critical element of the Democratic coalition, but despite their professional identification with the Democratic party, a majority defected to vote for President Reagan.

The Tennessee analysis found that dealignment and realignment were occurring simultaneously; the combined realignment to the Republican party (10%) and to the Democratic party (4%) equaled the proportion of the Volunteer State's voters who dealigned to become independents (14%). The Democratic party's traditional prominence in Tennessee, as well as the South, appears to be gradually eroding, but the Republican party fails to attract all these Democratic defectors. Instead, a plurality of Tennesseans now call themselves independents. The authors agree with Hopkins, Lyons, and Metcalf (1986:224) that the 1984 election did not herald a general partisan realignment in Tennessee or a permanent resurgence of the Democrats.

This finding of reduced partisan loyalty reveals the growing influence of such short-term factors as the personalities of candidates on voters' preferences. The 1984 ticket splitting between the Republican presidential candidate, Ronald Reagan, and the Democratic Senate nominee, Albert Gore, Jr., manifested the increasing unpredictability of the Tennessee electorate. Traditional regional partisan loyalties and party identification in Tennessee appear less robust as predictors of voting behavior. Voters increasingly defect not only from their historic Democratic loyalties in West and Middle Tennessee, but also desert GOP candidates in the eastern region. The Volunteer State's citizens respond to the televised images of candidates and react to local issues, not simply partisan labels.

Democratic and Republican strategists must increasingly target the volatile but crucial independents and ticket-splitting partisan voters to achieve electoral victories, particularly in statewide races for president, governor, or U.S. senator. At the courthouse and statehouse level, traditional party loyalties appear to retain much of their strength, clearly benefiting Democratic candidates.

The Democratic party's resilience stems largely from its image as the party of the average person and the unwavering support of black Democrats (Swansbrough and Brodsky, 1987). Furthermore, many independents view the Democrats as the party most willing to help them. While the apparent success of Reagan's economic program has embellished the GOP's image, the Republican party still suffers from a public perception of it as the party of the rich and of big business. Ronald Reagan's personal popularity and the perceived success of his economic programs contributed greatly to the GOP's increased party identification figures.

Although the Tennessee Republican party emerged as a serious competitor in the late 1960s, the electoral tide shifted by 1986 to again give the Democrats control over the state legislature, the governor's mansion, and the congressional delegations. The 1986 ABC News Exit Poll revealed that the Democratic party regained many of its former party identifiers, apparently with many independents returning to their traditional party. Almost half (47%) of Tennessee's 1986 voters called themselves Democrats, about a third (32%) self-identified as Republicans and the independent classification fell to 21%. The key issue for the GOP in future elections centers around whether they can retain their new Republican identifiers and attract independents without President Reagan heading the ballot. The volatility of partisan dealignment, rather than realignment, thus appears to best describe Tennessee's political life in the mid-1980s.

The Democrats face the challenge of attracting white southerners back to the party banner. The presidential candidacy of popular Tennessee Senator Albert Gore, Jr., certainly appeals to both white and black voters in the state. His presence on the 1988 national Democratic ticket, or that of another southern Democrat, would help keep Democrats faithful to their party while attracting many of the state's Independent voters. But although the Democrats now seem ascendent, they will need strong candidates and favorable issues to maintain their recent electoral dominance in Tennessee. Neither party can take the Tennessee voter for granted.

NOTES

1. A Democratic caucus challenge to the leadership of Senator John Wilder required a coalition of Democratic and Republican senators to reelect Wilder Speaker of the Senate and lieutenant governor.

2. The standardized regression coefficients (beta) for the seven variables follow: Presidential vote 1984 (.35**), Republican party is more likely to help people like you (.19***), Democratic party is more likely to help people like you (.11*), Republican party is more likely to keep the country prosperous (.12**), Republican party is more likely to get the country into war (.10**), Region of Tennessee residence (-.08*), Union household (.08*). Notations represent significance at the * .05 level, ** .01 level, and *** .001 level.

7

POLITICAL CHANGE IN
NORTH CAROLINA

Jack D. Fleer, Roger C. Lowery, and Charles L. Prysby

During the first two-thirds of the twentieth-century political party competition in North Carolina was clearly and regularly dominated by the Democratic party. Democratic candidates generally received two-thirds of the vote regardless of the office considered. The Republican party provided a modest but certain opposition based on the western region of the state. Analysts classified North Carolina as a modified one-party state (Key, 1949; Jacob and Vines, 1976), recognizing the considerable strength of the Democratic party and the persistent presence but relative weakness of the Republican party. Key (1949: 222) concluded: "The Republican party is strong enough to give North Carolina many earmarks of a two-party state yet not strong enough to threaten Democratic supremacy."

In statewide contests for federal and state offices, the strong support of voters for Democratic candidates was consistently assured throughout the first half of the century. Democratic dominance in presidential elections was interrupted only in 1928, when Al Smith faced intraparty divisions and failed to attract a majority of North Carolina voters. From 1900 (in gubernatorial elections) and 1914 (in U.S. senatorial elections) until 1960, Democratic candidates regularly received approximately two out of every three votes cast. Democratic solidarity was also present in elections to other offices including U.S. House of Representatives and state legislature (Fleer, 1968: chap. 5).

Democratic solidarity in North Carolina began to weaken for different offices at different times (see figure 7.1). In national presidential elections Republican party candidates became competitive beginning in 1952, when Dwight Eisenhower received 46 percent of the vote. The 1956 and 1960 presidential elections were also competitive, but a Republican candidate did not win a plurality of the state's votes until 1968, when American Independent party candidate George Wallace split the state's voters and allowed Richard Nixon to win with 40 percent. By 1972, with an avowed liberal Democratic candidate and an incumbent Republican running, a majority of North Carolinians cast

94

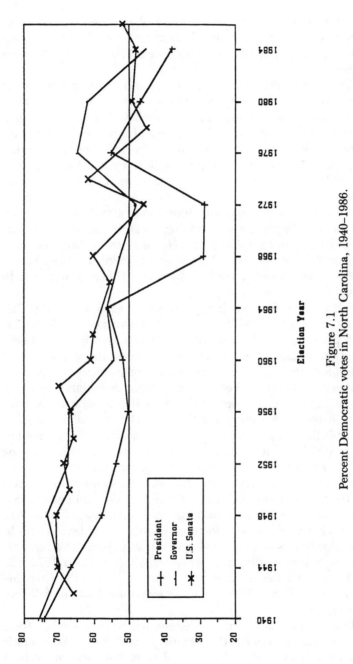

Figure 7.1

Percent Democratic votes in North Carolina, 1940–1986.

Source: North Carolina State Board of Elections, appropriate years.

their votes for the GOP standard bearer. In the five presidential elections from 1968 through 1984, Republicans have won four times, failing only when southerner Jimmy Carter headed the Democratic ticket (Fleer, 1986).

Republican competitiveness began to take hold in gubernatorial politics in 1960, and the party reaped the rewards of its new status with the 1972 and the 1984 victories of James Holshouser and James Martin, respectively. Both Republican candidates benefited from a divided state Democratic party, the simultaneous reelection bid of a Republican president, and a hard-fought U.S. Senate race. But the success of the historically minority party is due to more than short-term circumstances.

In 1972 former Democrat Jesse Helms won a seat in the United States Senate as a Republican, beginning a major change in the fortunes of the two parties for that office. Helms since has been reelected twice, and another Republican, John East, captured the other Senate seat in 1980. Recent Senate races have been very closely contested with Republicans winning four of six contests.

The relative party fortunes have changed in contests for the U.S. House of Representatives. While statewide figures mask significant differences in party competitiveness among districts, they do indicate declining support for Democratic congressional candidates similar to that which exists for other major offices. Several congressional districts remain relatively "safe" for either the Democratic or Republican party. Others have become quite competitive even if the same party wins repeatedly. Republican victory for the U.S. House first occurred in 1952. By 1985 the delegation stood at six Democrats and five Republicans, the largest Republican delegation from the state in the century. However in 1986, Democrats regained two House seats.

A lower level of Republican success has existed in contests for the two houses of the state General Assembly, although it should be noted that Republican candidates have received a greater percentage of votes than of seats. Even here, Democratic dominance has been eroded, as Republicans have slowly increased their victories in state legislative contests. Improvement began in the mid-1960s, reaching peaks in 1972 and again in 1984 when Republicans won 50 of the 170 seats. Creeping Republicanism is a fact of life even in this remaining bastion of Democratic dominance.

Republican success on the statewide level has been best when there have been divisions within the Democratic party, a liberal Democratic presidential candidate on the ballot, and races hard fought by both parties. Since 1972 presidential elections have been favorable to Republicans, while U.S. Senate races have been quite competitive though more often won by Republicans. In contrast gubernatorial contests usually have begun with a Democratic advantage although Republicans wound up winning two of the last four contests. In the politics of the U.S. House and North Carolina General Assembly, a Democratic advantage remains but with pockets of strong and durable Republican support.

Changes in the relative fortunes of the Democratic and Republican parties in winning major offices have been accompanied by changes in party identifications of voters. Table 7.1 provides data on party identification over the past two decades. Democratic party identification has declined, while Republican party identification has increased, although Democratic identifiers of all types remain the largest segment of the electorate. Perhaps surprisingly, the data show independence among North Carolinians has not grown. The portions of the electorate identifying as strong partisans, weak partisans, independent leaners, and independents are identical in the two surveys.

SOCIAL SOURCES OF INCREASED REPUBLICAN SUPPORT

Sources of Support: The Politics of Race

Analyses of the social bases of southern politics usually start with a consideration of the impact of race (Strong, 1971; Gatlin, 1975; Prysby,

Table 7.1

Party Identification in North Carolina, 1968 and 1986

Party Identification Category	Percent of Respondents	
	1968	1986
Strong Democrat	35	29
Weak Democrat	25	22
Independent Democrat	8	7
Independent	5	5
Independent Republican	6	7
Weak Republican	10	13
Strong Republican	11	17
	100	100
	(N = 718)	(N = 530)

Note: Respondents not expressing a party identification excluded.

Sources: Camparative State Elections Project Survey, 1968, and Carolina Poll data, 1986.

1980; Sundquist, 1983). Table 7.2 illustrates why that also should be the case in examining North Carolina politics. Race is strongly correlated with both party identification and vote choice. While black North Carolinians are overwhelmingly Democratic in both identification and voting, white North Carolinians are much more closely divided in party identification and vote choice. In this and other tables, we have drawn on the statewide Carolina Polls conducted by the School of Journalism at the University of North Carolina at Chapel Hill. These polls are uneven in their coverage. Questions generally were limited to presidential and senatorial races. None of the surveys asked about U.S. House races, for example. Fortunately, the U.S. Senate races in the state have been crucial contests that tell us much about electoral patterns. Consistency over time is lacking as well. Even party identification was not asked in all surveys, and when it was asked the item varied, being a three-, five-, or seven-point scale. Occupation also was not regularly ascertained.

In North Carolina, as in other southern states, voter registration increased significantly among the black population after the implementation of the Voting Rights Act of 1965. Unfortunately, we do not have a complete picture of this change because statewide data on voter registration were not compiled until 1968. Between 1968 and 1986, black voter registration almost doubled, from just over 300,000 to just under 600,000. However, during the same period, white voter registration increased from 1.7 million to 2.5 million. The resulting increase of blacks as a proportion of the total electorate was modest, from about one out of seven to one out of five.

The effects of region, class, age, and gender in structuring partisan loyalties among white North Carolinians are not nearly as strong or consistent as those of race. This is especially true if we examine white voters only, in order to eliminate the confounding influences of race. However, further examination of the data reveals some social bases of Republican support among white North Carolinians that are both significant and changing.

Sources of Support: Regional Politics

The geographical bases of Democratic and Republican party support are changing. The long-standing stronghold of the Republican party in North Carolina has been the western mountains (Key, 1949), which had the fewest slaves and were least dependent on a plantation economy. Mountain Republicanism enabled the minority party to have a dependable source of support for a wide variety of offices during most

Table 7.2

Partisanship among North Carolina Registered Voters by Race, 1982–1986
(in percent)

Date	Party Identification[a]										U.S. Senate Vote Intention[b]										
	White			Black			Total				White			Black			Total			
	Dem	Ind	Rep	Dem	Ind	Rep	Dem	Ind	Rep	(gamma)	Dem	Und	Rep	Dem	Und	Rep	Dem	Und	Rep	(gamma)
Oct' 82	45	26	29	79	18	3	49	27	24	−65*	47	11	42	72	11	17	51	11	38	−48*
Feb' 83	48	24	28	88	5	7	53	24	23	−73*	48	11	40	83	8	9	54	11	35	−66*
Feb' 84	45	19	36	82	11	8	51	19	30	−67*	38	7	55	90	4	6	47	7	46	−86*
Feb' 86	41	23	36	84	14	2	45	28	27	−78*	39	14	47	68	20	13	45	15	40	−55*
Oct' 86	46	19	35	80	14	6	48	24	28	−65*	44	6	50	78	6	16	50	6	44	−62*
Average	45	22	33	83	12	5	49	24	27		43	10	47	78	10	12	49	10	41	

[a]Ind. = all independent identifiers, including "learners."

[b]Und. = undecided, won't say, no answer. 1982–84 vote-intention data are for the Helms-Hunt election in 1984; 1986 vote-intention data are for the Broyhill-Sanford contest in 1986.

*P < .01

Source: Carolina Poll data, 1982–1986

of the twentieth century. Municipal, county, congressional, and state
legislative elections were won frequently by Republican candidates in
the mountains. The vitality and success of this base led Key (1949: 283)
to state that "(t)he strongest Republican state organization in the South
is that of North Carolina."

The eastern coastal plain tended to be the major sectional base of
Democratic strength. This region, essentially rural with a large black
population, consistently and dependably supported Democratic candidates. Not until the 1960s, as civil rights became a major issue and a
source of tension within the Democratic party and as black voting
rights became a regional and national issue, did this region begin to
change its pattern of voting for Democratic candidates at all levels of
the ballot. And even today, in municipal, county, state legislative, and
congressional elections, the Democrats are favored in the east.

Just as the timing of initial Republican victories varies by office, so
do the geographical bases of support. The most significant change has
occurred in presidential and U.S. Senate politics. As indicated by table
7.3, Republican candidates in the elections from 1972 through 1986
have received a disproportionate proportion of the vote from the mountains and the nonurban piedmont. The regional disparities are consistently larger for the office of governor. Recently, the piedmont has been
slightly more Republican than the mountains. Republican candidates
for each of the three major offices do least well in the coastal plain of
eastern North Carolina.

However, the Democratic advantage in eastern North Carolina has
been less in contests when Jesse Helms was a candidate (1972, 1978,
1984). Helms has been unusually attractive among voters in the coastal
plain in part due to his prior exposure on the Tobacco Network as a
radio and television commentator and in part due to his conservative
political philosophy (Snider, 1985). This support has led some observers
to refer to "Jessecrats," persons who normally vote Democratic except
when Jesse Helms is on the ballot.

While retaining its support in the mountains, the Republican party
has received increased support in the western and nonurban piedmont
and improved its standing in a growing number of eastern coastal
counties. While Democratic candidates have retained an advantage in
the coastal plain, the size of their margin in that region has been reduced. The competitiveness in the urban piedmont between the two
parties is striking. Overall, regional support differs less among the parties now than in earlier periods. The transformation of politics in the
state is made abundantly clear through this examination of the geo-

graphical bases of support for major party candidates for national and state offices.

The data in table 7.3 are aggregate vote totals, and some of the patterns may reflect the fact that blacks are unevenly divided across the regions of North Carolina (percentage of registrants who are black in each region: coastal plain, 28; urban piedmont, 22; nonurban piedmont, 14; and mountains, 3). Thus, it is useful to control for the effects of race when examining the relationship of region to partisan choice. Carolina Poll survey data reveal regional variations in partisanship among white North Carolinians. Among whites, the coastal plain averaged the highest margin of Democratic-to-Republican identifiers (49% to 28%). This region also reported the largest shift in white voter choice between the 1984 and 1986 U.S. Senate elections, from a 65% majority for Helms over Hunt to a 48% plurality for Sanford over

Table 7.3
Democratic Percent by Office and Region, 1972–1986

Office	Coastal Plain	Nonurban Piedmont	Urban Piedmont	Mountains	State Totals
President:					
1972	29	28	31	31	29
1976	61	55	51	53	55
1980	54	46	49	47	49*
1984	42	34	40	37	38
Governor:					
1972	58	45	47	45	48
1976	76	60	62	59	65
1980	68	57	67	56	62
1984	53	42	43	45	45
U.S. Senator:					
1972	47	43	50	47	46
1974	76	59	60	58	62
1978	47	45	44	47	45
1980	56	46	51	48	49
1984	51	43	53	47	48
1986	60	46	53	49	52

*Two-party percentage

Regions: Mountains, 17 counties; Urban Piedmont, 5 counties; Nonurban Piedmont, 37 counties; Coastal Plain, 41 counties.

Source: Data compiled by authors.

Broyhill (data are from preelection surveys, so there are some undecided voters). The whites in the urban piedmont shifted in the opposite
direction, from a 48% plurality for Hunt in 1984 to a 54% majority for
Broyhill in 1986. Nonurban piedmont whites were the most consistent
in their Republican vote preferences, in each of the five polls giving a
plurality or majority of their support to Helms or Broyhill. Party vote
choices were the most evenly balanced among whites in the mountain
region.

Geographical patterns also illustrate a basic dilemma facing the Republican party in the state and nation: the choice between the moderate and far-right wings of the party. In contemporary North Carolina,
this choice is between the Jesse Helms faction and the traditional party
organization headed by Governor Jim Martin and exemplified by
former U.S. Representative and Senator Jim Broyhill. Further compli-
cating the ideological and tactical differences between these two Republican factions are the regional differences in their bases of electoral
support. In the spring Carolina Poll preceding Helms's 1984 Senate
race, his strongest support among whites came from the coastal plain
while his poorest showing was in the urban piedmont. In the Carolina
Poll preceding Broyhill's 1986 race, his regional support among whites
reversed the pattern. Helms's strength is in the region that averages the
highest proportion of white Democratic party identifiers; thus, his attraction to Jessecrats carries great potential for erosion of that party's
traditional stronghold. However, the Martin-Broyhill wing of the Republican party, relative to the Helms wing, is much stronger among the
white voters living in the urban Piedmont, the more rapidly growing
and economically vital core of the state.

Sources of Support: Class Politics

The relevance of class polarization to southern politics has been suggested by a number of studies (Gatlin, 1975; Ladd, 1978; Lamis,
1984). In North Carolina, the Republican party's first and continuing
successes in congressional elections in the Charlotte area in the 1950s
underscored the importance of the growth of the urban middle class.
However the rise of the rural blue-collar Jessecrat vote in the coastal
plain in the 1970s indicated a new pattern of class voting.

Because of the strong interrelationship among class, race, and voting, it is necessary to examine white voters separately. Class polarization of partisan loyalty among white North Carolina voters is not
strong, clear-cut, or consistent across different class measures. Class
differences measured by income give one set of results; class differences

measured by education offer dissimilar patterns (table 7.4). In both cases, correlation coefficients are generally small and unstable indicating weak relationships between class and partisanship. A small but consistent polarization of two income groups (dichotomization of responses into those above and below the $20,000 level) is apparent in both party identification and U.S. Senate vote choice. Whites with more income were somewhat more likely to identify with and vote for the Republican party. The shrinking of this already small income polarization in the Helms-Hunt Senate matchup is probably explained by the defection of lower-income Jessecrats from the Democratic party, not evident two years later in the Broyhill-Sanford Senate race. In the spring 1984 survey, Helms outpolled Hunt 52% to 39% among lower-income whites, while in the fall 1986 survey, Sanford drew 51% to Broyhill's 43% among the same voters.

Table 7.4

Social Correlates[a] of Partisanship[b] among White North Carolina Registered Voters,
1982–1986
(cell entries are gammas)

Date	Income		Education		Age		Gender	
	PI	SV	PI	SV	PI	SV	PI	SV
Fall 82	−.06	.05	−.04	−.12	.35*	.13	−.15	−.23*
Spring 83	.17	.18*	.27*	.01	.15	−.04	−.20	−.12
Spring 84	.17*	.04	−.05	−.12	.27*	−.08	−.06	−.20*
Spring 86	.09	.15*	.03	.01	.39*	.14	−.20*	−.13
Fall 86	.27*	.21	.08	−.01	.37*	.25*	−.01	−.12

[a]Income, education, and age were dichotomized in order to maximize the number of white respondents in each subgroup.

Income = total family income before taxes in the preceding year, dichotomized at $20,000.

Education = years of formal education dichotomized at noncollege and college.

Age = year respondent turned 18 dichotomized at 1945.

[b]PI = party identification on a 3-point scale (Dem. Ind. Rep.)

SV = vote intention in US Senate election on a 3-point scale (Dem. Und. Rep.); 1982–84 vote-intention data are for the Helms-Hunt election in 1984. 1986 vote-intention data are for the Broyhill-Sanford election in 1986.

*P < .05

Source: Carolina Poll data, 1982–1986.

Sources of Support: Generational Replacement

A number of observers report or predict Republican success in appealing to younger white voters (Beck, 1977; Campbell, 1977). If this is accurate, the Democratic party will be hurt by the aging and eventual replacement of the New Deal generation. An analysis of the mean age of party identifiers among North Carolina's white electorate supports this prediction. Across the five Carolina Polls reported, the Democratic (but not Republican or independent) identifiers reported a steadily increasing average age. By 1986 the average age of white Democratic respondents (54) was significantly higher than that of white Republicans (46). Additional analysis reveals that in each of the five polls, those whites who turned 18 prior to 1946 are more likely to be Democratic identifiers, while younger whites more often express Republican identifications.

Age differences in vote choice are not so clear-cut. While younger whites are more likely than their elders to *identify* as Republicans, they are not consistently more likely to *vote* that way (table 7.4). Age differences were missing in the Helms-Hunt 1984 race but were significantly present in the Broyhill-Sanford contest two years later. Broyhill probably did worse among the older voters, compared to Helms, for largely the same reason that Broyhill did worse among the noncollege-educated and coastal plain whites compared to Helms—i.e., Broyhill's inability to attract the Jessecrat vote.

While Helms won in 1984 and Broyhill lost in 1986, to the extent that the moderate wing of the Republican party continues to better appeal to the young, upwardly mobile, urban, professional generation, so will that moderate faction improve its electoral fortunes as that younger generation of voters replaces the aging, blue-collar, rural conservatives that constitute the core of the Helms wing. However, this strategy will be successful for the Republican party as a whole only if those younger voters become and remain loyal Republican voters, a characteristic that they did not exhibit in the five Carolina Polls analyzed.

Sources of Support: The Gender Gap

Some research in the 1970s reported evidence of strong gender effects among party activists and leaders (McGrath and Soule, 1974; Margolis, 1979). However, analysts in the 1980s disagree over the potential of women's issues to generate significant patterns of political behavior in the larger American electorate. (Poole and Zeigler, 1985; Darcey et al., 1987).

The evidence from North Carolina is that gender differences are weak in structuring party identification among whites but do have a somewhat stronger and more consistent effect on vote choice (table 7.4). Across the 1980s, white females were only slightly more likely than males to identify with the Democratic party, but white females were more likely than males to favor Democrats in the polls prior to the 1984 and 1986 U.S. Senate elections. Gender differences were especially large in the 1984 Hunt-Helms contest. In the Sanford-Broyhill contest, gender differences in vote choice were considerably weaker.

In summary the sources of support for increased Republican success vary. The racial base of Democratic and Republican support is clear. Beyond racial differences, there are modest class and regional differences in party support among whites. Age and gender differences are less clear. Additionally, the two wings of the Republican party differ in their bases of support.

ATTITUDINAL SOURCES OF PARTISAN CHOICE

Republicans and Democrats are more sharply differentiated in their political attitudes than in their social characteristics. Two basic attitudinal sources of partisan choice can be examined: (a) retrospective evaluations of governmental performance; and (b) orientations on specific issues of public policy. Both may be important in explaining increased Republican voting in North Carolina. One hypothesis is that increased Republican voting during the 1980s resulted from a combination of unfavorable evaluations of government performance during the Carter administration and favorable assessments under the Reagan administration. Another explanation is that the increased Republican support resulted from conservative voters becoming increasingly disenchanted with the issue positions of Democrats and/or pleased with Republican positions.

The available data do not permit a thorough testing of both hypotheses. We can, however, piece together information from a variety of surveys in order to provide a picture of the North Carolina electorate's political attitudes.

Retrospective Evaluation and the Vote

The importance of retrospective evaluations as an influence on the vote has received considerable recent emphasis (Fiorina, 1981). The effects of such evaluations on partisan choice in North Carolina can be examined by focusing on vote intentions in the 1984 senatorial election from 1981 through 1984. The polls also measured ratings of Reagan's job performance (in terms of excellent, good, fair, or poor). If retrospective evaluations play a significant role in determining the partisan direction of the vote, then: (a) there should be a strong connection between senatorial vote intention and presidential job rating at each point in time; and (b) as the overall rating of Reagan's performance rises or falls, support for Helms likewise should change. The relevant data are in table 7.5 and show support for both expectations. As Reagan's job rating declined and then increased, support for Helms over Hunt similarly fell and rose. The pattern is not identical in both cases—the low point for Helms was the spring of 1983, whereas for Reagan it was the fall of 1982—but the general shape of the curve is similar. And in each year there is a strong relationship between the two items, with the gammas ranging from .50 to .71. Moreover, the strong association between the two items is not simply due to their both being connected to party identification. Even if Republican and Democratic identifiers are examined separately, support for Helms and assessment of Reagan's performance remain strongly related.

Issues and the Vote

While retrospective evaluations about government performance, espe-

Table 7.5

Senate Election Vote Intentions and Reagan Job Ratings, 1981–1984

Survey Date	(A) % for Helms	(B) % with favorable Reagan job rating	relationship between A and B (gamma)
Spring 1984	49	63	.65*
Fall 1983	39	57	.64*
Spring 1983	37	48	.55*
Fall 1982	41	47	.50*
Spring 1982	39	49	.71*
Fall 1981	45	63	.66*

Entries in the first column are the percent of respondents who preferred Helms over Hunt for the U.S. Senate (respondents not expressing a preference for either candidate are excluded from the analysis). Entries in the second column are the percent of respondents who gave Reagan an excellent or good job rating (respondents not expressing a rating are excluded from the analysis). Entries in the third column are gammas for the association between senatorial candidate preferrence and Reagan job rating.

Source: Carolina Poll data, 1981–1984.

cially concerning the economy, are important, orientations on issues of public policy also are related to partisan choice. In fact, there is good reason to believe that issue voting is greater in the post-civil-rights period of southern politics than in previous periods (Nie et al., 1979). Table 7.6 presents the relationships among a variety of issue items and three different measures of partisanship across some polls.

In every case where we have data, individuals with more conservative issue positions were more likely to express a Republican preference. However, the relationships are extremely weak in a number of cases. In some cases, the weak association (e.g., the balanced budget item asked in the spring of 1984) extends across all three measures of partisanship.

Table 7.6

Issue Positions and Partisanship, 1981–1984

Issue	1984 President Vote	1984 Senate Vote	Party I.D.
Economic Issues:			
Social security (spring 1984)	.45*	.07	.23*
Tax increase for schools (spring 1984)	.09	.26*	.09
Balanced budget (spring 1984)	.03	.04	.04
Budget cuts (fall 1981)	n.a.	.60*	n.a.
Social issues:			
Abortion (spring 1984)	.09	.17*	.06
Abortion (fall 1982)	n.a.	.20*	n.a.
School prayer (fall 1982)	n.a.	.41*	n.a.
Women's rights (spring 1984)	.23*	.27*	.07
Death penalty (spring 1984)	.53*	.49*	.32*
Gun control (fall 1981)	n.a.	.42*	n.a.
Civil Rights issues:			
School integration (spring 1984)	.16*	.45*	.08*
King holiday (spring 1984)	.54*	.62*	.26*
Foreign and defense issues:			
Nuclear freeze (fall 1982)	n.a.	.19*	n.a.
Defense budget (fall 1981)	n.a.	.45*	n.a.

Entries are gammas for the association between the specified issue and the measure of partisanship. A positive gamma indicates that a more conservative position is associated with a Republican preference. An "n.a." indicates that the relationship could not be ascertained due to the absence of data.

*$p < .05$

Source: Carolina Poll data, 1981–1984

In other cases, the association (e.g., the abortion item asked in the spring of 1984) varies considerably in strength, depending on the measure of partisanship. These observations suggest that while Republican voters tend to be more conservative than Democratic voters, the differences often are not that great and what deeply divides voters varies across elections. Also, issue orientations are more strongly related to vote intention than to party identification, which is consistent with the exception that Republican candidates tend to draw votes from more conservative Democrats identifiers.

Issue versus Retrospective Voting

In sum, both retrospective evaluations and issue orientations affect partisan choice. However, retrospective evaluations are much more volatile and thus have a greater effect on short-term vote changes. Ideological orientations are less likely to shift dramatically in the short run and thus are less crucial in producing electoral swings. Republican candidates will receive votes disproportionately from more conservative voters, regardless of whether these candidates receive 40 percent or 60 percent of the total vote. Whether Republican candidates win or lose, however, will depend very much on the nature of voter evaluations of government performance.

On a broader note, the nature of future evaluations of government performance may determine what future party realignment or dealignment occurs. During the first six years of the Reagan administration, evaluations generally were quite positive, particularly in comparison to the final two years of the Carter administration. If the remainder of the Reagan administration and subsequent Republican administrations display the same pattern, or if future Democratic administrations repeat the Carter performance, party loyalties are likely to shift toward the Republicans. But if a more mixed set of evaluations characterizes the next several years, the North Carolina electorate is likely to remain in its present condition. Future partisan alignments in North Carolina, then, may be affected as much by what happens nationally as by particular events and individuals within the state. The latter factors are important, of course, but they usually operate within parameters established by national forces, especially since state and national elections coincide in North Carolina.

REALIGNMENT VERSUS DEALIGNMENT

Two basic ideas about the changes in electoral patterns in North Carolina can be considered. One view is that a realignment is occurring, with voters shifting their partisan loyalties from the Democratic to the Republican party (Sundquist, 1983). To be sure, this realignment is not a critical realignment, marked by a fundamental, thorough, and rapid transformation of loyalties. Instead, it bears more similarities to what Key (1959) referred to as a secular realignment. But even though it may be gradual, incomplete, and even erratic, the cumulative impact is significant.

An alternative position is that dealignment is occurring. Voters, especially those who considered themselves Democrats, are becoming more detached from the parties (Beck, 1977). Generational replacement adds to the dealignment by bringing into the electorate younger voters, who feel little of the loyalty to the Democratic party that their parents did (Campbell, 1977). The result of this dealignment is an electorate that is more willing to vote Republican for specific reasons, but not one that is particularly loyal to the Republican party. It is a more volatile electorate, responsive much more to the short-term forces specific to an election than to general notions of partisanship (Wattenberg, 1984). Behaviorally, such an electorate should display substantial levels of ticket splitting, switching over time and defections from partisan loyalty.

The realignment and dealignment explanations are not mutually exclusive. Some of both may have occurred. The data previously presented in table 7.1 do not indicate any dealignment over the last twenty years, at least in terms of party identification. However, voting behavior may be less guided by party identification now than in the recent past, even if there is not a greater tendency to identify as an independent. This leads us to consider voting defections among party identifiers. In fact, voting defections among Democratic identifiers must play a significant role, as increases in Republican voting have outstripped increases in Republican identification.

Carolina Poll data on the voting intentions of Democratic and Republican identifiers in presidential and senatorial elections, can be examined, although it should be realized that the items dealt with voting intentions sometimes as much as two years before the actual election. While defections in intentions may differ from what ultimately occurs in the election, it seems legitimate to look at intentions as a measure of the willingness of voters to deviate from their stated partisan loyalties. Voting defection rates among Democrats appear especially great, ranging from 16% to 37%, with a mean of 24% (data not presented). Republican defection rates, by comparison, are somewhat lower. For each race, up to a third of the Republicans expressed an intention to vote for a Democratic candidate, with the mean figure across the seven polls being 20%. Overall, these data indicate substantial willingness on the part of party identifiers, including Republicans, to cast a ballot for a candidate of the other party, even for offices at the top of the ticket. Moreover, the partisan groups exclude independent leaners, and if they had been included in these calculations, the defection rates undoubtedly would be higher.

Another attribute of a dealigned electorate is substantial ticket splitting. Almost one-third of the 1984 electorate indicated an intention to vote for a mix for Democrats and Republicans for the top three statewide races (president, senator, governor). Moreover, this ballot splitting is not simply a matter of Democratic voters casting a ballot only for Reagan but not for other Republican candidates; less than one-fifth of the ticket splitters fell into this category. In 1980 a comparable proportion of the electorate cast split ballots. Just considering the top of the ballot reveals considerable change. If the entire ballot were considered, ticket splitting undoubtedly would have been far higher for both years.

Finally, we can look at the extent to which voters cross party lines over time. Carolina Poll data on voting for the U.S. Senate in 1984 and 1986 show that while there is a strong relationship between the two votes, as expected, considerable numbers of both Hunt and Helms voters changed the partisan direction of their votes when casting a ballot for Sanford or Broyhill. About one-fifth of the Helms voters in 1984 indicated they would vote for Sanford, and a similar proportion of Hunt voters indicated they would vote for Broyhill. While this is only one instance (data on other vote pairs were unavailable), it suggests that there is significant switching over time even for the same office in subsequent elections.

This brief look at defectors, ticket splitters, and switchers suggests that there is substantial dealignment of the electorate. Much of the Republican vote has come from voters who are not consistently loyal to the Republican party. Of course, the same is true for the Democratic party. A significant portion of the electorate cannot be counted on to vote for either party; rather, these voters respond to short-term forces associated with particular elections. But while dealignment characterizes the North Carolina electorate, some realignment has occurred. Republicans have developed a more solid base of support. Even more realignment may occur in the future. Some of the dealigned sectors of the electorate may realign with the Republican party (Hadley and Howell, 1980). Whether that happens, of course, depends on future events.

CONCLUSION

Political change in North Carolina is pervasive. The emergence of more intense competition for a wide variety of offices is a fact. While increased competition began at different times for the several offices, it became a certainty for all offices in the 1980s. These changes derive from numerous sources, including erosion of the long-established regional support for the parties and the presence of a more diverse electorate. Regional, racial, and socio-economic differences affect competition between the major parties and between the wings of the Republican party. However, political change derives also from the impact of national political forces on the state's politics. Retrospective performance evaluations and issue orientation differences are especially important. The influence of national politics in North Carolina both reflects and contributes to the volatility and fluidity of the state's electorate and political competition.

The 1986 congressional elections provide the latest evidence of increased competitiveness and growing electoral dealignment. Recent elections for the state's delegation in Congress include a significant number of marginal results. In recent years there have been more competitive U.S. House and Senate races in North Carolina than in any other state. The volatility of the state's electorate is illustrated by findings on ticket splitting, party defectors, and cross-over voters. The uneven influence of short-term forces (i.e., President Reagan, varying issues, campaign resources) contribute to uncertain election results. Two major groups of "floating" voters are the Jessecrats (eastern conservative Democrats) and the young piedmont professionals. Voters in these and other groups shift their voting preferences from party to party, faction to faction, and year to year.

The competitive politics, marginal elections and volatile electorate have drawn major attention to the state's politics. The state has experienced both significant dealignment of many voters and important realignment of other voters, both weakening the traditional advantage of the Democratic party especially for national offices. Republican candidates and the party have benefited from many of these changes but that benefit rests precariously on short-term forces. The future alignment of parties and politics in North Carolina is uncertain but in part will be a product of the changes that have been analyzed in this research and of future developments in the nation and state.

8

PARTISANSHIP IN KENTUCKY: 1979–1986

Malcolm E. Jewell and Phillip W. Roeder

HISTORICAL VOTING PATTERNS

Kentucky, like most other border states, is a traditionally Democratic state. In this century the Democratic party has elected its candidate in all but five of the gubernatorial elections (exceptions being in 1907, 1919, 1927, 1943, and 1961), and it has consistently controlled both houses of the legislature except for the 1919–20 period (see Jewell and Cunningham, 1968; Shannon and McQuown, 1950; Clark, 1960; Blanchard, 1984).

Despite the Democratic advantage, the two parties were highly competitive from the mid-1890s until 1932. Kentucky elected its first Republican governor in 1895 and voted for William McKinley in 1896. Many so-called gold Democrats defected from their party over the issue of Populism and did not return to their party for many years. Most presidential elections form 1896 to 1924 were very close, and there was frequent alternation in partisan control of the governorship.

The administration of Franklin Roosevelt had the effect of reestablishing the Democrats as the dominant party in both state and national elections. From 1932 through 1951 the Democrats won every presidential race, usually by comfortable margins; won all but one governor's race; and controlled both Senate seats for all but two years. Throughout this period, however, the Republican party remained competitive. It ran candidates in nearly every race for statewide office, and it rarely fell below 40% of the vote in these contests.

Kentucky, like Tennessee and North Carolina, has a bloc of "mountain Republican" counties in the southeastern part of the state (adjoining the similar Republican counties in those two states). The Republican loyalty of these counties was an outgrowth of the conflicts in the state over slavery and the Civil War, and the simple fact that it was not feasible to grow crops requiring slave labor on the steep slopes of southeastern Kentucky. The persistent Republican voting pattern of these counties is a major reason for the maintenance of a relatively high level of two-party competition in the state.

The fact that today's party loyalties and voting patterns are still shaped by events of 125 years ago illustrates the importance of tradition and custom in Kentucky politics. There has been a high degree of stability in the voting patterns of most rural counties. While the Republicans have controlled most of the southeast, the Democrats have dominated most rural counties in the western, central, and northeastern areas, and some coal counties in the southeast. Most of the competitive rural counties are located along the boundaries between the Democratic and Republican blocs.

In most of these rural counties one party has dominated local politics for long periods of time; serious competition has occurred in the majority party primary; and the minority party has run candidates intermittently if at all—and with very little success.

It is the urban counties of Kentucky that have been politically the most volatile and unpredictable. In these counties for a long time there has been closer partisan competition, but usually Democratic majorities. In the cities, of course, the population has been more heterogeneous, with immigration from both the Democratic and Republican sections of the state and from out of state.

There are, of course, no voting surveys available to document the patterns of partisan identification in Kentucky during the first half of this century. But the stability of county and state voting patterns strongly suggests that there has been a high degree of stability in individual party identification, that most voters have been loyal to a party rather than being independents, and that, among partisans, Democrats have outnumbered Republicans by about a three-to-two margin.

Kentucky is typical of the other border states in another important respect. Beginning with the first presidential election of Dwight Eisenhower, the national Republican party has made major inroads in the state. The Republican party barely lost the 1952 presidential election, and won those in 1956, 1960, 1968, 1972, 1980, and 1984. It held both U.S. Senate seats from 1957 to 1972, and regained one in the 1984 election. In the U.S. House the Republicans have consistently held the "mountain Republican" seat; since the mid-1960s they have consistently held at least one seat based on suburbs of Louisville and northern Kentucky; and since 1978 they have held a Bluegrass seat centered in Lexington.

Table 8.1 shows the proportion of total votes won by the Democratic party in each major statewide race from 1976 through 1986. This illustrates the point that the Democrats are usually much stronger in gubernatorial and senatorial races than in presidential contests. The lopsided Democratic senatorial victory in 1986 was atypical. The Republican party ran an unusually weak candidate against incumbent Democratic Senator Wendell Ford, a consistently powerful vote getter.

It is evident that a large number of Kentuckians, and frequently a majority, have been voting Republican for presidential, senatorial, and congressional candidates. The size of the Republican majority reached 65% for Senator John Sherman Cooper in 1966; it reached 60% or more for Richard Nixon in 1972 and Ronald Reagan in 1984. In these respects, Kentucky is very much like the other border states.

But the 50% to 60% of Kentuckians who have been voting Republican in national elections have not demonstrated similar support for Republican candidates at the state, legislative, or local levels. Kentucky has elected only one Republican governor since the 1943 race: Louie Nunn in 1967. In recent years the Republican party has consistently won between 20% and 30% of the state legislative seats—approximately the same number it held during the 1940s and 1950s, and considerably less than it held during the Nunn administration. Despite some success in metropolitan and urban counties and cities, the Republican party has not made significant inroads into local offices in Democratic counties.

Commentators on southern politics recently have begun to talk about "dual partisanship," the voting pattern in which Republicans win presidential and many congressional races while the Democrats maintain their political control most of the time in state, legislative, and local

Table 8.1
Democratic Proportion of the Vote in Statewide Elections in Kentucky

Year	Presidential (%)	Senatorial (%)	Gubernatorial (%)
1976	52.8		
1978		61.0	
1979			59.4
1980	47.6	65.1	
1983			54.6
1984	39.4	49.5	
1986		74.4	

races. Kentucky politics looks more like the dual partisanship of the South than it resembles the more consistently competitive politics of such border states as Tennessee, Virginia, and North Carolina.

PARTY IDENTIFICATION AND REGISTRATION

The empirical base for this study of partisanship in Kentucky is the semiannual statewide polls conducted by the Survey Research Center of the University of Kentucky from 1979 through 1986. In addition to standard demographic questions, these surveys include (with a few gaps) questions on party identification, liberalism-conservatism and party registration. A few of these surveys also include information on attitudes toward controversial issues, ratings of state and national officials, and voting in several state and national races.

In most of our analysis, we will present pooled data, drawn from two or more semiannual surveys. This has the advantage of increasing the number of respondents and permitting us to examine attitudes and characteristics of subgroups. When data were available for a large number of surveys, we have usually used the data from one survey a year for the more recent years. For the most part, we do not present trend data, because there is very little evidence of change over the eight-year period in the attitudes of respondents or in the relationship between attitudes and other characteristics.

For our purposes, the most important variable in the survey is party identification. We want to measure trends in party identification, examine variables that may explain it, and determine whether identification has an effect on political attitudes and behavior.

Voters have been asked their party identification repeatedly from 1979 through 1986 (with a break in 1984). With one or two exceptions, the question was administered so as to produce a seven-way classification, but we will use the three-way categorization of Democrats, independents, and Republicans for the sake of continuity and simplicity in correlating party identification with other variables. In the three-way classification, independents who say they lean toward one party or the other are classified as independents. We will also omit the small number of those who failed to respond with an identification in one of the three categories.

Figure 8.1 shows the trend in party identification from 1979 through 1986; for each year the data from the fall and spring surveys have been

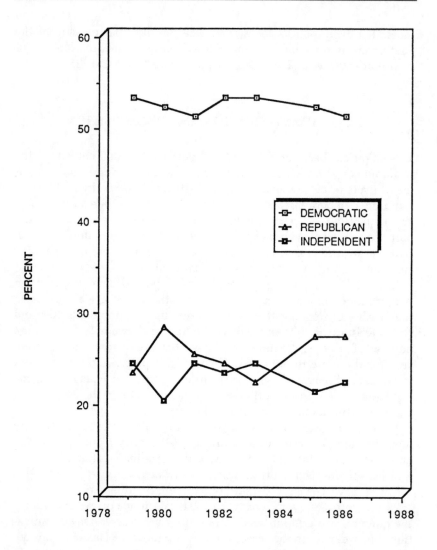

Figure 8.1
Kentucky party identification, 1979–1986.*

*The data are based on two surveys by the Survey Research Center at the University of
Kentucky for each year except for 1984, which are missing.

averaged to reduce variations caused by sampling error. The chart reveals a surprising pattern of consistency over the eight-year period. Partisan identification has ranged between 51% and 53% for Democrats, between 22% and 28% for Republicans, and between 20% and 24% for independents. Republican identification was lowest in 1979 and 1983, years of gubernatorial primaries and elections. By 1985 and 1986 the Republicans had regained the position they held in the presidential election year of 1980. Republican gains have come largely at the expense of independents rather than of Democrats. There is no evidence of the large-scale gains in Republican identification during the 1984–86 period reported by surveys in some Southern states for the period since 1983.

An examination of the seven-way breakdown of party identification (available for the 1980–86 period) also shows remarkable consistency over time. When the 1985 and 1986 data are pooled, they show the following breakdown:

23% strong Democratic
28% weak Democratic
 7% independent, leaning Democratic
 9% independent
 6% independent, leaning Republican
15% weak Republican
12% strong Republican.

These are almost identical to the figures for 1980. The only change worth mentioning is a gain in strong Republicans from 9% to 12%.

The conclusion from these tables is unmistakable. If there is a realignment, or a dealignment, going on in Kentucky politics, it cannot be discerned from the data on party identification over the 1979–86 period.

It is possible that we can partially explain the stability of party identification by examining the stability of party registration, and the relationship between the two. Kentucky is one of the few southern or border states with closed primaries. In order to vote in a partisan primary, a voter must be registered with that party; if the voter wishes to change parties to vote in the next primary, he or she must make the change thirty days before the general election that precedes the primary (or almost eight months in advance).

Between 1980 and 1986 the proportion of voters registering as Democrats rose from 67.9% to 68.1%; the proportion of independents dropped from 3.5% to 3.3%; the proportion of Republicans remained unchanged at 28.6%. After six years of a Republican administration in Washington and registration drives organized by both parties, nothing changed. (The percentages in the intervening years were almost identical).

These registration figures are noteworthy in several respects, in addition to their remarkable consistency. The proportion registering independent, while very small, is comparable to that in other southern and border states that require registration by party. The Democratic registration margin of approximately seven to three over the Republicans is huge, but it is also misleading as a measure of partisan strength. No Democratic presidential, senatorial, or gubernatorial candidate in this century has carried Kentucky by more than 65% of the vote.

We are interested in comparing party identification and party registration in Kentucky as a step toward determining whether one may have an effect on the other. Table 8.2 provides a crosstabulation of party identification and registration for the 1982–83 period. (Because some respondents are not registered, the totals are less than those for all identifiers, increasing the proportion of Democrats and decreasing the proportion of independents). Examining the top section, we find that almost all Democratic identifiers are registered as Democrats and over 90% of Republican identifiers are registered Republican. Those who identify as independents are twice as likely to register Democrat than Republican, while one-fifth of them register as independent—virtually the only voters to do so.

There are basically two reasons for a person to register Democratic or Republican. The first is a sense of loyalty, and the second is a desire to vote in the Democratic or Republican primary. In Kentucky, as in most southern and border states, the Democratic statewide primaries are often close and exciting, while the Republicans rarely have closely contested statewide primaries. We might expect to find Republican identifiers registering as Democrats in order to vote in state primaries, but our survey suggests that only 8% of Republicans do so.

Locally, the party with a majority in a county frequently has close primaries, while the minority party seldom has contests and sometimes does not even run candidates. Consequently, registration patterns (particularly in rural counties) are affected by the party balance at the county level. In 1981 there were 46 counties (out of 120) where the Democrats had at least 90% of the partisan registration, but in most of them the normal Democratic vote in statewide races was only 60% to 70%. It would appear that 20% to 30% of the voters in these counties

Table 8.2

Relationship between Party Identification and Party Registration in Kentucky

Party Identification	Numbers of Persons			% Across Party Registration			Percentage Down		
	Dem.	Ind.	Rep.	Dem.	Ind.	Rep.	Dem.	Ind.	Rep.
Statewide Totals:									
Dem.	991	9	20	97	1	2	82	11	4
Ind.	183	71	96	52	20	27	15	86	19
Rep.	36	3	385	8	1	91	3	3	77
Rural Republican counties:									
Dem.	51	1	5	89	2	9	91	14	6
Ind.	5	6	12	22	26	52	9	86	13
Rep.	0	0	72	0	0	100	0	0	81
Rural Democratic counties:									
Dem.	178	2	5	96	1	3	85	18	6
Ind.	26	8	15	53	16	31	12	73	17
Rep.	5	1	67	7	1	92	3	9	77
Rural strong Democratic counties:									
Dem.	248	0	2	99	0	1	80	0	3
Ind.	55	11	16	67	13	20	18	100	26
Rep.	6	0	44	12	0	88	2	0	71
Metropolitan counties:									
Dem.	210	2	2	98	1	1	76	8	1
Ind.	52	20	21	56	21	23	19	83	20
Rep.	13	2	81	14	2	84	5	8	79

Note: The statewide data are based on two surveys in 1983 and the fall 1982 survey conducted by the Survey Research Center at the University of Kentucky.

were registered Democratic but were usually voting Republican. There were also 11 counties where 75% to 88% of the two-party registration was Republican though the normal Republican vote was 10% to 20% less than that.

Given these registration patterns, we might expect to find that the relationship between party identification and registration is different in various types of counties. The lower section of table 8.2 shows this relationship for four types of counties: rural Republican, rural Democratic, rural strongly Democratic, and metropolitan. The partisan categories for rural counties are based on voting in statewide races. (All Republican counties are combined to generate enough respondents. The data only include two surveys in 1982.)

An examination of the data shows that about 13% of Republicans in strongly Democratic and metropolitan counties register Democratic but (particularly in strongly Democratic counties) the absolute numbers of these voters are very small. Much more important are the differences in registration by those who identify as independent. They are much more likely to register Republican in Republican counties and to register Democratic in the other three categories of counties. In all four types of counties it is largely the independents who account for the gap in partisan balance between registration and identification. Consequently, it is presumably the independents who largely account for the difference between voting patterns and registration.

What do these data tell us about the meaning of party identification to voters in Kentucky? One possible explanation is that some voters do not think of themselves in terms of party identification until asked to do so by an interviewer. Some of them may confuse identification with registration, and give the same answer for both; others, who recognize a contradiction between how they register and participate in primaries and how they vote in general elections, may decide on the spur of the moment to tell an interviewer that they are independents.

There are also substantive explanations for this phenomenon. More than half of those voters identifying as independents are registered as Democrats, and presumably vote in the Democratic primary. But, as we will demonstrate later, many of them frequently vote Republican. In fact, among independent identifiers, those registered as Democrats are just as likely to vote Republican as are those who register independent. It appears that a number of voters think of themselves as independents because they are registered Democratic and vote in that primary, but frequently vote Republican—at least in national elections. If such voters did not have to register with a party and were not limited to voting in one party's primary, many of them might think of themselves as Republicans.

One more clue to understanding party identification in Kentucky comes from a survey conducted in 1986 in one of the major metropolitan centers in Kentucky (Fayette county and two adjoining counties). The respondents were asked the traditional party identification question, and then were asked "when it comes to national politics," which party they identified with, and "when it comes to state and local politics" what was their identification.

Substantial numbers of voters made a distinction between the two levels of identification. The most important difference was that almost one-fifth of those with a national Republican identification thought of themselves as Democrats at the state level. Patterns of registration reported by the respondents were more closely correlated with state party than with national party identifications. Among the registered Democrats, 48% identified as national-level Democrats and 60% as state-level Democrats; 14% identified as national Republicans and only 4% as state Republicans.

We suggest that the prominence of the Democratic primary in Kentucky and the party registration requirements result in there being a number of persons who think of themselves as independents and yet vote Republican. The structure of the Democratic primary thus makes it unlikely that the proportion of Republican party identifiers will grow as much as the proportion of actual Republican voters. An electorate that identifies itself as about one-fourth Republican and about one-fourth independent is frequently producing comfortable majorities for national Republican candidates. Thus it is difficult to measure the degree of realignment in Kentucky by changes in party identification.

CHARACTERISTICS AND ATTITUDES OF PARTY IDENTIFIERS

The stability of partisan identification is obvious, and the explanations offered are plausible; however we will explore other factors relating to partisanship that have the potential to improve our understanding of party identification in Kentucky. The previous sections do not focus in any detail on the social or political content of party identification; rather the focus is on historical patterns and traditional loyalties reinforced by the political/governmental structure of closed primaries and the subsequent importance of the statewide Democratic primary and the relative unimportance of the Republican primary in Kentucky. In the next sections we examine the demographic, ideological, and issue content of party identification.

What types of Kentuckians identify with the Democratic and Republican parties or identify themselves as independents? What social and economic groups comprise these groups of party identifiers? Table 8.3 provides some answers to these questions. This table examines age, education, income, gender, and race of respondents who identify themselves as Democrats, Republicans, or independents based on four separate surveys in the period 1982–1986. With the exception of race, differences are slight. Democrat identifiers tend to be slightly less educated, slightly older, somewhat poorer and female, and black. Independents tend to be somewhat younger and male and slightly more

Table 8.3

Party Identification and Demographic Characteristics 1982–1986*

Characteristic	Total (%) Down	Dem.	Ind.	Rep.
Education:				
Less than HS	26	54	20	26
High school	38	53	24	23
College	35	47	25	28
Age:				
18–24	10	49	26	26
25–40	38	48	27	25
41–65	35	55	21	25
65 +	14	55	16	30
Income (000s):				
Less than $10	23	56	21	24
$10–20	29	51	24	25
$20–30	25	50	25	26
$30 +	23	51	21	27
Gender:				
Male	46	50	25	25
Female	54	53	20	27
Race:				
Black	6	69	20	11
White	94	51	23	27
Total % Across		52	23	26

*The data are combined from four surveys conducted by the Survey Research Center of the University of Kentucky, in the period 1982–1986.

educated, while Republicans are slightly older, female and wealthier, and white. Although blacks tend to identify strongly with the Democratic party, it is important to be cautious in racial comparisons because of the small percentage of blacks in the sample.

Examination of these data over time shows patterns of stability with little or no change in the demographic make-up of party identifiers from one year to another. It is interesting to note that in apparent contrast to many southern states, younger Kentuckians are not turning to the Republican party, at least in terms of identification. Independents tend to be younger, while Democrats and Republicans tend to be somewhat older.

In addition to demographic characteristics, we also examine whether party identifiers differ in their political ideologies. Previous research based on these same data (1981 surveys only) suggests that, although Kentucky is like most southern states in that it prefers the Democratic party, in terms of political ideology, Kentuckians tend to identify themselves as more moderate and less conservative than those in a number of southern states (Baer, Roeder, Sigelman, 1984). Also, since we suggested previously that party identification in Kentucky is a product of historical developments and party registration based on closed primaries, we should not expect to find significant differences among party identifiers in relation to their ideological identification as conservative, liberal, or middle of the road.

A comparison of statewide surveys in 1981 and 1985 finds that Democrats are somewhat more liberal and Republicans are more strongly conservative, while independents slightly prefer the ideological middle of the road in both 1981 and 1985. There is one major shift occurring in this period, and that is a significant increase in people identifying themselves as middle of the road. Democrats and independents become less liberal and more moderate, while Republicans become less conservative and more moderate in the period 1981–1985. The proportion of ideological moderates (not leaning toward liberal or conservative) increased steadily from 1981 to 1985 for all groups of party identifiers, but then decreased slightly for independents and fell back to 1982–1983 levels for Democrats and Republicans in 1986. These findings suggest that, although party identification has remained stable in this time period, Kentuckians have become much more moderate in terms of stated political ideology. Kentuckians cling to traditional party ties at the same time they appear to be moving toward the ideological center. This suggests explanations relating to the importance of identification with political parties based on historical patterns, the role of close primaries and party registration, or the irrelevance of political ideology to issues of partisanship in Kentucky. We attempt to explore these possible explanations further by examining partisanship relative to political and social issues.

A major question that often distinguishes Democrats and Republicans as well as liberals and conservatives is the extent of support for spending more money on certain government programs. When asked whether they think state and local governments should be spending more, less, or about the same as now for certain public programs, Kentuckians tend to differ over time and by party identification. An examination of data from three separate surveys (1981, 1983, 1985) and for three program areas (public grade schools and high schools, programs for the poor, and environmental programs) shows that support

for more spending on programs for the poor increased from 1981 to
1985; however Republicans were less supportive than Democrats, and
these differences were relatively consistent over time. Although there
were similar differences between party identifiers in support of spending more public schools, the changes over time were less pronounced
than for programs for the poor. The partisan patterns changed somewhat for environmental programs in that independents tended to be
more supportive of increased spending in this area; however, there was
an increased level of support over time similar to the other two policy
areas.

Other issues that may be related to partisan identification are social
issues such as abortion, capital punishment, gun control, and the Equal
Rights Amendment. In 1981, support for the ERA did vary by party
identification in that independents tended to be more supportive than
either Democrat or Republican identifiers. Independents also tended to
be more supportive of abortion than either Democrat or Republican
identifiers. In the fall of 1986, Democrats were less supportive of the
death penalty for convicted murderers than both independents and Republicans; and more supportive of stricter laws concerning the sale of
handguns.

Support for elected public officials also may help clarify the role of
partisanship in Kentucky. Comparisons of support for Governor Collins
and President Reagan in 1985 and 1986 by party identifiers shows clear
partisan differences in evaluations of these two officials. Although the
differences are sometimes slight, Democrats tend to be more supportive
of the Democratic governor than either independents and Republicans.
In contrast, Republicans tend to be significantly more supportive of
President Reagan in this period than either independents or Democrats. These findings lend some support to the concept of separate state
and national party identifications discussed previously; however, there
are too many confounding factors to advance this idea with any degree
of confidence.

Finally, comparing respondent voting choices to party identification
in a number of elections shows expected partisan patterns for Democrats and Republicans. Although we have only one statewide election
(1979 governor's race) to compare to three presidential elections, there
are substantial differences in the preferences of independents in those
elections. Independents favored Reagan by a significant margin in
1984, were evenly divided between Carter and Ford in 1976, and only
slightly favored Reagan over Carter in 1980. In contrast, in the 1979

gubernatorial contest independents preferred Democratic candidate Brown by a significant margin over his Republican opponent.

SUMMARY AND CONCLUSIONS

There are a number of conclusions to be drawn from this analysis of party identification in Kentucky. First, we find no evidence of party realignment or dealignment in the period 1979–1986. Kentuckians continue to prefer the Democratic party by almost a two-to-one margin over the Republican party. The major reason for this stability of party loyalties appears to be the closed primary system, which encourages voter registration in the more competitive primaries.

Although the Democratic party remains dominant in both identification and actual voting in state, legislative, and local races, the Republican party is competitive in Kentucky; and in fact, has been relatively successful in presidential, senatorial, and certain congressional races in the postwar period. Again, the major explanation for Democratic dominance seems to be the existence of the closed primary and the importance of registration for the statewide Democratic primaries, which tend to be consistently more competitive than Republican primaries. Comparison of party identifiers and registrants in counties that vary in dominance by one or the other party demonstrates that independents largely account for differences between voting patterns, registration, and identification.

Despite these conclusions suggesting substantial numbers of voters who may be identifying with one party and registering and voting with the other, or perhaps confusing identification and registration, party identification apparently is not without meaning to many voters. First, in a local public opinion survey we do find some evidence in support of the concept of "dual partisanship." Second, we find evidence of ideological and issue differences among party identifiers. Finally, we believe that given these findings, it is unlikely in the near future that the proportion of Republican party identifiers will grow to anywhere near the proportion of actual Republican voters in presidential and many statewide elections in Kentucky.

9

THE APPEARANCES OF REALIGNMENT AND DEALIGNMENT IN ARKANSAS

Diane D. Blair and Robert L. Savage

In a volume focusing on realignment and dealignment in partisanship among southerners, a chapter on Arkansas is obligatory. Although Arkansas is a Rim or Border rather than Deep South state, with some interesting strains of both Midwestern Populism and the Western Frontier culture, in terms of voting behavior it was the most loyally Democratic of all the states of the Old Confederacy. Arkansas' presidential votes went more consistently and heavily Democratic than did those of any other state, and Democrats traditionally swept state and local offices as well, usually uncontested. Arkansas, then, is something of a hard-core test of realignment or dealignment in the South.

Since realignment is generally defined as a durable alteration in the partisan balance of identifiers (Stanley, 1986), the testing requirements are clear: changes in attitudinal affiliation as evidenced in surveys and in voting behavior as evidenced in elections. Dealignment, involving a "decline in the centrality of parties to citizen political orientations and behavior" (Stanley, 1986) is somewhat more problematic. The best evidence for dealignment would be surveys tracking the degrees of party loyalty and the intensity of feelings for the party of choice over time, but such are not available in Arkansas. Still, it is possible to trace what partisan changes have and have not been occurring in Arkansas and to comment with some certainty on the multiple meanings and portents of these changes.

THE ELECTORAL EVIDENCE FOR PARTISAN CHANGE IN ARKANSAS

The strongest electoral evidence for partisan change in Arkansas is the sharply decreasing support for Democratic presidential candidates. In 1968, Arkansas became the last southern state to deny its electoral votes to the Democratic presidential candidate in the post-Reconstruction era, supporting Wallace over Nixon by a slim plurality with Humphrey running third. In 1972, it became the last southern state to actually vote Republican for president, supporting Nixon over McGovern. However, having voted consistently Democratic from statehood in 1836 until 1968 (with the artificial exceptions of the Civil War and Reconstruction years), Arkansas has gone Democratic only once in recent times, giving Carter his second largest majority (66%) outside his home state of Georgia in 1976, but supporting Reagan in both 1980 and 1984.

If the last twenty elections are divided into twenty-year cycles, the decline in Democratic presidential fortunes is a dramatic one. From 1908 through 1924, a period of Republican dominance nationally, the Democratic candidates averaged 59.6% of the state's votes. With the coming realignment that made the Democrats dominant nationally, their candidates from 1928 through 1944 averaged a whopping 75.4%. From 1948 through 1964, Arkansans continued to give their electoral votes to Democrats, but the margins generally were much less to cheer about, averaging 55.4%, a full twenty percentage points less than the preceding period. In the latest cycle, the Democrats have actually become the minority party in presidential elections. Given Carter's landslide victory in 1976, the average Democratic vote of only 42.6% from 1968 through 1984 is all the more a dramatic movement. This seems compelling evidence for partisan realignment in Arkansas, but for any strong assertion of that realignment as measured by election outcomes, Arkansas Republicans must exhibit increasing support in other contests as well.

U.S. Senate races have become distinctively more competitive and, in a clear break from tradition, that competition has shifted to the general election. Dale Bumpers, for example, after a fierce primary victory over incumbent Senator J. W. Fulbright in 1974, then gained his Senate seat with 85% of the vote in a virtually effortless general election campaign. Seeking reelection in 1980 and 1986, however, he had no primary opposition, but much narrower general election margins of 59% and 62%. Similarly, David Pryor, after a close and bruising Democratic primary in 1978 for the open seat created by Senator John L. McClellan's death, cruised through the general election with 76%. Seeking reelection in 1984, however, he was unchallenged in the Democratic primary but had to spend over $1.5 million and campaign nonstop for a year to win a 57% victory in the fall contest. Still, U.S. Senate races to date have been won only by Democrats, and by margins that, compared to competitive-party states, appear comfortable.

The evidence from U.S. House elections in Arkansas is somewhat more complex but only marginally more indicative of rising Republicanism. In 1966, Republican John Paul Hammerschmidt captured the Third Congressional District seat and has held it safely since (his only serious challenge coming in 1974 from young Bill Clinton). The Third District is largely extant with the Ozarks in Arkansas, the hill country not unlike that in several other southern states that has been the historical base of the Republican party in the region. The central Second District, containing the state's largest metropolitan center, was won by Republican Ed Bethune in 1978 after a divisive Democratic primary. When Bethune gave up his seat in an unsuccessful challenge to Senator Pryor in 1984, however, it was recaptured by a Democrat, Tommy Robinson, leaving Hammerschmidt once again the lone Republican in Arkansas' four-person House delegation. If effort is to be counted, the Republicans have made strides: the first time in the twentieth century that all the state's U.S. House seats were contested in the general election came only in 1982, and this was repeated in 1986. However, all incumbents were easily reelected in 1986 by margins ranging from a "low" of 64% to more than 80%.

The gubernatorial general election has also become more competitive than in the traditional one-party past, and here the Republicans have had their most dramatic successes. Winthrop Rockefeller's victories in 1966 and 1968, as well as Frank White's stunning upset of Bill Clinton in 1980, have been the defeats that have shaken the Democrats most, in part because both Republicans' victories can be attributed to the support they drew from disaffected Democrats. Still, these setbacks seem to have had a temporary impact. When the Democratic party threw off the remnants of the Orval Faubus machine and began nominating younger, cleaner, more progressive candidates (Bumpers in 1970 and 1972, Pryor in 1974 and 1976, Clinton in 1978), Republican gubernatorial candidates were reduced again to an average 30% of the general election vote. And when Clinton apologized for the economic pain he had caused and insensitivity he had shown by sponsoring sharp increases in vehicle license and registration fees, he recaptured both the governorship and the Democrats he had temporarily alienated. Clinton was reelected with relative ease in 1984 and 1986. This last Clinton victory gives him a four-year term following a constitutional change in the tenure for elected executives in Arkansas. Dramatic as their victories have been, then, Republicans will have occupied the State House only six years in the twenty-four-year period, 1967-1991.

The Democratic percentage of the vote in major statewide contests in recent years is given in table 9.1, which shows increased Republican competition but, aside from the presidency, little electoral success. Republicans have had even less success in contesting for other state offices. Of the lesser statewide executive posts, only the lieutenant governor's office has fallen to a Republican in this century, the two terms won by Maurice "Footsie" Britt as Rockefeller's running mate. Indeed, in no year have Republicans even contested for all six constitutionally mandated executive offices. Similar patterns are to be found in state legislative races. Less than 10% of the state legislative seats are presently held by Republicans: 9 of 100 in the House; 4 of 35 in the Senate. Moreover, the overwhelming majority of legislative seats are uncontested in the biennial general elections. In 1986, there were only sixteen general elections contests and no incumbent defeats.

One final piece of electoral evidence is especially illuminating: the enormous difference between the usual turnout in Arkansas Democratic and Republican primaries. In 1982, for example, 567,125 persons voted in the Democratic primary and only 13,147 in the Republican. In 1984, while Republican turnout increased nearly 50%, that still resulted in only 19,562 Republican primary voters while 492,595 were voting in the Democratic primary. In 1986, despite a four-person gubernatorial contest in the Republican primary, only 22,346 voters chose to cast their ballots therein compared to 520,628 voters in the Democratic primary. If Arkansas had party registration and closed primaries, this would be conclusive evidence of the continued dominance of the Democrats in Arkansas. Since Arkansas has neither, however, this inferential leap from primary participation to partisan identification is an especially large one. For a much more

Table 9.1

Democratic Voting for President, Governor, and U.S. Senator, 1976–1986

	Democratic Percentage of Total Vote for:		
Year	President	Governor	U.S. Senator
1976	65.0	83.2	
1978		63.4	76.6
1980	47.5	48.1	59.1
1982		54.7	
1984	39.6	57.3	57.3
1986		63.9	62.2

reliable test of partisan affiliation, survey responses are a necessary supplement to election outcomes.

ATTITUDINAL EVIDENCE OF REALIGNMENT

The findings arrayed in table 9.2 have been gleaned from a number of sample surveys conducted over the past quarter-century. Because they were conducted by different organizations for varying purposes and utilizing methods also highly variable, they must be treated with some caution. Still, they provide the longitudinal perspective essential in determining any movement toward realignment, and there is a comforting consistency across the findings.

Certain obvious conclusions leap from the table. While it may be disputed as to whether the Democratic party continues to be a majority party, its general dominance in partisan identification is inescapable. On the other hand, the party has just as inescapably declined over the period. The second "party" in Arkansas, however, is not the Republican party. Even with the severe stricture of categorizing "leaners" as partisans, independents outnumber the Republicans in twelve of the seventeen surveys reported here. Still, the Republican party exhibits notable growth over the period. If (and we recognize that statistically it is a dubious process) we average the pre-1980 surveys and compare that value with the other surveys, the Democrats fall from 59% to 54%, the independents remain stable at 28%, and the Republicans increase from 13% to 19%. For the eleven post-1980 surveys, the averages are 53% for the Democrats, 26% for the independents, and 22% for the Republicans. If these are considered pre- and post-Reagan years, then the popularity of Reagan may well have helped legitimize the decision to identify oneself as a Republican.[1] Still, only slightly more than one in five adult Arkansas identify themselves as Republicans.

Taken together, the election data and the survey data combine to suggest some modest realignment in Arkansas. However, the data also serve to raise more questions than answers. There are major mitigating factors that shape present, and no doubt future, party politics in Arkansas. The five factors that seem most important include two that, according to contemporary political folklore, should support continuing Republican growth; migration patterns, and generational change; one whose outcome is unclear for partisan advantage, ideological complexity among voters; and two that presumably afford a Democratic advantage, the comparative strength of the parties as political organizations and regional patterns in the state.

Table 9.2

Partisan Identification among Arkansans, 1962–1986

Poll and Source	Date	% Identifying Themselves as:		
		Democrat[a]	Independent	Republican[a]
Rockefeller poll (Kielhorn, 1973: 108)	1962	66[b]	23	11
Ibid.	1966	58	34	8
Ibid.	1970	53	32	15
Action Research (Ranchino, 1972: 11)	Oct. 1970	59	24	17
Precision Research (unpublished)	Oct. 1980	59	28	13
Ibid.	Nov. 1980	49	35	16
Arkansas Household Research Panel (Savage & Blair, 1984: 81)[c]	Apr. 1982	49.9	14.3	28.3
ABC Exit Poll (Finkel & Scarrow, 1985: 642)[c]	Nov. 1982	60.0	30.0	6.7
Precision Research ("Report . . . ," 1983)	May 1983	59.9	23.5	16.7
Arkansas Senatorial Polls for Senator David Pryor (unpublished)	Apr. 1984	59.6	18.7	21.7
Ibid.	Sept. 1984	57.0	16.5	26.5
Ibid. [c]	Nov. 1984	53.2	18.0	28.0
Bailey Poll of Arkansas (Bailey, 1986)[c]	Aug. 1985	51	30	16
Ibid. [c]	Oct. 1985	44	35	19
Ibid. [c]	Aug. 1986	47	35	13
Ibid. [c]	Sept. 1986	43	41	13
Private poll for Governor Bill Clinton (unpublished)[c]	Nov. 1986	53	21	21

[a] Includes "leaners," not identified separately.

[b] Polls conducted for nonacademic purposes typically report results using figures that are rounded off without fractional components. Consequently, we report the values from such polls without decimals to avoid any illusion of false precision.

[c] The reported values total noticeably less than 100% due to other responses and to refusals. Indeed, we suspect the other poll reports simply excluded such respondents in their analyses.

MITIGATING FACTORS IN ARKANSAS PARTY POLITICS

Migration and generational change would seem to enhance Republican electoral prospects in Arkansas given that the older, stable population has been so strongly committed to the Democratic party. Any change in the relative numbers of the old Democratic base must be looked upon with optimism by Republicans.

At first glance, migration patterns into and from Arkansas would seem especially propitious for Republican fortunes. Many of the in-migrants are retirees who presumably retain the social and political values of their former lives. Many of these people are from the urban Midwest and are settling in the northwestern region of Arkansas, that part of the state where Republican partisan identification is more likely to be reinforced by longstanding community values. In contrast, the out-migrants are blacks from the Delta area, a group whose political emergence was associated with Republican Win Rockefeller but, since his passing from the scene, has become solidly Democratic as with southern blacks generally. Two qualifications are to be noted here, however. One is the obvious regional basis of these migration patterns, and the other is that the in-migrants are not so reflective of the stereo-type of retirees as one might imagine.

Regionalism will be more fully examined later, but it suffices here to say that these regional relocations at most tend to reinforce existing patterns of partisan cleavage. While Republicans may gain a net advantage for statewide elections, the party is not expanding its base to become a truly statewide party. Its strength has traditionally centered in the Ozarks, and whatever number of blacks leave the Delta, that region largely remains committed to the Democratic party for the fore-seeable future.

The stereotype of the retiree as a Midwestern middle-management person coming to Arkansas for its climate and its low cost of living has only a limited validity. Indeed, many of these retirees are former skilled blue-collar workers who bring their Democratic affiliations with them. Moreover, retirees or not, many of the recent in-migrants are people who have roots in the state, such as second- or third-generation "Arkies" whose families had left the state during the Great Depression. As Donald Voth (1984), a rural sociologist, has argued, the state's "migration experience has been at least as much a source of continuity and stability as of change." In sum, migration patterns have probably fostered the growth of Republicanism in Arkansas, but more nearly as a trickle rather than as a flood.

Admittedly, there is little direct evidence by way of survey data. The one study that provides such evidence was a mail survey in 1982 with the usual sampling biases found in such surveys.[2] Still, that study found that of long-term residents of the state (twenty years or more), nearly 55% were Democratic identifiers. Among those living in the state ten years or less, only about 35% were Democratic identifiers. This difference does suggest a continuing weakening of the Democratic party in Arkansas if the state's demographic profile continues to be changed by present migration patterns.

Examination of generational differences is likewise hampered by slight data resources. The only early study that might permit a longitudinal perspective, carried out in 1970, found that Arkansans of age 20 to 35 were similar to all other age groups in partisan identification (Kielhorn, 1973). Still, more recent evidence does suggest that generational turnover has at some point begun. An indirect measure to be treated with all due circumspection is support for Ronald Reagan in the 1984 presidential election. A statewide survey on election eve found that younger voters were much more supportive of the Republican candidate: by 63.4% for those under 30 and 71.7% of those 30–44, versus 59% of the 45–59 age group and 57.1% of the over-60 age group.[3] A more direct measure—but for only the state's Second Congressional District—asking for voters' partisan preferences in national politics in 1986 provides comparable results (Davis, 1987).[4] While Democrats noticeably outnumber Republicans for all age groups, that advantage is decidedly less for younger voters. Generally, among voters under 50, about 40% identify as Democrats and about 25% as Republicans. For those over 50, the percentages are about 50% and 10% respectively.

The Second District study potentially allows some examination of the question of whether younger Arkansans reflect the national tendency of partisan dealignment among the new political generation. However, the results are inconclusive. The age groups showing the highest percentages of independence are those 50–59 and 30–39 at 37.7% and 37.3% respectively. In any event, the available survey evidence confirms the conventional wisdom that Republicanism will find more fertile soil among younger rather than older people. It also confirms, however, the strong sense of those teaching today's younger people that they are without the politically relevant historical events that guide their parents and grandparents: the Civil War, Reconstruction, two world wars, the New Deal, the civil rights movement, Watergate, and VietNam.

Interestingly, neither migration patterns nor generational differences necessarily reflect what has the oldest "credentials" as a basis for partisan change in the South—individual conversion. Indeed, in Arkansas at least, such conversion does not seem particularly common. The phenomenon can only be approached indirectly by examining what is probably the most usual rationale for expected realignment through conversion, the belief that southern whites will gravitate to the Republican party as they recognize its affinity to their own inherent conservatism. There are several problems with this argument, however, the two chief ones being the assumptions that southerners share a common ideology and that this ideology is political conservatism. In reverse order, let's briefly examine the assumption that southerners are conservatives.

Assuredly, the race question and the suspiciousness with which southerners view action by the national government (and indeed, most large-scale collective action) mark the region as politically conservative. At the same time, one could point to many examples of political "liberalism" in the South, perhaps most notably the prominent role played by many political leaders of the region in Franklin Roosevelt's New Deal. In any case, the historical record of southern politics is hardly one of unallayed commitment to conservatism. More germane to Arkansas is its own recent record in gubernatorial politics during a time when Republican voting has been generally increasing. In only two of the state's last eleven gubernatorial elections have voters failed to elect the clearly more progressive candidate. And one of those two exceptions was 1970 when both parties' candidates were recognized as progressives. Even the bloc voting of blacks in support of these winners does not detract from the assertion that the historical record does not show unmitigated and unrectified conservatism among white Arkansans. The black vote has been a critical factor assuredly, but the demographic reality (21.7% black population in 1960 declining to 16.9% in 1970 and 16.3% in 1980) is that a majority of the votes for a winning gubernatorial candidate in Arkansas must come from whites.

More important than the myth of southern white conservatism for partisan change, however, is the actual lack of ideological consistency among voters. As Maddox and Lilie (1984) have persuasively argued, students of American politics need to move beyond the simplistic typology that divides Americans along a single ideological continuum distinguishing liberals from conservatives. Their fourfold typology based on two cross-cutting continua—support or opposition to government intervention in the economy and to its intervention in social issues—more realistically describes the complexity that citizens face in assessing governmental action and their response to it. Put succinctly, a person may independently assess the appropriateness of governmental action with respect to economic matters and to social or life-style issues. Summarily, then, Maddox and Lilie point to the Populist who supports intervention in both dimensions, the Libertarian who supports neither, as well as the more traditional persuasions of the Liberal who supports intervention in the economy but not life-styles, and the Conservative who reverses that pattern.

One study has attempted to replicate their examination in Arkansas (Savage and Blair, 1982).[5] While findings regarding the number of adherents of each persuasion varied considerably from their national results, those findings nonetheless show that ideological pluralism characterizes Arkansans rather than any consensus, conservative or otherwise.[6] The leaders of the two parties in Arkansas are faced with the same problem that confronts their national counterparts—how to develop a consistent stance on political issues that will attract and sustain a voting majority when public opinion is in such disarray.

Even if the Republicans should prove to have an edge on issue appeals among white Arkansans, they nonetheless face two problems that will likely forestall their hegemony in the state for many years to come. One is their institutional weakness, and the other is the continuing regional cleavage in partisan support.

The widely recognized weakness of the southern Democratic parties as organized entities would suggest that Republicans have still another edge for making advances. In Arkansas, however, both political parties are notably weak (Gibson et al., 1985: 152). Yet, the Democratic party can be likened to a drafty old mansion through which many come to gawk, to frolic, or, much more rarely, to work. The Republican party, on the other hand, is a cottage in great disrepair, its foundation seemingly strong but with few building blocks available for expansion.

The Republicans of Arkansas, as noted, have their base in the Ozarks. They have had only very modest success in expanding from the old mountain Republicanism to include a wing of urban Republicanism, and, like the Republican party nationally, they have all but lost any hope of attracting significant numbers of blacks. The party in this state, then, has not been successful in laying the other cornerstones that Key saw as the most likely building materials for creating a two-party South. One need not look much beyond the surface to see that for all the new competitiveness, Arkansas remains for nearly all practical purposes a one-party state. While Republicans have had little to cheer about in competing for all statewide offices and their contingent in the state legislature seems frozen at about 10 percent, the problem is not just that they have not yet been successful in contesting elections. The problem is that they have so few gladiators, outside the Ozarks, willing to enter the lists throughout the state.[7]

The minute turnout in the Republican state primary (about one-twentieth that of the Democratic primary) has been discussed. More than that, many counties have not even a semblance of local Republican organization, further aggravating the primary turnout problem; and in the most recent Republican administration, Governor Frank White faced a chronic problem of finding partisans to fill all the major appointive positions. The most telling fact, however, lies not with the party's ability to compete for power in state politics but its largely moribund role in local politics outside the mountain region. In the 1986 general election, Republicans contested Democrats in only 117 local races. True, most municipal elections, by law or by local tradition, are nonpartisan. Yet, with a minimum of 16 elective posts across 75 counties, the Republican effort is clearly minuscule. Further compounding their problems, they won in only slightly more than 20 percent of these races, and most of these victories occurred in mountain counties.[8]

The regional character of the Republican party is especially evident in these local contests. Using a typology that divides the state's counties into three categories—Ozark, Delta, Urban—Republicans faced Democrats in 79, 17, and 21 local races, respectively.[9] Ironically, the Republicans won as often in Delta races as in Ozark races, about 18%. They won one-third of the races in Urban counties, but they contested for much less than a quarter of the available posts in those counties.

Assuredly, in the contemporary media age of American electoral politics, the old-style party organization is not as essential to winning state and national elections, and Arkansas parties have never had such organization even among the Democrats. What is at issue is the control of government, and with all their visible successes and increasing general competitiveness in presidential and gubernatorial contests, Arkansas Republicans have not advanced in their prospects for sharing power with the Democrats very much beyond what Key found here in the 1940s. At the same time, their prospects for the future are brighter, but changes in partisan identification have little to do necessarily with whatever partisan realignment may occur.

PARTISANSHIP IN ARKANSAS' FUTURE

The brighter Republican prospects in Arkansas for the foreseeable future remain very much with candidacies for offices at the top of the ticket, and those prospects in the short run depend upon the continuing likelihood of split-ticket voting. That Arkansas voters are both willing and able to split their tickets is clear (see *Arkansas Votes*, 1973; Blair and Savage, 1981). Indeed, in what is probably the most oft-noted anomaly of Arkansas politics, voters in 1968 simultaneously selected George Wallace, candidate of the American Independent party, for president, Republican Winthrop Rockefeller for governor, and Democrat J. W. Fulbright for the U.S. Senate. A more recent example comes from Sebastian County, the state's most notable hotbed of Republicanism in recent years. In 1980, the Republicans Ronald Reagan and Frank White easily carried the presidential and gubernatorial elections there, but the leading vote getter by a very large margin was the Democratic candidate for county sheriff, who captured 82% of the vote in that race.

As this example illustrates, ticket splitting is especially endemic in that part of the state, the northwestern region, where Republican identifiers are most numerous, and it reflects persistent Republican difficulty in fielding an acceptable slate of candidates down the length of the ticket. In the short term, then, one, two, and more rarely three Republican candidates at the top of the ticket may be favored in some years, but in all but a few locales the "lesser" races are won by Democrats. Such a pattern suggests a *tradition of independence* but is not necessarily evidence that voters have become dealigned, either at the micro- or the macrolevel. What might be advantageous to Republican political fortunes, at least in the short run, would be the development of what Charles Hadley (1985) has called "dual identification."

The root of dual identification lies in what V. O. Key (1949: 278–279) labeled as "presidential Republicanism." He found this propensity among some southerners to split their presidential vote decision from all other voting decisions. What Hadley points to is a more generalized tendency to distinguish between national and state levels in voting. There is some evidence that many Arkansans may be doing just this, but it is a relatively recent phenomenon. Kielhorn (1973) reports pertinent statewide survey results from 1970 that strongly indicate little propensity to make such a distinction. In that year over 95% of Arkansans proclaimed the same partisan identification at both levels. The 1986 Second Congressional District survey, on the other hand, found 391 voters who indicated a partisan preference at each of three levels— national, state, local—and nearly 27% of these were dual identifiers (Maggiotto and Wekkin, 1987). Most interesting is the fact that younger voters are more prone to adopt such dual orientations. Of the voters 18–29 years of age, 34.9% were dual identifiers. Voters of ages 30–49 were slightly more likely than the average to take this stance, while voters over 50 were much less likely to profess a dual identification (Davis, 1987). These results from an exit poll in an election where the presidency was not at stake suggest all the more that dual identification is likely to have a significant impact on the state's politics, a prospect enhanced all the more by the stronger tendency of the youngest partisans to identify themselves in this fashion.

Dual identification, however, is a stance at least as akin to political independence as it is to political partisanship. Such a duality may sit well with some Arkansans. Most, however, will likely find it too strict a commitment when the partisan label they have most often worn, Democratic, was no real commitment at all. Not so long ago, after all, "everyone" was a Democrat, at least outside the Ozarks. Real choices were made in the Democratic primary, where party affiliation was meaningless. The primary offered a menu where all selections were à la carte, and the voters made choices in terms of their own tastes, highly personalistic choices. The basic impact of the new competitiveness is to make the general election an opportunity for a second course. The menu is more selective, but the choice for Arkansans, as it traditionally had been, is one to be made on the basis of their personalistic responses to the candidates offered up to them. Ideologies and programs have little to do with such images. Indeed, those are largely alien to the one-party, which is to say no-party, tradition. On the other hand, that is not to say that issues have no pertinence. Stands on particular issues are very much part of the candidates' images, but the voters typically define the issues. Frank White used issues (the car tag fee increases as well as the location of thousands of fiercely unwelcome Cuban refugees at Fort Chaffee) to upset Bill Clinton's bid for reelection in 1980. Those issues, however, were ones that many Arkansans were centrally concerned with and also ones that could be linked to widely recognized personal and leadership traits of Governor Clinton, a negative linkage.

This essentially personalistic style of voter decision making suggests, then, that Republicans can and will win particular races in Arkansas when one or another of three conditions are met. They can win when the Democratic candidate is just clearly an unacceptable alternative. This is a negative comparative judgment and does not build toward Republican partisanship in itself. For example, most Arkansans found McGovern as the Democratic presidential candidate in 1972 an altogether unpalatable item on the menu. Republicans can also win, typically in situations involving a Democratic incumbent, when the voters are angered by past actions of that candidate. Again, this is a negative judgment. Clinton's unsuccessful campaign in 1980 is a classic instance, but a contrite and repentant Clinton regained the office two years later. Finally, Republicans can win if they offer a distinctly palatable candidate. Reagan's victory in 1984 is a good example of this. Yet, even such a positive basis for voter choice helps little to build any firm partisan commitment where that choice is clearly independent of any other choices. That independence of choice, not independence of party as such, is the typical Arkansan's habit.

In the long run, then, a thorough realignment resulting in firm partisan attachments depends upon changes in the demographic profile of Arkansas that produce clear-cut political cleavages resulting in more consistent demands for programmatic stances from candidates and their parties. There are some trends that point to such a possibility, but projecting demographic trends in any systematic fashion would require as much space as has already been consumed. Moreover, if, as one political scientist has argued, the media age has produced a "Southernization of America politics"—i.e., made campaign politics and voting more personalistic—then the demographic changes would be for nought. Arkansans would be right back where they have always really been (Jackson, 1986).

Where Arkansans have been is a standing decision to be Democrats. Now that Republican candidates are generally considered to be at least potentially palatable items on the election menu, the Democratic party is simply standing on less firm ground.

NOTES

1. The Reagan impact in Arkansas on both Republican electoral choices and partisan identification is discussed in more detail in Blair (1986).

2. The survey was conducted for the authors by the Arkansas Household Research Panel, University of Arkansas, during April 1982.

3. These findings are form the Arkansas Senatorial Polls for 1984, graciously made available by Senator David Pryor. For further information on this and the 1984 presidential election in Arkansas generally, see Blair (1986).

4. Davis's study is based on exit polls taken in the district on General Election Day. Voters were also asked about partisan identification in state and in local politics, focusing on the intriguing question of "dual identification," a matter we address later.

5. This study did not presage Maddox and Lilie; it followed directly from the earlier Lilie and Maddox (1981).

6. Much of the divergence of the findings are no doubt due to the typical biases to be expected from a mail survey. For the record, the respondents' national orientations were divided as follows: Conservative, 31.4%; Libertarian, 15.1%; Liberal, 7.3%; Populist, 6.5%; mixed, 38.0%; other, 1.7%.

7. For a more detailed analysis of party organization in Arkansas, see Blair (forthcoming), chapter 5.

8. Republican candidates did win all four races in which their opponents ran as independents, however.

9. The typology is from Savage and Gallagher (1977).

THE
DEEP SOUTH

10

Party Identification and Political Change in Alabama

Patrick R. Cotter and James Glen Stovall

The Alabama in which V. O. Key worked and wrote while preparing *Southern Politics* (1949) was among the bedrocks of the Solid Democratic South. Indeed, one-partyism was so solidly ingrained within the state that Alabama voters did not wander far from their staunch support for the Democratic party even when Al Smith was nominated in 1928.

The state and local politics described by Key also placed Alabama at the center of the region. In particular, Alabama's pre-Second Reconstruction politics featured a considerable level of multifactionalism and friends-and-neighbors voting. Occasionally the disorganized politics of the state would transform itself into a bifactional conflict between the Populist and agrarian interests found in northern and southeastern Alabama against a coalition composed of black-belt planters and the "big mule" industrialists and financiers of Birmingham and Mobile (see also Hackney, 1969).

Since the time of Key's writing, Alabama has experienced substantial changes in its politics, particularly at the national level (for discussions of more recent electoral politics in Alabama, see Burnham, 1964; Strong, 1972; Bass and DeVries, 1976; and Lamis, 1984). As seen in figure 10.1, only once since 1960 has a Democratic presidential candidate carried the state. Ronald Reagan won in Alabama by a narrow margin in 1980 and by a substantial amount in 1984. The Republican party won its first U.S. Senate seat since Reconstruction in 1980, but the Democrats narrowly reclaimed the seat in 1986.

Alabama has experienced less change in its state and local politics than in its national inclinations. The reason for the slower pace is the extended presence of George Wallace, a politician who was elected (or had a surrogate elected) governor five times between 1962 and 1986. In establishing himself as a durable force in the state, Wallace broke the mold of the discontinuous electoral politics described by Key (1949). Wallace's continued support within Alabama was the result of his abil-

142

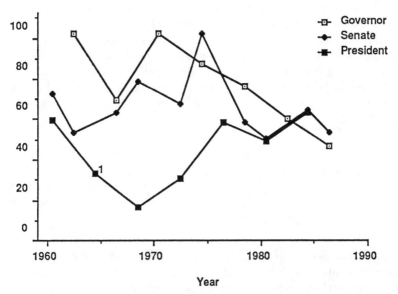

Figure 10.1
Percentage of Democratic vote in Alabama since 1960.

[1] Democratic electors not pledged to Lyndon B. Johnson

ity to cut across the state's traditional cleavages, appealing to voters both as a Populist and liberal on economic issues and as a conservative on race. (For discussions of Wallace in Alabama, see Black and Black, 1973a, 1973b, and Carlson, 1981). By shifting his emphasis from one set of issues to another, Wallace continued to win the governorship despite massive changes in the state's political environment.

Even at the state and local levels, however, the Republican party has made some gains in recent years. The largest breakthrough occurred in 1986 when, after a divisive nomination battle within the Democratic party involving a dispute over the outcome of the runoff election, Guy Hunt was elected the first Republican governor in Alabama this century.

TYPES OF POLITICAL CHANGE

While a review of recent election results supports a conclusion that Alabama politics have changed, the type and direction of this change is not known. The purpose of this chapter is to examine what type of change has occurred in Alabama politics. This will be done by investigating the party identifications of the state's citizens. Because of its stability and influence on other dispositions and behaviors, party identification is a measure often used to study political change.

Examining the party identifications of Alabamians over the last several years can produce evidence about three possible movements in the state's politics[1]:

Dealignment—a weakening of partisan attachments within the electorate, indicated by a large, and possibly growing, number of independents in the state (Beck, 1977, 1979). A dealignment is also indicated if Alabamians not are using their party identifications to form political dispositions or to guide political behavior.

Realignment—a durable shift in the composition of the parties, typically resulting in a change in the partisan balance within the electorate.[2] Researchers who have examined political realignments have suggested several different lines along which the composition of the parties may change. These include social status (Converse, 1966; Gatlin, 1975), political ideologies (Beck, 1982), and opinions on racial issues (Carmines and Stimson, 1981).

Impact of short-term forces. Some recent research has shown that not only does party identification influence an individual's opinions about short-term forces in the political environment, such as issues or candidates, but also that these opinions can in turn influence party identification. (For examples of this line of research, see Shively, 1980; Dobson and St. Angelo, 1975; Marcus and Converse, 1979; Page and Jones, 1979; Howell, 1981; and Franklin and Jackson, 1983.) That is, the relationships between party identification and such things as issue opinions or evaluations of candidates or political leaders are reciprocal. One object within the political environment that may have an important impact on the distribution of party identification is the performance of political leaders, such as the president (Franklin, and Jackson, 1983; see also Clarke and Stewart, 1984). Thus, the occurrence of a "short-term force" type of change is indicated if shifts in the party identification of Alabamians parallel changes in opinions about objects within the political environment, such as the performance of the president. Whether changes in party identification resulting from short-term forces are the first indicators of a more stable realignment can be determined only after a longer period of time.

DATA AND METHODS

The data used in this study were collected in a series of semiannual surveys conducted by the University of Alabama's Capstone Poll beginning in the spring of 1981. The surveys are based on telephone interviews with random samples of adult Alabama citizens. A random digit-dialing method of sampling was used in the studies. Each study is based on a sample of approximately 500 respondents.

Party identification is measured by responses to a question which asked, "When it comes to national politics, do you consider yourself a Republican, a Democrat, an Independent or what?" Those saying that they were either a Democrat or Republican were then asked how strongly they identify with their party. Those saying that they were independents were asked if they lean toward either the Republican or Democratic party. Combining the results of these items produces the standard seven-point party identification scale ranging from Strong Republicans to Strong Democrats. Respondents who said that they identified with a minor party were placed into the missing data category of the party identification scale measure. Respondents who initially said that they did not identify with any party, or did not know which party they identified with, were classified as independents if they showed some interest in either state or national politics. Otherwise they were placed in the missing data category.[3]

Some researchers (for example Beck, 1977, 1979, Anderson, 1979) believe that younger citizens (who are less firmly attached to the existing parties) are the major source of change in either a dealignment or realignment. Others (for example, Erickson and Tedin, 1981) believe that electoral change can occur through the conversion of individuals already well established within the electorate. Because of possible differences between generations, we will separately examine younger and older citizens.

Also, much of the discussion of political change in the South has focused on the dispositions and behaviors of whites. Black citizens have shown more uniformity and stability in their political preferences than have whites. Consequently, in investigating changes in Alabama's politics, we will separately examine the party identifications of whites.[4]

RESULTS

Distribution of Party Identification

The results of the party identification measure for the twelve surveys conducted between the spring of 1981 and the fall of 1986 are presented in table 10.1. Throughout this period Democrats outnumbered Republicans. However, the ratio of Democratic to Republican identifiers has varied considerably over time. The spring 1981 survey found that 34% of Alabamians identified with the Republican party (treating "leaners" as identifiers) and 51% thought of themselves as Democrats. Subsequent surveys show a decline in the number of Republican identifiers (and an increase in Democratic identifiers) so that by the fall of 1982, only 24% of the state's citizens declared that they were Republicans. This percentage slowly increased until by the fall of 1984 the number of Republican identifiers (40%) was slightly less than the number of Democrats (46%). Since then the number of Republicans identifiers first declined slightly and then increased to its present 40% level. The number of Democrats has moved in the opposite direction. In the latest survey (conducted shortly after the 1986 general election), about 46% of the respondents identified themselves as Democrats.

A similar fluctuation in the relative number of Republican and Democratic identifiers is found when the party identifications of black and white Alabamians are examined separately (table 10.2). Blacks overwhelmingly identify with the Democratic party throughout the period. Even among these citizens, however, some changes in the ratio of Democrats and Republicans are observed. In the fall of 1982, about 88% of black Alabamians identified themselves as Democrats compared with only 3% who said that they were Republicans. However, in the fall 1986 survey, Democrats "only" outnumbered Republicans by a 85% to 11% margin.

Among whites there is a more equal, though still fluctuating, distribution of party identifiers. Indeed, in the most recent survey, Republicans outnumber Democrats by a slight 46% to 39% margin. Republicans and Democrats were also about equal in strength in the early part of the period under study. For example, in the spring of 1981 Democrats outnumber Republicans by a 44% to 40% margin. However, in the fall of 1982 the number of Democrats (51%) was substantially greater that the number of Republicans (29%).

Changes in the ratio of Republicans and Democrats have also occurred among younger Alabamians (40 years of age or less) (table 10.3). The number of Republicans and Democrats was about equal at the beginning and end of the period examined. Indeed, in the fall of

Table 10.1
Party Identification in Alabama*

Party	Spring 1981	Fall 1981	Spring 1982	Fall 1982	Spring 1983	Fall 1983	Spring 1984	Fall 1984	Spring 1985	Fall 1985	Spring 1986	Fall 1986
Strong Republican	12%	10%	6%	6%	9%	8%	10%	16%	13%	12%	14%	14%
Weak Republican	13	11	12	10	10	11	12	13	15	14	12	13
Independent Republican	9	10	8	8	10	10	11	11	10	10	12	13
Independent	14	9	11	18	14	14	17	14	11	12	14	13
Independent Democrat	10	10	11	8	11	10	9	4	10	10	8	10
Weak Democrat	18	23	25	21	22	22	21	17	19	19	18	14
Strong Democrat	23	26	28	29	25	25	20	25	22	23	23	22
Total	100%	100%	100%	100%	100%	100%	100%	100%	100%	100%	100%	100%
N	500	451	491	490	485	469	484	478	484	483	488	476

*Missing data deleted. Percentages in tables may not sum to 100 percent because of rounding error.

Table 10.2

Party Identification among White and Black Alabamians*

Party	Spring 1981	Fall 1981	Spring 1982	Fall 1982	Spring 1983	Fall 1983	Spring 1984	Fall 1984	Spring 1985	Fall 1985	Spring 1986	Fall 1986
White Alabamians												
Strong Republican	14%	12%	8%	7%	10%	9%	11%	19%	16%	14%	16%	16%
Weak Republican	16	13	15	12	11	14	14	16	16	17	14	15
Independent Republican	10	11	10	10	12	12	12	13	12	11	14	15
Independent	16	10	11	20	16	16	19	15	12	14	14	15
Independent Democrat	11	11	12	9	11	12	10	3	10	9	7	10
Weak Democrat	17	23	25	21	20	22	20	17	18	18	18	13
Strong Democrat	16	20	20	21	20	17	14	17	16	16	17	16
Total	100%	100%	100%	100%	100%	100%	100%	100%	100%	100%	100%	100%
N	395	344	363	390	393	363	388	379	383	378	414	395
Black Alabamians												
Strong Republican	2%	6%	3%	0%	2%	3%	2%	5%	2%	6%	3%	7%
Weak Republican	2	6	4	2	2	1	4	2	4	4	3	3
Independent Republican	4	7	2	1	0	3	2	1	2	3	0	1
Independent	9	1	8	9	6	7	9	7	5	3	9	4
Independent Democrat	8	10	6	5	10	3	6	3	12	12	10	8
Weak Democrat	22	21	24	22	32	26	26	21	25	22	18	22
Strong Democrat	52	48	52	61	46	57	51	61	51	50	57	55
Total	100%	100%	100%	100%	100%	100%	100%	100%	100%	100%	100%	100%
N	90	95	111	93	80	90	85	87	85	95	68	73

*Missing data deleted.

Table 10.3

Party Identification among Younger and Older Alabamians*

Party	Spring 1981	Fall 1981	Spring 1982	Fall 1982	Spring 1983	Fall 1983	Spring 1984	Fall 1984	Spring 1985	Fall 1985	Spring 1986	Fall 1986
						Younger Alabamians						
Strong Republican	14%	10%	6%	7%	11%	7%	11%	16%	14%	15%	16%	15%
Weak Republican	17	16	13	12	11	16	16	18	19	17	11	18
Independent Republican	9	10	9	11	9	11	12	10	10	10	12	14
Independent	18	8	9	16	15	16	16	13	11	12	16	11
Independent Democrat	12	12	12	8	12	10	12	5	12	11	10	9
Weak Democrat	14	25	28	22	22	20	19	16	19	18	18	16
Strong Democrat	16	18	24	24	20	20	16	21	16	17	16	17
Total	100%	100%	100%	100%	100%	100%	100%	100%	100%	100%	100%	100%
N	269	237	246	255	246	256	226	230	235	264	233	247
						Older Alabamians						
Strong Republican	10%	10%	8%	5%	7%	8%	9%	16%	13%	9%	12%	14%
Weak Republican	9	7	12	7	8	6	8	9	11	11	13	8
Independent Republican	9	10	6	6	10	9	10	12	10	10	12	11
Independent	10	10	12	20	14	12	18	14	11	11	10	16
Independent Democrat	9	8	9	9	10	9	6	2	8	8	5	11
Weak Democrat	21	20	22	20	22	25	24	18	20	20	19	11
Strong Democrat	31	35	32	33	29	31	25	29	27	30	29	28
Total	100%	100%	100%	100%	100%	100%	100%	100%	100%	100%	100%	100%
N	225	211	240	225	237	205	250	239	246	213	249	228

*Missing data deleted. Younger Alabamians are defined as respondents 40 years of age or less.

1986 younger Alabamians were more likely to say that they were Republicans (43%) than Democrats (42%). However, in the fall of 1982 Democrats outnumbered Republicans among younger citizens by a 54% to 30% margin.

The distribution of party identification is more stable among older Alabamians. Even among these respondents, however, the ratio of Republicans to Democrats has changed during the period examined here. In the fall of 1982, Democrats outnumbered Republicans among older citizens by a 61% to 18% margin. In the fall of 1986, the ratio was a closer 50% to 33%. Throughout the period under study, older citizens are more likely to identify with the Democratic party than are younger respondents.

In summary, between 1981 and 1986 more of the state's citizens have identified themselves as Democrats than as Republicans. The results of the Capstone Poll surveys have also consistently shown that blacks and older citizens are more likely than white or younger respondents to identify themselves as Democrats. However, within the entire electorate, as well as within each of the subgroups examined, the ratio of Republicans and Democrats has fluctuated. Beginning in 1981 the number of Republicans declined and then increased, declined slightly again, and then experienced a final increase.

The fluctuations that have taken place in the party identifications of Alabamians support a conclusion that the state has experienced political change during recent years. In order to identify what type of change has occurred, we shall now examine the nature of party identifications of Alabamians.

Nature of Change

Dealignment.

One indicator of a dealignment is the presence of a large and possibly increasing number of independents. Such a situation is not found in Alabama. Rather, the number of independents has remained relatively stable since 1981, regardless of whether attention is focused on "pure" independents alone, or on both "leaning" and pure independents. A substantial majority of Alabamians do identify themselves as either Democrats or Republicans.

A dealignment is also indicated if individuals do not use their party identification as a guide to forming other political dispositions, especially those related to elections. However, a strong relationship is found between party identification and evaluations of Ronald Reagan's performance as president. The correlations (r's) between these measures range in size from .46 to .62 (results not shown). Party identification is also strongly related to the results of a number of "trial heat" or "horse race" questions asking about potential candidates in the 1984 presidential election (correlations range from .44 for Reagan-Jackson to .65 for Reagan-McGovern).[5]

It is not possible to determine if the relationships between party identification and evaluations of presidential performance or candidate preferences were stronger among Alabama citizens at an earlier time. Thus it is not possible to say that citizens are now using their party identification to a greater or lesser extent in forming dispositions than they once did. It is apparent, however, that party identification at the present time does have a substantial impact on individuals' political attitudes and preferences. This, in conjunction with the presence of a relatively small and stable number of independents (even among younger respondents) within the state's electorate, leads to the conclusion that Alabama is not experiencing a political dealignment.[6]

Realignment: social status.

Several researchers (Converse, 1966; Gatlin, 1975, for example) have speculated that the breakup of the South's traditional, racially based politics will result in the development of increasingly stronger relationships between citizens' social status and their party affiliations. As a result, the region's politics will come to resemble the post-New Deal patterns found in the remainder of the country.

The results of the analysis show that an individual's social status (as measured by education) is related to his/her party identification. More-educated individuals tend to identify themselves as Republicans while less-educated respondents are more Democratic (correlations (r's) range from −.10 to −.23, all statistically significant at the .05 level).[7] The strength of the relationship between education and party identification varies over time. It is generally stronger when the number of Republican identifiers is the smallest.

Overall these results indicate that there is some status difference in party identification. However, while there may be a greater relationship between Alabamians' social status and their party identifications now than in the past (Cotter, 1983), the results of the present analysis show that this relationship is not exceptionally strong. In addition, when the number of Republicans increases, the relationship between status and party identification declines. These findings suggest that the relationship will not grow in strength. As a result, it is difficult to argue that a status-based realignment has occurred within Alabama during the last several years.

Realignment: ideology.

Another indicator of a possible realignment is a growing distinctiveness of party identifiers on the grounds of political ideology (Beck, 1982). A relationship between self-described political ideology and party identification is found in Alabama (correlations (r's) range from –.15 to –.32). Those who say that they are conservative tend to identify themselves as Republicans, while liberals think of themselves as Democrats. It is important to remember, however, that a significant portion (about one-third) of the respondents in each sample do not classify themselves on the ideological scale.

The results of the analysis also show that a relationship between self-described ideology and party identification is found among white respondents (average $r = -.20$), and among both older (average $r = -.26$) and younger citizens (average r = $-.23$). The relationship between party identification and self-described ideology, however, is not consistently stronger among younger or older respondents. Finally, the strength of the relationship between party identification and self-described political ideology fluctuates over time. Generally the relationship between party identification and self-described ideology is highest when the number of Republicans is lowest. For example, the correlation between party identification and self-described political ideology is –.32 in the fall of 1982, but only –.15 in the spring of 1981.

Overall, these results give only modest support to the notion that a realignment is occurring on the basis of political ideology. There is a relationship between ideology and party identification. However, this relationship is neither consistent nor growing. Nor is it stronger among these (younger respondents) expected to be most influenced by a realignment.

Realignment: issues.

Carmines and Stimson argue "that issues can bring about significant political change by producing slow, steady shifts in the partisan complexion of the electorate." (1981: 108). These shifts were sparked by the racial issues of the mid-1960s. They document their argument by showing a growing difference in racial attitudes between new Democratic and Republican party identifiers.

It is possible to give only a partial test to the Carmine and Stimpson argument because questions about racial issues have not been included in each of the Capstone Poll surveys. However, one of the studies did include several questions asking respondents' opinions on racial issues. As seen in table 10.4, questions about racial issues are generally unrelated or are only weakly related to party identification. This is true even when only white respondents or only younger respondents are examined. The only racial issue question even modestly related to party identification asks about actions of the government in Washington. This suggests that the observed relationship may reflect some other disposition besides or in addition to opinions about civil rights.

Impact of short-term forces.

Researchers have recently shown that party identification is influenced by the opinions that individuals have about "short-term" forces, such as the president, in the political environment. We have already shown that a strong relationship exists between party identification and attitudes about Ronald Reagan's performance as president. It is also the case that, just as the distribution of party identification has changed during the last several years, so too have Alabamians' opinions about Ronald Reagan. For instance, in 1981 Alabamians evaluated Ronald Reagan very favorably (55% saying he was doing an "excellent" or "good" job). Evaluations of Reagan's performance, however, declined during 1982 (in the fall of 1982 only 37% said that he was doing an excellent or good job) and then increased. In the fall of 1986 about 27% of the respondents rated Reagan as excellent, and an additional 34% said he was doing a good job.

What is immediately obvious in examining changes in Reagan's job ratings is that the fluctuations in his public support closely parallel increases and decreases in the number of Republican identifiers. This close relationship is clearly illustrated in figure 10.2. Similarly, when the different surveys are treated as the unit of analysis, a very strong correlation is found between the proportion rating Reagan as excellent or good and the number of Republican identifiers (r = .93). These findings suggest that what we have labeled as a "short-term force" change is occurring in Alabama.[8]

DISCUSSION

The results presented in this chapter point toward the following conclusions:

1. A dealignment does not seem to be occurring in Alabama; voters

Table 10.4
Correlation (r) between Party Identification and Opinions on Racial Issue Questions

Opinion	Total	Whites	Younger	Older
Achieving racial integration is so important that it justifies busing children to schools out of their own neighborhood.	−.15*	−.05	−.18*	−.16*
Should white people have the right to keep black people out of their neighborhoods if they want to, or should black people have the right to live wherever they can afford to, just like anybody else?	.05	.00	.05	.07
Are you in favor of desegregation, segregation, or something in between?	.02	.02	.05	.01
Do you strongly agree, agree, disagree, or strongly disagree that the government in Washington should make every possible effort to improve the social and economic position of blacks and other minorities?	−.29*	−.21*	−.34*	−.26*
Do you strongly agree, agree, disagree, or strongly disagree that it is a good thing for the country that blacks are now allowed to vote?	−.06	.00	−.14*	.01
Some say that the civil rights people have been trying to push too fast. Others feel that they haven't pushed fast enough. How about you—do you think that civil rights leaders are trying to push too fast, are going too slowly, or are they moving at about the right speed?	.15*	−.03	.22*	.14*

*Questions were asked in the spring of 1983. Some items were recoded in conducting the analysis. p .05

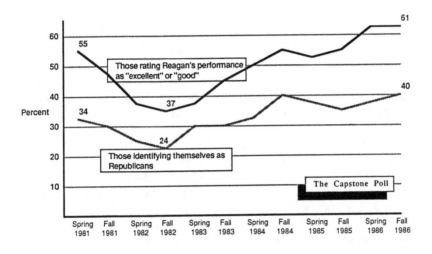

Figure 10.2
Evaluation of Reagan as president and Republican Party identification in
Alabama, 1981–1986.

still readily identify with political parties, the number of independents
is not growing, and the analysis shows that Alabamians use their party
identifications to make political judgments.

2. A realignment, to some degree, may be occurring because of political ideology, but there is little evidence that it is happening because
of long-term political issues.

3. The strongest evidence involving change among Alabama voters is
based on the relationship between Ronald Reagan's performance ratings and Republican party identification; in other words, political
change in Alabama has a distinctive "short-term force" hue.

The results presented in figure 10.2 clearly show that the distribution
of opinions about Ronald Reagan is related to the distribution of party
identifiers in the state. Determining how much of an influence a
change in one of these dispositions has on the other is not easy with the
available data. The results of recent research do suggest, however, that
the relationship between evaluation of Reagan and party identification
is reciprocal (for example, Franklin and Jackson, 1983). Thus, the conditions that influence the public's evaluations of Reagan probably also
influence their party identifications. Consequently, the results of the
analysis suggest that recent changes in the balance of party identifica-

tion in Alabama have occurred because of events and conditions within the political environment.

In the short run, the findings of this study suggest that whatever is good for Ronald Reagan is also good for the Alabama Republican party. The results, however, give no indication about what will happen when Ronald Reagan leaves the political scene. Only time will tell if the Reagan presidency has allowed the Republican party to build a significant base of support within the state, or if the absence of a popular Republican in the White House will relegate the GOP to its traditional minority status.

Unfortunately, the results of the 1986 election provide few insights into the future of the state's politics. Despite a strong effort by Reagan, incumbent Republican U.S. Senator Jeremiah Denton lost his seat to Congressmen Richard Shelby. To some this defeat may indicate that the public's approval of Reagan, while helpful to the local GOP, is not resulting in a political realignment within Alabama. However, the narrow defeat of Denton, despite his weaknesses as a candidate, indicates that the state's Republican party may have significantly improved its position in recent years and that the GOP has a real future in Alabama.

Like Denton's defeat, Guy Hunt's election as governor does not say much about future partisan politics in the state. Hunt's victory was less his own doing than the result of the bitter struggle over the outcome of the runoff election. In this dispute, a Democratic party committee selected the "loser" of the runoff to be the party's nominee because the "winner" of the runoff had illegally encouraged those who had voted in the Republican primary election to "cross over" and vote in the Democratic runoff. The public's anger at the party's decision led directly to Hunt's victory.

Capstone Poll surveys conducted during the election campaign show that the distribution of party identifiers at the end of the campaign was almost exactly what it was at the beginning of the contest. However, the potential of Hunt's victory (through its possible impact in areas such as candidate recruitment and fund raising) to spark a long-term realignment remains unclear.

NOTES

1. It is possible that Republican victories in recent elections may simply represent the influence of factors peculiar to these contests and not a shift in the long-term political preferences of Alabamians. If this is the case, then, as

suggested by Brady (1985), there should be substantial stability both in the distribution of party identification within Alabama and in the composition of the parties. As will be shown, party identification has experienced more than enough fluctuation within the last several years to rule out the possibility that Alabama has undergone no real change.

2. Among the major works examining political realignments are Beck, 1979; Sundquist, 1973; Clubb, Flanigan, and Zingale, 1980; Kleppner, et al., 1981; Campbell and Trilling, 1980; and Key, 1955, 1959.

3. Miller and Wattenberg (1983) report that a similar procedure is used to construct the party-identification scale found in the National Election Study surveys. Interest in politics was indicated by whether respondents were either "interested" or "very interested" in either national or Alabama state politics. For further discussion of the use of this procedure in constructing the party-identification scale, see Craig (1985). Similar questions and procedures were used to construct measures of state party identification. The measures of state and national party identification are strongly related to one another (average r equal approximately .7) Results also indicate that there are slightly more Democratic identifiers and fewer Republicans on the state than the national party identification measure. (For further information about party identification at multiple levels of government, see Jennings and Niemi, 1966; Perkins and Guynes, 1976; and Hadley, 1985).

4. Data are not available to study the influence of migration on political change in Alabama.

5. Overall, the relationships involving party identification are somewhat weaker among younger than older respondents. Strong relationships are, however, found among both groups.

6. A high level of split-ticket voting is another indicator of a dealignment. The split results in the 1984 (president-U.S. Senate) and the 1986 (governor-U.S. Senate) elections clearly shows that a considerable amount of split-ticket voting occurs in Alabama. Analysis of the 1984 election found that at least one-third of the electorate cast a split ballot (Cotter, 1985). Unfortunately, a lack of comparable information for other states makes it difficult to conclude whether the level of split-ticket voting in Alabama is high or low.

7. A relationship between education and party identification is found when only white respondents are examined. It is also found among both younger and older Alabamians, though status is more closely related to party identification among older than younger respondents.

8. Another indication that the distribution of party identification in Alabama is influenced by outside, short-term forces and events is found in the results of the spring 1984 study. This survey was in the field at the time of the bombing of the Marine headquarters in Beirut and the U.S. "invasion" of Grenada. When respondents are divided into those interviewed before or after October 22 (the day of the Beirut bombing and the day before the Grenada invasion), a small, but statistically significant relationship ($r = .11$ $p. .05$) is found. Those interviewed after this day are more Republican and less Democratic in their party identification than are others. It is also important to note that Reagan's job performance rating is higher among those interviewed after October 22 compared to those interviewed earlier in the study.

11

Partisan Change in South Carolina

Cole Blease Graham, Jr.

This chapter concentrates on presidential and gubernatorial elections in South Carolina since 1964. The voting patterns in elections for these two statewide executive offices reveal contrasts in partisan change and partisan choice. Republicans have dominated presidential elections, but Democrats have generally won in gubernatorial contests.

The opening sections briefly describe South Carolina historical developments, current population characteristics, and general economic features. The ensuing analysis relates differing county-level electoral patterns to selected population and socioeconomic variables. Public opinion poll findings are the basis of a concluding discussion of the dimensions and prospects for partisan political change in the state.

THE POLITICAL SETTING

From the Civil War through the general economic depression of the 1930s, South Carolina was a static society. The earlier political dominance of South Carolina's plantation owners had generally faded with the political rise of white supremacists in the late 1800s. But, when unified under the Democratic party banner, rich and poor white Democrats did not need black voters to win statewide elections (Key, 1949: 131). A die-hard States' Rights view, one crop-cotton agriculture, racial segregation, and a general intellectual malaise kept the state isolated from the nation well into the twentieth century.

Yet, these conditions were a challenge to the established traditions of aristocratic propriety and control. For example, *The State* newspaper in Columbia was founded by relatives of Confederate General Wade Hampton and has consistently editorialized against racial violence and undirected economic change. While simultaneously vulnerable to criticisms of paternalism, especially of blacks, and to collusion with the white, working class, Populist politics that they outwardly opposed,

South Carolina's traditional political elite have generally advocated a deliberate and moderate approach to social and political developments.

The onset of consistent and lasting legislative leadership by Solomon Blatt, who was House Speaker in 1935–1945 and 1951–1973 (Cauthen, 1965), and Edgar Brown, who was a state senator from 1929 to 1973 (Workman, 1963), coincided with the efforts of the state's emerging business elite to promote economic development during and after World War II (Lander, 1970: 211–230). The new, business-based leadership, in an appeal to the state's earlier "Golden Age," revived South Carolina traditionalism.

These long-standing values provided a base for slowly developing public policies with an emphasis on persuasion and "change with dignity and purpose." Though perhaps more in tune with the narrower interests of business and large-scale developers than the social problems of a broader population, South Carolina's elected leadership nevertheless positively confronted new political forces and demands. Today, fiscal responsibility, educational improvement, especially technical training, and economic growth and development have replaced white supremacy and white resistance as the state's dominant political issues.

Active, self-directed economic growth and development have been the bases for the transition of the relatively static social and economic structure of South Carolina; it is "fossil no more" (Pierce, 1983: 383). And, in the process, the old Democratic political alliances have eroded and the new electoral results tend to be more partisan. Republicans have won all but one presidential vote in South Carolina since 1964, while Republican governors have been elected twice. Political observers and street-level opinion attribute Republican ascendancy in presidential voting to the alienation of long-time Democrats by the positive civil rights position of the national Democratic party and the enactment of the Civil Rights Act and the Voting Rights Act. So far, these issues have not affected the governor's elections in the same partisan way, although the 1986 governor's race may foretell a deeper partisan shift.

MAJOR STATEWIDE ELECTIONS, 1964–1986

A quick look at statewide elections shows that Democrats won seven of eight presidential votes from 1932 through 1960. The only exception was Strom Thurmond's Dixiecrat victory in 1948. Franklin Roosevelt carried South Carolina by overwhelming majorities in the Depression and during the World War II years with as much as 95% of the vote in South Carolina. By 1960, John Kennedy was able to beat Richard

Nixon by fewer than 10,000 votes. The Republican party won its first South Carolina presidential election in 1964, when Barry Goldwater won over Lyndon Johnson by 18 percent. South Carolina was one of only six states carried nationally by Goldwater.

As illustrated in table 11.1, Republicans have won every presidential election since 1964 with the exception of Jimmy Carty in 1976. Carter defeated Ford by roughly the same percentage (12 percent) as Nixon had won in 1968. Ford won only three South Carolina counties— Aiken, Greenville, and Lexington, although he lost narrowly in Charleston, Beaufort, Kershaw, and Pickens. In 1980, Ronald Reagan had about 2% more votes than Carter, but Reagan stretched the margin to 27.8% over Mondale in 1984. In contrast, table 11.1 also shows that Democrats have more often been elected governor. Republicans won only in 1974 and 1986 and by narrow margins.

Results in contested elections for United States senator since 1964 also illustrate the demise of Democratic exclusiveness. Senator Strom Thurmond, first elected as a Democrat, switched to the Republican party in September 1964. Senator Ernest Hollings fought off early Republican opposition and both have been easily reelected since, indicating perhaps an "unspoken" compromise to share the seats. While it is possible to identify Thurmond with upstate conservative values and Hollings with the more traditional coastal interests, in fact each has carved out a statewide power base. Thurmond has emphasized constituency service and the value of his seniority in the Senate; Hollings has stressed economic growth and his active leadership in national legislation to deregulate business.

These partisan political tendencies have been accompanied by population growth and redistribution and the emergence of urban centers more like mainstream national ones. Economic developments have broadened manufacturing beyond textiles and enlarged the productive capacity of the state. The next section summarizes these broad demographic and economic changes as a basis for a more informed description of the contrasting election outcomes.

DESCRIPTORS OF CHANGE

Population Growth and Distribution

The population of South Carolina increased 8.7% in the 1960s and 20.5% between 1970 and 1980 to a total of 3,112,814 in 1980. The population density of the state has jumped 31% since 1960 to 103 persons per square mile. Net migration into South Carolina between 1975

Table 11.1
Election Outcomes in South Carolina for President, Governor, and United
States Senator, 1964–1984

Year	Democrat		Republican	
	Number	Percent	Number	Percent
President				
1964	215,723	41.1	309,048	58.9
1968	197,486	29.6	254,062	38.1
1972	186,824	27.7	477,044	70.8
1976	450,807	56.2	346,149	43.1
1980	417,117	48.9	421,117	49.4
1984	344,470	35.6	615,539	63.4
Governor				
1966	255,854	58.2	184,088	41.8
1970	250,551	51.7	221,233	45.6
1974	248,938	47.6	266,109	50.9
1978	384,896	62.2	236,946	37.8
1982	466,347	70.0	201,002	30.0
1986	354,897	47.9	368,636	51.1
United States Senator				
1966	164,955	37.8	271,295	62.2
1966	223,790	51.3	212,032	48.7
1968	404,060	61.9	248,780	38.1
1972	241,056	36.7	415,806	63.3
1974	356,126	69.5	146,645	28.6
1978	281,119	44.4	351,733	55.6
1980	512,554	70.4	257,946	29.6
1984	306,982	32.3	644,814	67.7
1986	465,500	63.9	262,886	36.1

Source: South Carolina Election Commission Reports for all years except 1986, which is compiled from newspaper reports.

Note: There was no election for U.S. Senator in 1964. There were two contested races in 1966. Incumbent Strom Thurmond (R) defeated a Democratic challenger, and Ernest F. Hollings (D) won the remaining two years of Senator Olin Johnston's term. Hollings ran again in 1968 and won a full six-year term. Each incumbent has won in subsequent races: Thurmond in 1972, 1978, and 1984; Hollings in 1974, 1980, and 1986.

and 1980 showed a gain of 93,726 people (South Carolina *Statistical Abstract*, 1985: 307, 325).

The black population of the state has also changed in number and distribution (South Carolina *Statistical Abstract*, 1985: 311, 327). From a black majority of 60.7% in 1880, the state's proportion of blacks slipped to 30% in 1980. Today, many black citizens live in rural counties like Allendale (62.8% black), Williamsburg (62.3%), Lee (61.2%), and Jasper (51%). Black voter registration made notable advances in the 1960s (Bain, 1972: 560–565), so that some counties with a majority black population also have a registered voting majority of blacks.

The general population distribution is often characterized by comparison of up-country and low-country South Carolina. The "up" and "low" designations originate geologically from a fall line that bisects the state from northeast to southwest. The section above the line has falling water as a basis for textile manufacturing and electricity production, clay soils as a basis for small farms, and a "backwoods" settlement pattern of later arrivals, who tend to be more politically conservative as well as more fundamental in religious views. The low-country was settled earlier by large land owners who were more loyal to the Church of England and who organized the blackwater rivers and loam soils into large agricultural operations. Of course, such generalizations are misleading to some extent. Aristocratic entrepreneurs developed large plantations in the river "bottoms" or valleys of the up-country (Banner, 1974: 77). Low-country manufacturing was stimulated in the 1930s by the development of man-made lakes for electricity generation (Edgar, 1984).

The Emergence of Metropolitan Centers

While the older sectional differences are useful background for understanding South Carolina politics, a contemporary South Carolina is more nearly split between urban and rural interests. The urban portion increased from 36.7% in 1950 to 41.2% in 1970 and 54.1% in 1980. By 1983, more than half (59.9%) of the state's population level in metropolitan statistical areas (MSAs), although compared to 75.8% in MSAs nationally, South Carolina still has rural characteristics. The state's MSAs contain 13 of its 46 counties.

The metropolitan areas are distributed across the entire state. The established metropolitan areas are in the northwest (Greenville–Spartanburg), in the center (Columbia), and to the southeast (Charleston). These areas have been MSAs since federal definition began.

Anderson (near Greenville–Spartanburg) and Florence in the eastern PeeDee region are recently designated metropolitan counties. York County is near the Charlotte, North Carolina, MSA, and Aiken County has long been in the Augusta, Georgia, MSA. All of these growing urban centers have developed around the interstate highway system that criss-crosses the state and Columbia, at the center, is within eighty to one hundred miles of each.

Economic Developments

The textile industry, South Carolina's original industry, developed basically because of an abundant supply of cheap labor and a friendly reception by the state government. Since the 1930s, the state has had an industrial development board that encourages the location of new investments and that tries to get existing industry to stay and expand.

Governors, along with business and local officials, regularly participate in organized "industry hunting" and economic development missions. Governors annually measure the success of their administration by the amount of new business investment. The state's manufacturing base is linked to the housing and automotive sectors of the national economy. Automobile supplies, especially carpeting, have long been a part of the value of the state's manufactures. The relocation in 1985 from Pennsylvania of a Mack Truck assembly facility boosted the economic base.

Workers who produce textile mill products have steadily declined from 12.4% of the state's work force in 1976 to 8.2% in 1984. In less than a decade, the textile mill industry lost more than 30,000 jobs. Recent increases in numbers of employees since 1979 have been in the construction (+ 8.500), retail trade (+ 36,500), and services (+ 44,200) sectors of the South Carolina economy. In sum, nonagricultural employment makes up 92.4% of the state's work force (South Carolina *Statistical Abstract*, 1985: 67, 74).

These broad characteristics allow selection of more specific measures for more detailed analysis. Three measures appear feasible. The number of blacks is a population measure that relates to voting patterns, the proportion of rural dwellers reflects the impact of metropolitan areas, and per capita income is a measure of economic change. The relationship of these measures to election outcomes and the implications for partisan shifts in South Carolina are discussed in the following section.

ANALYSIS OF PRESIDENTIAL AND GUBERNATORIAL ELECTIONS

The election results given in table 11.1 are measurable at the county level. County-level election results conform to county-based census measures of population and other characteristics such as per capita income. While the associations among these measures do not relate to an investigation of individual voting preferences, statistically significant relationships between voting outcomes and these selected social characteristics do describe aspects of partisan choice in the state.

The county is an identifiable political subdivision, and it is used in South Carolina as a way of organizing the vote. Political campaign managers target specific counties, and every South Carolina county has an election commission for identifying precincts and reporting election returns. Even though campaigns today are also directed at precincts and functional groups of voters, changing precinct boundaries, the volume of analysis implied to track their changing population composition, and the relative vagueness of the specific politics of a precinct suggest that this level of analysis will be appropriate in other, more detailed studies.

County Rankings

By using the established division into up-country (Piedmont) and low-country (Coastal Plain) along the geological fall line, twenty Piedmont counties and twenty-six Coastal Plain counties may be identified. Consistency of county preference may be found by ranking the top half, or 23 of 46 counties, by level of support for Democratic candidates. The results are displayed in table 11.2.

More counties are consistently Democratic in elections for governor than for president. Only six counties are in the top half in all twelve elections. These counties are typically small and have large proportions of black citizens. By population number and percent black population, they are: Chester (30,148—38.6); Fairfield (17,528—58.5); Allendale (10,700—62.8); Hampton (18,519—52.7); Marion (34,179—52.2); and Marlboro (31,634—47.1). Collectively, these counties include only 4.6% of the state's total population, but they have 7.6% of the black citizens (South Carolina *Statistical Abstract*, 1985: 319).

By comparison Democrats did not rank in the top half in any of the twelve elections in three counties—Kershaw, Aiken, and Lexington. These three counties have 39,015, 105,625, and 140,353 citizens respectively, but they average only 18.3% black. Six metropolitan counties are included in the group that ranked consistently in the lower half (six out of six elections) of county support for Democratic candidates for president or governor. Only Anderson County showed high Democratic support, ranking in the top half five of six times in gubernatorial races. The exception was the 1986 election, which was won by the Republican

Table 11.2

Counties Ranking in Top 23 Counties in Democratic Support for President and Governor in South Carolina, 1964–1986

Presidential Elections		Gubernatorial Elections	
Up-Country	Low-Country	Up-Country	Low-Country
Six Times			
Chester	Allendale*	Abbeville	Allendale*
Fairfield*	Georgetown	Cherokee	Hampton*
	Hampton*	Chester	Marion*
	Marion*	Chesterfield	Marlboro
	Marlboro	Fairfield*	
		Greenwood	
		McCormick*	
		Union	
Five Times			
Chesterfield	Bamberg*	Anderson**	Jasper*
McCormick*	Clarendon*		
	Jasper*		
	Williamsburg*		
One Time			
Spartanburg**	Charleston	Greenville**	Beaufort
	Darlington	Newberry	Colleton
	Horry	Saluda	Dorchester**
			Horry
			Lee*
			Richland**
None of Six Possible Times			
Greenville**	Aiken**	Kershaw	Aiken**
Kershaw	Barnwell	Spartanburg*	Calhoun*
Newberry	Lexington**		Charleston**
Pickens**			Lexington**
Saluda			Sumter

* = black majority population county

** = metropolitan (MSA) county

Source: Calculated from official and newspaper election reports.

candidate, Carroll Campbell. South Carolina Democrats do not seem to do as well as Republicans in metropolitan counties whether they are promoting a candidate for president or for governor.

Associations among County Rankings

The consistency of county voting patterns may be discussed more broadly by comparing the percentages of votes by county for the Democratic candidates over time. Each election may be compared with other elections to see how much continuity there is in county voting patterns. A high correlation of the rankings of the counties between different elections shows the similarity of their ordinal positions. A low or negative correlation value shows dissimilarity. Kendall's Tau-b is the coefficient that measures correlations of ordinal data in square tables. The value, called a coefficient of concordance, measures the general cohesion between several ranked orders. As used here, it indicates the overall consistency in voting strength by county for Democratic candidates. At the value of zero, the concordant pairs exactly equal the discordant pairs. As the values approach + 1, the suggestion is that the ranks of a county are more nearly alike in the situations that are compared.

The Tau-b coefficients for presidential elections in South Carolina demonstrate that counties with high rankings in their support for Carter in 1976 also tended to rank high in their support for him in 1980 (+ .702). While counties that ranked high for Humphrey also ranked high in their support for McGovern (+ .814), Carter did not draw similar levels of support from them. The Humphrey rankings reappeared in some strength in the 1984 ranking of support for Mondale, and there appears to be some spillover of Carter's relative support as well. The most discordant comparisons result from the 1964 rankings for Lyndon Johnson's candidacy. If partisan change is measured from the 1964 presidential election base for Johnson, South Carolina Democrats seem to have abandoned national Democratic nominees.

The values for the gubernatorial elections do not show the clear differences found in presidential support rankings. The highest value (+ .619) is in the concordance between Riley's second campaign and Daniel's 1986 candidacy. Daniel campaigned on a platform of continuing Riley's "excellence," especially in education, but the victorious Republican Carroll Campbell mired the Daniel effort with charges of lackluster leadership and cronyism. Riley's 1978 rankings correlate favorably with his 1982 levels (+ .480), but not as strongly as might be expected for the state's first incumbent four-year governor. While Riley won in 1978 by a convincing margin, he won even more handily in the 1982 so that the calculations probably reflect the increased support expected for an incumbent in areas where there was not as much support as before. The sharp drop by Daniel's rankings in 1986 compared to Riley in 1978 (+ .297) may be the most telling value. The state's first two term, eight-year governor may have benefited from incumbency as a resource in 1982, but the advantage did not extend to a designated successor. Protégés of previously successful Democratic governors may now be imperiled by partisan shifts. Two earlier, successful candidates were protégés of traditional South Carolina leaders; Robert McNair followed long-term Speaker Solomon Blatt, and John West understudied State Senator Edgar Brown. All of the Democratic gubernatorial candidates had "paid their dues" by extensive service in elected office before running for governor.

The Tau-b values suggest a weakening in both McNair's and West's support bases in 1986 and hint at partisan change. The success of the 1986 Republican campaign in adjoining up-country counties like Greenville (the Republican candidate's home country), Spartanburg, and Anderson may only imply a recurrence of "friends and neighbors" voting. But, Riley is from Greenville County also. Whether his strength there sprang from a strong home-county base or partisan loyalty, it did not carry over to Daniel, who comes from a small county (Cherokee) that is next to Spartanburg. The neighborly vote should have helped Daniel, but it did not. Whether a similar deterioration in the Democratic vote for governor becomes definable as a partisan reorientation that transcends local geographic loyalties will have to be seen in future elections.

From these general findings, the next section moves to a discussion of the association of selected socioeconomic variables and Democratic support.

Associations with County Socioeconomic Characteristics

The selected independent variables for association with support for Democratic candidates are county per capita income, black population by county, and percent rural in each county. Hypothetically, there should be an inverse relationship between per capita income and Democratic support and positive associations between black or rural population levels and the percentage of votes for Democratic candidates.

As per capita income increases, Democratic support should fall because of increased disapproval of taxing and spending programs attributed at least to national Democrats. As a sidewalk observer put it,

"New Deal Democrats in the South become Republicans when taxes on their income amount to 25 percent." This "tax bracket creep" suggests that as South Carolinians do better economically, the support for Democrats should fall.

County black population size is one way to deal with the racial issue in South Carolina politics. Voting data in South Carolina are reported by black and white categories. As a consequence, there are some identifiable all-black precincts. A general inspection of these precinct results shows that blacks still tend to vote in blocs for national and state Democrats in South Carolina. As the number of blacks in a county increases, there should be a corresponding increase in support for Democrats.

Counties with high rural populations will tend to support Democratic candidates because these counties tend to be poorer and thus potential beneficiaries of federal and state spending programs. These counties, however, may be more fearful of racial developments, ideologically opposed to public spending, and less educated. A negative association indicates that this population segment may defect from Democratic positions if these issues are prominent.

Pearson correlation coefficients are shown for presidential and gubernatorial elections in table 11.3. As expected, Democratic presiden-

Table 11.3

Pearson Correlation Coefficients for Selected County Characteristics and Support for Democratic Candidate

Year	Candidate	Per Capita Income	Number Black	Percent Rural
1964	Johnson	.238	−.124	.152
1966	McNair	−.072	−.214	−.212
1968	Humphrey	−.629**	.048	−.447**
1970	West	−.148	−.175	−.254
1972	McGovern	−.683**	−.004	−.503**
1974	Dorn	−.432**	−.467**	−.509**
1976	Carter	−.644**	−.425**	−.445**
1978	Riley	−.179	−.276	−.212
1980	Carter	−.670**	−.403**	−.581**
1982	Riley	−.519**	−.282	−.355
1984	Mondale	−.719**	−.168	−.622**
1986	Daniel	−.659**	−.195	−.522**

Source: Calculated from official and newspaper election reports.

** = significant at .01 level.

tial candidates do poorly among counties with higher per capita income. The consistently high negative values suggest that "pocketbook" issues are especially important for areas with higher affluence and that national Democrats have simply not been appealing in these sections of South Carolina.

Surprisingly, the measures of black and rural population levels do not show the expected positive associations. Carter's higher negative values suggest that he also received support from the counties with higher levels of white population. Black voters make up 30% of the state's general electorate, but the black population is low in many counties and less than 10% in Oconee, Pickens, and Lexington counties. Perhaps the fact that Carter was a southerner helps explain his broader attraction.

The rural defection is a potentially compelling descriptor of a general partisan shift. The first major negative value (-.447) is in Humphrey's 1968 campaign. Large numbers of South Carolina rural, white voters in fact supported George Wallace's American Independent party that year. These counties did not return to the Democrats in 1972 and later as the negative values for McGovern, Carter, and Mondale indicate. Since there were no other significant third-party presidential candidates in the period of this study, much rural support must have become Republican in subsequent presidential votes.

The Pearson values for Democratic gubernatorial candidates show a pattern similar to the presidential candidates. Economic issues surfaced strongly in 1974, 1982, and 1986. A Republican candidate, James Edwards, won in 1974 during a time of economic recession and the oil supply crisis. Governor Edwards' most effective political advertisement portrayed him in a kitchen with two bagsful of groceries along with the promise that, were he the governor, the same full bags would be in a South Carolina kitchen four years in the future. The Democrat Dorn had retired from Congress and was identified with federal spending and the "old boy" network. His candidacy was complicated by the disqualification of the Democratic primary nominee, Charles "Pug" Ravenel, in a residency dispute that put the state Democrats in disarray. Increased spending for education improvement by Riley (1982) and Daniel's promise to continue Riley's policies (1986) perhaps underlie the negative values for them.

Congressmen Dorn did not do well in counties with higher numbers of black citizens, perhaps because his congressional district is composed of up-country counties with higher percentage of white population. The negative value implies that Dorn did well in counties with higher numbers of whites, but, more realistically, it may be an example of the candidate's support by people who knew him and who had voted for him before.

Though not as high as in the presidential races, the lack of rural support for other Democratic gubernatorial candidates is also evident. Dorn and Daniel did poorer the higher the percentage of rural population. John West has a slightly negative score. He was involved in the last gubernatorial campaign expressly involving racial rhetoric and the racial issue (Black, 1976: 84–85). His opponent, Republican Congressman Albert Watson, had a campaign marred by a school fight among black and white students allegedly staged by his campaign staff. West ran as a moderate and was the first governor to declare the state "color blind."

Arrests of rural whites for racial violence, for example, for overturning school buses at Lamar in Darlington County during the McNair administration, may give some basis to rural disaffection with Democrats on the racial issue. But, economic conditions and state government spending practices may be the more important issues today for rural and affluent counties alike. Financing the state's Education Improvement Act may have added current complications for Democratic candidates. The act is associated with a 1-cent increase in the state sales tax and a perceived increase in personal property tax rates. Fears of increased state centralization of public school administration and the exploitation of confidence in the financial administration of the state by the Republican candidate Campbell in the 1986 campaign no doubt added to rural losses for the Democratic candidate. A discussion of public opinion survey data and the pivotal importance of taxing and spending issues to South Carolina voters follows.

A LOOK AT SOUTH CAROLINA
THROUGH PUBLIC OPINION POLLS

In addition to the study of election results by county, another way to conceptualize partisan change is through comparison of individual evaluations of partisan loyalties. As shown as table 11.4, blacks and citizens with lower education levels are more likely to be Democrats in South Carolina. Generally, about two-thirds of blacks, one-half of families with less than $13,000 annual income, and one-half of the group with less than a high school education see themselves as Democrats. Republicans draw identification from about one-third of whites, citi-

Table 11.4

Selected Demographics of Partisan Identification in South Carolina

	Percent Partisan Identification					
	Democrat		Independent		Republican	
Demographic	1980	1986	1980	1986	1980	1986
State total	41	36	25	38	34	26
Race:						
Black	82	63	10	29	8	8
White	31	26	28	41	41	34
Education:						
Not high school graduate	57	56	15	30	28	14
High school graduate	44	39	25	36	31	25
Some college	34	27	28	38	39	35
College graduate	25	27	33	44	42	29
Income:						
Under $13,000	*	55	*	33	*	12
Over $13,000	*	40	*	43	*	16
Under $25,000	*	43	*	30	*	27
Over $25,000	*	24	*	40	*	35

Sources: University of South Carolina survey (Tyer, 1980) and *The State* Poll (1986)

Notes: Not all rows add to 100 due to rounding.

*Figures not available

zens with some college and college graduates, and families with annual income of over $25,000. The associations between partisan choice and measures of social status suggest that South Carolinians meet the general national pattern that finds Democrats as working-class people with lower incomes and lower educational levels. Republicans in the state are more likely to be white and have higher educational levels and incomes.

Partisan shifts typically occur because of declining interest in a specific party or because people do not like it anymore. The comparison of two public opinion surveys in table 11.4 shows only a slight loss of Democratic identity by blacks and a slight increase in Democratic partisanship in less educated categories. Except for some erosion in Republican strength among citizens with less than a high school education, the major contrast in the two surveys is an increase in independent strength. The comparison is clouded by the large number of undecided respondents in the 1980 survey. Even so, it is reasonable to conclude that about one-half of South Carolina voters do not identify clearly with either party.

The shift away from Democratic identification among whites, high school and college graduates, and higher income groups is the significant feature in table 11.4. South Carolina Democrats have a proportional majority following only among blacks, the lowest income category, and citizens who are not high school graduates. Given the strong Democratic character of pre-1964 voting results, the broader electorate at that time was far more identified with the state or national Democratic party than in the 1980s. The reduction of the traditionally solid Democratic majority to a support base only among the relatively disadvantaged demonstrates extensive partisan dealignment in South Carolina.

The relatively large independent strength suggests that issues are more important than party ideology in voter choice and that party realignment, at least on state issues, is variable. The independents swing back and forth depending on individual party and candidate appeal. In the 1986 survey, 40% who rated the state as an excellent place to live and work were independents, but 25% of independents also ranked it as fair or poor. The excellence rating by independents is almost the same as that for Republicans, but the fair or poor rating is twice as much. The independent disapproval rate suggests some reservations about Republican solutions as well. Comprehensive partisan realignment in South Carolina will not be a fact until the percentage of independent voters is small.

In general, South Carolinians have held fairly uniform approval ratings for business growth and economic development policies and fairly uniform negative ratings on taxing policies. A Harris Poll (1971) highlights the opinions of state citizens about its economic climate. The results reflect support for economic improvement in contrast to positions that may reflect a principle or a popular cause. For example, when asked whether it was more important to bring in new industry or to preserve the environment and character of the state in its present form, 65 percent said new industry was more important. Forty-six percent identified factors such as "more and better jobs, higher pay and wages, and improved salaries as the elements of an improved state economy" (1971: 6–7).

South Carolinians are as negative about taxes as they are positive about business development. Harris's study of state taxing policy (1971: 93–115) and the University of South Carolina survey (Tyer, 1980: 13–16) found negative feelings about the federal income tax, state income taxes, and the local property tax. In *The State*'s January 1986 poll, only 9% of South Carolinians agreed that an increase in federal taxes was a good way to reduce the national debt, while 60% thought it more appropriate to cut spending. South Carolina Republicans and independents advocated spending cuts by two-thirds in each case. Whether federal tax cuts are really the issue or whether the negative views simply mask objection to federal domestic policies that may benefit the poor or the black minority is unclear. What is clear is that South Carolina Democrats cannot carry the state for any national candidate who does not advocate restraint in federal taxing and spending policies.

Citizen sensitivity on taxation issues has also forced the gubernatorial candidates from both parties to walk a tightwire between adequate state revenues and more state spending, for example, to improve public education. Spending and taxing issues define the patterns of partisan dealignment at the state level. In *The State*'s October 1985 poll, blacks "Agreed Strongly" at about twice the rate as whites (45.8% to 19.8%) in their response to the statement: "Now that South Carolina is spending more money on public education, the overall quality of public education has improved over the past year." When comparing views on building more prisons or developing a release program for nonviolent prisoners, only 14.6% of black respondents favored more prisons, but 45.8% of whites did. The suggestion of these responses is that voters may become more dealigned, maybe even realigned over specific issues requiring more or continued state revenues and outlays.

CONCLUSIONS

Since the onset of active federal civil rights and domestic spending policies, South Carolinians have almost overwhelmingly abandoned their support of Democratic party candidates for president. Democrats have not fared as badly in governor's races, but they have lost relative support in metropolitan counties. The stronghold of Democratic gubernatorial candidates is no longer a consistent majority of the state's population. They must battle with independents and Republicans to win elections.

The future successes of Democratic candidates for governor will depend on how they are perceived to deal with taxing and spending issues. They will have to convince a skeptical majority of the fairness of their fiscal policies. If they do not, they can expect continued dealignment to result in the same partisan devastation for them as for Democratic presidential candidates. A Democrat is faced in 1990 with the new problem of winning the State House back from a Republican governor who may be running as an incumbent. The two-term feature, put in place perhaps as a tactic by Democrats to give them the advantage of incumbency in 1982, now potentially works against them.

Prospects for the 1988 presidential choice in the state suggest no changes in Republican preference. The Reagan victories in 1980 and 1984 indicate widespread acceptance of a national platform that reduces federal taxes and enhances state control over spending. Only a significant turn down in the national economy could redirect Republican and independent support back to the Democrats. Even a fresh, moderate, or southern Democratic presidential candidate will be hard-pressed to overcome the lasting effects of South Carolina's realignment with the national Republican party's White House design.

12

GEORGIA:
Political Realignment or Partisan Evolution

Michael B. Binford

The state of Georgia has long been recognized as a bastion of Democratic strength. The state usually provides an easy general election campaign for state Democratic nominees, after hard-fought party primaries, but recent Democratic presidential nominees have not always fared so easily. Ideology appears to influence strongly the partisan defections in the presidential elections of 1964, 1968, 1972, and 1984; in fact, in the last twenty-six years, only a favorite son on the ticket seems to have overcome this conservative and pro-Republican trend in presidential voting. At first glance, Georgia appears to have a strongly bifurcated electoral system, with presidential elections showing a surprising degree of Republican support, but with Democrats firmly in control at other levels. Table 12.1 presents the recent partisan vote distributions for presidential, senatorial, and gubernatorial races in Georgia. These data underscore the strong Democratic advantage at the Senate and governor's levels, and the divergent tendency at the presidential level. Georgia Republicans have been trying to convert their support at one level to stronger support across all types of elections. So far, they have met with only limited success.

Table 12.1

Party Identification in Georgia

Party	Wright, Erikson, McIver (1974–82)	ABC Exit Polls 1982	ABC Exit Polls 1986	Roper Poll 1987
Democrats	55.5	55.6	51	51.3
Independents	25.4	25.1	24	26.2*
Republicans	12.4	16.0	25	23.1

*includes Independents, Other Party, and No Particular Party responses. The Roper question was: "Regardless of how you have voted in the past, what do you usually consider yourself—a Democrat, a Republican, some other party, or what?"

Survey data indicate rapidly eroding support across the South for the Democratic party among white southerners, and especially among young white voters. The CBS-*New York Times* polls report a shift from 52% Democratic, 19% Republican in 1980 to 33% Democratic, 36% Republican in 1986 (Toner, 1986). Carmines and Stanley (1986) found increasing congruency between conservative ideology and Republican identification among young white southerners. They conclude: "the ideological realignment now occurring in the South is being brought about mainly through immigration and population replacement. The effects of these processes should lead to a steady diminution of that peculiar species of southern politics, the conservative Democrat. Once a dominant feature of southern political life, he is more likely in the future to find himself on the list of endangered species" (Carmines and Stanley, 1986, p. 9). Their implication is that the conservative Democrat will be replaced by his cousin, the conservative Republican. While the changes described by Carmines and Stanley certainly are in process, we may also be seeing the reemergence of the Populist-Progressive Democrat, based upon more evenly distributed components of the traditional New Deal coalition (Stanley, Bianco, and Niemi, 1986).

Recent nationwide studies of party identification and voting behavior support the description of Georgia as a highly partisan, pro-Democratic state that is beginning to see modest Republican growth. Using aggregated CBS-*New York Times* survey data from 1974 to 1982, Wright, Erikson, and McIver (1985) estimate that 55.5% of Georgia voters identify themselves as Democrats, and only 12.4% call themselves Republicans (Wright, Erikson, and McIver, 1985, p. 476). Only Louisiana has a higher Democratic rate of identification, and only Rhode Island has a lower level of Republicans. These figures show the strong tilt in the favor of the Democratic party. Ideologically, Georgians appear moderately conservative, with 31.8% saying they are conservative, 38.7% moderate, and 16.9% liberal. In a 1982 ABC poll, 55.6% claimed Democratic allegiance, 16% were Republican, and 25.1% were independent. The March 1987 Roper Poll of the 1988 southern primary states indicated Republican gains in Georgia, with 23.1% reporting Republican identification, but still 51% calling themselves Democrats. These figures indicate evolutionary development rather than a rapid shift in partisanship. Clearly, the Republicans are beginning to erode the solid Democratic claim in Georgia, as table 12.1 indicates.

Using presidential voting returns from 1944 to 1980, Rabinowitz and McDonald (1986) found that long-term relative support for presidential candidates is based on a combination of ideology and partisanship, and Georgia lies in the conservative, highly Democratic area of the voting space. Contemporary analyses of party organizations, such as Bibby et al. (1983), Feigert (1983), and Jewell and Olson (1982), all classify Georgia as a one-party (Democratic) dominant system. Given this consistent designation, any evidence of Republican gains or partisan realignment would be quite noteworthy and would seem to require a strong national or regional trend as a catalyst; the Republican party of Georgia does not have the power or the resources to stimulate such a realignment on its own, although it has been consistently more active in recent years.

Contemporary Georgian electoral history is not without its Republican successes. After a near loss in the governor's race in 1966, in which the Republican candidate actually won a plurality of votes, Republicans had to wait until 1980 to win a statewide, nonpresidential election. The incumbent Democratic Senator, Herman Talmadge, after a long investigation and eventual censure by the Senate, was narrowly defeated by a political newcomer, Mack Mattingly. Mattingly was the first Republican senator from Georgia since Reconstruction, but his narrow defeat in 1986 indicates that a second Reconstruction is not necessarily at hand. Table 12.2 shows the recent electoral returns for statewide races in Georgia. In the state legislature, small, incremental growth in the number of Republican legislators has been made. The post-Watergate period set back this progress, but those losses have been recouped. Currently, 10 state senators and 27 representatives are from the GOP. The question to explore here is, have these Republican victories been idiosyncratic aberrations from deeply rooted Democratic

Table 12.2

Percent of Votes for Democratic Candidates

Year	President	Senate	Governor
1972	24.7	54.0	
1974		71.9	69.1
1976	66.9		
1978		83.1	80.6
1980	57.6	49.4	
1982			62.8
1984	39.8	79.9	
1986		50.9	70.5

Source: Data from Georgia secretary of state

habits, or have the more national trends of dealignment, or indeed, realignment begun to penetrate into Georgian electoral behavior?

The traditional analyses of Georgia's electoral behavior clearly begin with V. O. Key's classic, *Southern Politics* (1949). Written during the heyday of Eugene Talmadge's influence on state politics, Key's analysis describes the one overriding dimension or faultline of Georgia politics: region. Based on the county-unit system, which gave the winner of the county's popular vote two, four, or, at most, six county unit votes, state politics were easily dominated by the numerous rural counties. The county-unit system explains the large number (159) of counties in the state. Both Eugene and Herman Talmadge continually based their electoral coalitions on rural constituencies and ran against "those lying Atlanta newspapers." The rural counties have dominated the leadership positions of the state legislature and have provided almost all statewide Democratic candidates. The demise of the county-unit system, court-ordered corrections to malapportionment, and tremendous demographic and economic changes have reversed the traditional power relationship between rural and urban areas in Georgia. Now, the urban portion of the state, particularly the spreading Atlanta metropolitan area, is perceived as the economic, and increasingly, the political engine of the state.

Numan Bartley's analysis of the period from 1948 to 1968, *From Thurmond to Wallace* (1970), chronicles early Republican successes at the presidential level and the near victory of the GOP in the 1966 governor's race. Bartley conducts a thorough aggregate analysis of several geographic categories of counties, and he emphasizes the potential partisan-ideological tension by noting that the "tendency for Georgia's most conservative voters in state politics to be the most liberal voters in national politics was a political absurdity that could not forever endure" (Bartley, 1970, p. 33). The tension was relieved, and the tight control by the Democratic party was weakened by non-Democratic victories in the presidential elections in 1964, 1968, 1972, and 1984. Ideology and racial appeals seem to have superseded partisanship as the dominant influence on presidential voting decisions in Georgia.

Bartley describes the alliance between black voters and affluent urban whites, and he foresees three eventual political alternatives: (1) large-scale political realignment with a homogeneous, white Republican party in control; (2) dominance by the states' rights wing of the Democrats, with Republicans as conservative challengers; or (3) a restored Progressive-Democratic coalition. All three alternatives are pertinent to our investigation of party realignment. Given the 1986 Senate

results, Bartley's description of the third alternative is especially presci-
ent. "The Democrats will ultimately have to make a major effort to
restore the progressive coalition. A moderately progressive Democrat
could count on the votes of Negroes, would be in a favorable position to
recapture the north Georgia towns, and would have to make a substantial showing in affluent urban-suburban neighborhoods" (Bartley,
1970, p. 109). This description serves well as a summary of Wyche
Fowler's 1986 victorious coalition, which defeated the only statewide
elected Republican since Reconstruction.

Two analyses conducted in the mid-1970s provide updates on electoral politics in Georgia: Joseph Bernd's chapter in the *Changing Politics of the South* entitled "Georgia: Static and Dynamic" (1972), and
"Georgia: Politics of Consensus" in *The Transformation of Southern
Politics* (1976) by Jack Bass and Walter DeVries. Bernd shows the dramatic changes coming from the growth and expansion of the urban
sector and the declining power and prosperity of the rural portion of
the state. His work supports the enduring effects of the rural-urban
split, but he also notes the growing influence of race, with conservative
states' rights candidates doing well, regardless of party affiliation.
Overt and covert racial appeals have been evident in Georgia elections
for some time, and racial themes were important parts of Goldwater's
1964 victory, Maddox's 1966 victory, and Wallace's 1968 success.
Bernd's analysis concludes that elective office was open to "city candidates with rural values," but as of 1972, Georgia's politics were neither
city-dominated nor liberal.

Bass and DeVries chronicle the growth of consensus politics in Georgia, especially in the Democratic party, based on a coalition of rural
Democratic strongholds, affluent urban whites, and blacks. They see
Jimmy Carter, George Busbee, and Sam Nunn as successful examples of
Democratic consensus politics. Racially moderate, with small town
roots, these politicians have clearly added to the continued Democratic
dominance in the state, with Carter going on to become the only Democrat to break the pattern of Republican strength in presidential elections. For these candidates, and one may add the current Governor Joe
Frank Harris to this list, the "Democratic coalition consists of blacks,
courthouse Democrats who have learned the benefits of black allegiance to the Democratic party, a developing role for organized labor,
rural whites with a Democratic heritage who remain suspicious of urban Republicans and their country club image, a few white liberals,
and the top echelon of the business and financial community, who tend
to view Georgia Republicans as somewhat unstable political amateurs.

The self-interest of the business elite merges with blacks and working-class whites in the broad quest for modernization and economic development" (Bass and DeVries, 1976, p. 150).

Black voters, whose registration rose dramatically in the mid-1960s, have become a crucial bloc of votes in urban areas and in several black-belt counties. They are the basis for any enduring support for the national, liberal Democratic party candidates, such as Humphrey, McGovern, and Mondale. Their consistent Democratic support has made black voters an essential component of the Democratic coalition and has allowed them to counterbalance, but not necessarily outweigh, the influence of rural white voters. As Alex Lamis (1984) concludes, consensus Democratic candidates must appeal to the "night and day" alliance of blacks and rural white voters in order to win. Candidates basing their campaigns on only one or the other component may be successful in a Democratic primary, but both types of voters are necessary for general election success.

With an understanding of the rural-urban split and of the growing role of black voters, Herman Talmadge's 1980 defeat and Wyche Fowler's 1986 victory can be more clearly understood. In 1980, Talmadge lost badly in urban areas, and he forfeited the traditionally high level of support for Democratic nominees among black voters (Lamis, 1984, p. 103). Mattingly developed a coalition of suburban Republican voters, dissatisfied urban Democrats, and blacks, and narrowly defeated the vulnerable incumbent. Coinciding with a presidential election increased the turnout, and Mattingly probably attracted support among the less politically interested, less partisan voters who tend to turn out only in presidential elections. Young, white voters may have been particularly important to his coalition, given the research that indicates growing Republican strength and President Reagan's high popularity among this group (Ladd, 1985; Wolfinger and Hagen, 1985; Carmines and Stanley, 1986).

However, the Republican party was unable to maintain this fragile coalition in its next statewide contest, the 1982 governor's race. The Republican, a respected state legislator, Bob Bell, received only 37% of the vote, with most of it concentrated in the growing suburban Republican strongholds. Urban voters, rural voters, and blacks returned to the Democratic party en masse. In 1986, Mattingly's narrow defeat demonstrated that his 1980 coalition could not be easily reassembled, and his efforts to develop a rural, conservative coalition were not enough to overcome the "night and day" Democratic alliance. With over 355,000 fewer voters in 1986 than in 1980, turnout was of particular importance. While the correlation of Mattingly's vote percentages in 1980 and 1986 is .60, indicating a moderately consistent pattern of returns throughout the state, his lower total votes and lower turnout were sufficient to narrowly defeat him. A vigorous, traditional campaign by a consensus Democratic candidate was enough to overcome the incumbency, the substantial (five to two) financial advantage, and the presidential endorsement and campaigning of Ronald Reagan for the Republican candidate. Reagan's personal popularity was not converted into a sizeable Republican vote for Mattingly, and it remains to be seen if future Republican presidential candidates can augment or solidify the growth of Georgia's Republican party.

Using census data on population and official voting returns and registration data from the Georgia secretary of state's office, we can outline the broad patterns of partisan voting behavior across the state, as well as analyze the activity in such key areas as urban counties, black-belt counties, and the Atlanta suburban ring.

Figure 12.1 highlights the urban and black-belt counties based on 1980 census figures. The ten urban counties had populations of over

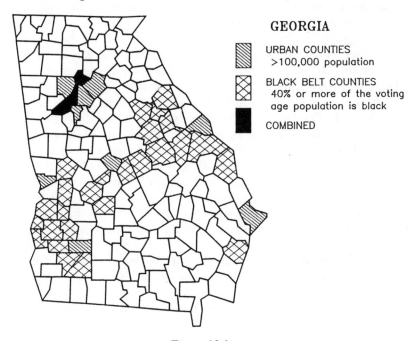

Figure 12.1
Urban and black-belt counties in Georgia.

100,000, and in the 28 black-belt counties, 40% or more of the voting age population was black. Recent analyses indicate that the rural black population of Georgia is migrating out of the black belt and into urban areas or into other states in substantial numbers. Black majority population counties have declined from 77 in 1910, to 48 in 1930, and finally, to 19 in 1980. Only 17.8% of the state's registered voters live in black-belt counties, and only 36.7% of the state's registered black voters live there. In contrast, 34% of the state's black voters live in the core Atlanta area covered by Fulton and DeKalb counties.

The ten largest urban counties presently hold 47% of the state's registered voters and 55.1% of Georgia's black voters. In 1972, 44% of the registered voters lived in these same urban counties. The urban-suburban portion of Georgia is rapidly growing, primarily from the influx of out-of-state people. Since 1980, 75% of the state's job growth has occurred in metropolitan Atlanta, and 72% of all the state's jobs are in the seven metropolitan areas of the state (Walker, 1987). These areas include both urban and suburban counties. Fifty-one percent of the state's nonagricultural jobs are in the 18 county metropolitan Atlanta area. The rapid growth and in-migration in the suburban areas provide ample recruits for the Republican party.

The greatest political growth in Georgia is focused in the urban and suburban areas, too. Fourteen of these counties increased their 1972 registration figures by at least 50%. By far, the greatest growth was in the urban-suburban ring or "doughnut" around the metropolitan Atlanta area. Gwinnett County increased its registration numbers by 250%, while Fayette County increased by over 300%. Only two black-belt counties increased by at least 50%, Burke and Marion counties. Eleven black-belt counties had fewer voters in 1986 than in 1972.

Following Shively (1982) and Binford (1986), Stability Scores were calculated for all Georgia counties based on consecutive pairs of presidential, senatorial, and gubernatorial elections. Basically, these scores indicate the contribution to the winning vote margin that can be attributed to stable (i.e., consistent) party voters across the two elections. The sign of the Stability Score indicates in which partisan direction the stable voting goes; the Democratic direction receives a positive score and the Republican direction a negative one. If a county appeared among the fifteen most stable Democratic or Republican counties for two of the three types of elections, that county was categorized as stable for the party.

Table 12.3 reports the summary statistics for these stability measures. The clearest impression drawn from the table is that the strong pro-

Table 12.3
Stability Scores for Georgia Counties

Stability	Governor (1982–86)	President (1980–84)	Senate (1980–86)
Maximum (M o s t Democratic)	28.6	39.7	27.0
Minimum (Most Republican)	–24.7	–24.7	–0.0
Mean	2.6	9.0	21.4
Standard Deviation	10.0	10.3	6.7
Correlations (r):			
Senate/President	.74		
Senate/Governor	.65		
President/Governor	.58		

Democratic tendency in Georgia varies from the most extreme case of gubernatorial elections, where no county showed a measurable stable Republican advantage, to a less robust tendency in the senatorial elections and a modest level in presidential elections. These data emphasize the decided Democratic edge in Georgia's electorate.

Correlations between pairs of stability measures for the same office over time are quite high (i.e., gubernatorial .82, presidential .78); the strength of these correlations indicates that the stable tendencies are long lasting. The correlations among the stability scores for different types of elections are moderately strong, ranging from .58 to .74, indicating relative consistency across types of elections. The correlations between percentage of registered voters who are black and the Stability Scores are .67 for presidential stability, .51 for senatorial stability, and .37 for gubernatorial stability. Having a substantial proportion of black voters in the county is related to support for presidential and congressional Democrats, and less related to stable voting for state-level offices. The Stability Scores are negatively correlated with change in registration; growing counties tend to have a stable Republican advantage.

Figure 12.2 presents visually the stable Republican counties (Walker, Catoosa, Fannin, Cherokee, Cobb, Douglas, Gwinnett, Rockdale, Clayton, Fayette, and Columbia) and the most stable Democratic counties (Greene, Taliferro, Twiggs, Macon, Wheeler, Turner, Randolph, and Clay). Figure 12.2 indicates the concentration of Republi-

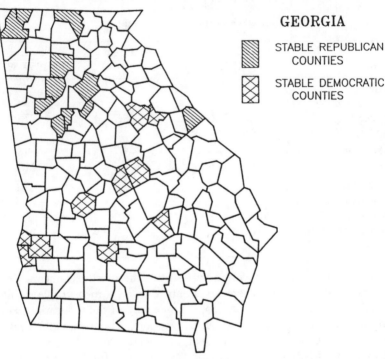

Figure 12.2
Stable Republican and Democratic counties in Georgia.

can strength in the northern mountain counties, in the suburban Atlanta doughnut, and in Augusta. Democratic strongholds fall in the state's rural black belt.

While Republican counties tend to be more consistently, strongly Republican across types of elections (or at least across the senatorial and presidential elections), the Democratic stable advantage is much more broadly spread across the state and across the types of elections. Of particular note is the total lack of a geographic base for Republicans seeking the governor's office. Twenty-two counties fell into the fifteen most stable Republican counties over all three types of elections; thirty-one counties fell into the top fifteen stable Democratic counties, with Macon, Twiggs, and Greene being in the top for all three election types. Obviously, Democratic stability is spread more broadly across the state, but Republican stability is concentrated in larger, faster-growing counties, such as the metropolitan Atlanta ring.

The dynamics of these two groups of counties can be seen by noting that the census indicates that Georgia's population increased by 19.1%

between 1970 and 1980. In the Republican stable counties, the mean change was 71.1%, with three counties reporting over a 100% increase. Democratic counties reported a mean change of 8.6%, including one county which declined by 16%. Likewise, the census reports that 71% of the people were born in the state. The Republican counties have an average of 62% native-born Georgians; the Democratic stable counties report an average of 87.5% born in Georgia. Recent estimates show that the growth in the two largest Republican counties continues unabated. Between 1980 and 1987, Cobb County showed an increase of 38.9%, and Gwinnett County increased 78.7%. For the past three years, Gwinnett has been named the fastest-growing county in the nation.

Political analysts and activists have come to pay increasing attention to the metropolitan Atlanta ring when studying Republican strength and growth in Georgia. The doughnut consists of Cobb, Gwinnett, Clayton, Fayette, Douglas, and Rockdale counties. All of these counties are growing rapidly, increasing their total population 33.7% between 1980 and 1987, and Republicans are regularly winning local elections. Most of the Republicans in the state legislature come from this area of the state. Collectively, these six counties represent 14.9% of the registered voters in the state, but their high turnout rates magnify their electoral impact. In the 1986 Senate election, 17.2% of the total votes came from the doughnut. Senator Mattingly took 62% of the 1986 vote, for a 50,190 edge over Fowler. In 1980, against Talmadge, he received 66.6% of the vote for a 75,127 vote edge.

Fulton and DeKalb counties are the "hole" of the doughnut. Fulton, with its large black voter population, is usually a Democratic stronghold, but DeKalb's voting tends to be more volatile. Together, the two counties contain 22.4% of the state's registered voters, but voter turnout is often lower than in the surrounding doughnut. Between 1980 and 1987, the population of these two largest counties increased by 15.4%. In 1986, 22.9% of the Senate votes came from these two counties. Fowler received 61.3% of the vote, leading Mattingly by 62,798 votes. Therefore, the combined doughnut and hole cast 40.1% of the Senate vote, and Fowler received 51.3% of the vote in these eight counties. In the 1986 election, the absolute number of voters and the comparatively high turnout of voters in the center of the doughnut overcame the higher turnout but relatively lower total votes in the doughnut itself. In 1980, Mattingly won 62.7% of the vote in Fulton and DeKalb counties. He received 44.4% of his 1980 votes in the eight county area; in 1986, only 37.3% of his votes came from this area. In 1980, Mattingly had a 166,789 vote edge from the combined doughnut and hole, an advantage that helped him overcome Talmadge's strong showing in rural areas. The dramatic reversal of the voting in Fulton and DeKalb played a very crucial role in Mattingly's defeat and marked the reemergence of the "day and night" coalition.

Fowler, the progressive Democrat whose entire political career has been centered in the Atlanta metropolitan area, was able to cut into the potential Republican vote in the suburbs and to hold the urban core. With the help of state party leaders, he expanded his core of support to include the traditional, rural Democratic voters. In this respect, he is very different from the other consensus Democrats, who had rural roots and yet developed a following in the urban area; Fowler's strength was always in the urban area. In fact, Fowler's primary vote percentages statewide did not correlate well with any other Democratic candidate in a general election campaign, but his votes correlated well (.49) with Mattingly's 1980 general election vote. By the general election, his coalition had expanded, and his vote distribution more closely resembled earlier Democratic candidates. His vote percentage correlated .59 with Governor Harris's 1986 and 1982 returns, .79 with Carter's 1980 votes and Mondale's 1984 percentages, and .60 with Talmadge's 1980 general election votes.

The correlations of candidate vote percentages since 1972 show moderately strong consistency among Democrats and Republicans, with the exception of the 1974 elections. Coefficients range from .54 to .79. Based on these votes, hardly any enduring partisan realignment has occurred. More likely, party dealignment and a demographic partisan evolution are in process.

The dealignment is shown by the tendency to support Republicans at the national or local level, but not for statewide offices; by the volatility of voting behavior between 1984 and 1986; and by the weakening impact of party identification on voting behavior. This dealignment and evolutionary growth for the Republicans has had two clear consequences: Republicans are having consistent success in winning local office in the suburban areas, and the power of the Republican party is sufficient to have caused the Democrats to work much harder at reestablishing the "night and day" coalition. With the 1986 election, Georgia Democrats appeared to emphasize partisanship over ideology by embracing more liberal Democrats, like Fowler, for statewide office. Only time will tell if this renewed Democratic cohesion can face a growing Republican party.

The diminishing impact of partisan identification on voting has been widely noted, and much remains to be seen about how shifting partisan attitudinal identification translates into partisan votes. After the 1984 election, there was a great deal of journalistic and scholarly discussion about partisan realignment and the new Republican majority. The 1986 elections have raised many doubts about that realignment, in the South, as well as throughout the nation. The *New York Times* reports that in the 1986 elections, 56% of the southern respondents, and 50% of the white respondents from the South voted for Democratic candidates for the House of Representatives. If the data on party identification are accurate, a growing number of new Republican identifiers voted for Democratic candidates. Such anomalous behavior, while fairly common in the South in the other direction, may play a significant role in preventing the solidifying or crystalizing of the party identification of young voters. Party identification is often based on partisan attitudes and partisan behavior. By failing to produce full slates of competitive candidates for all statewide offices in Georgia and thereby denying the voter the opportunity of "behaving" like a Republican voter, the Republican party may be inhibiting the political realignment it so fervently seeks.

As this analysis shows, Georgia does not appear to be undergoing a fundamental political realignment. Nevertheless, that party system is evolving, based on substantial demographic changes and the active suburban recruitment of the Republican party. In-migration and a convergence between conservative ideology and Republican identification among young white voters could be at the root of this growth. Ronald Reagan's strong personal popularity has not drastically altered the partisan distribution, perhaps because of the unease in many parts of the state toward his agricultural policies and his reluctance to protect the textile industry. Personal sympathies combined with policy discomfort have not facilitated partisan realignment.

In 1986, the Republicans kept the two congressional seats they held (one narrowly), but they lost the statewide race for senator. Republican strength is highly concentrated geographically, not widely distributed. This concentration may abet Republican local victories, but not substantially improve their statewide chances. However, the concentration is centered in the most rapidly growing counties of the state.

The Democratic party has not been complacent and is reacting to the growing Republican potential in the state. Democrats are cooperating to produce consensus candidates who are firmly based in the traditional "day and night" coalition. If the evolution described above produces an ideologically conservative, cohesive Republican party, moderates and liberals (especially those aligned with black voters) may gain in strength in the Democratic coalition.

Given the open primary system and the degree of competition in the

1988 presidential race, the 1988 presidential primary may prove to be a good test for assessing the extent of partisan evolution in Georgia. The primary will show many voters in which parts of the state choose to participate in Republican party competition rather than in the Democratic contest. The general election will test the volatility of the Georgia electorate, assessing the extent of stable Republican and Democratic behavior. Sizeable and stable Republican activity in both the primary and general election could indicate that the partisan evolution is moving in the direction of partisan realignment. Low or volatile Republican activity would indicate continued evolution, but not realignment.

13

CHANGING PARTY POLITICS IN MISSISSIPPI

Stephen D. Shaffer

Mississippi has traditionally been a very Democratic state, and a state in which politics has alternated between a concern with economic issues and an obsession with race. It is instructive to briefly examine its history in order to better understand the nature of party politics today.

After the Civil War, the Republican party controlled the Reconstruction government of Mississippi until 1876, because of election boycotts by many whites who opposed congressional Reconstruction laws. The Reconstruction government stressed progressive economic policies, such as building public works and facilities and establishing a public school system. Due to federal protection of the right of blacks to vote, blacks, who constituted a majority of the population, participated freely in government, resulting in both of the black U.S. senators during this era being from Mississippi (Loewen and Sallis, 1974, p. 152–154).

As Reconstruction ended, whites employed tactics of intimidation, violence, and voter fraud to establish conservative (Bourbon) Democratic control of state government. When the Populist movement threatened to unite lower income whites and blacks, the endangered Bourbons raised the race issue to divide the races. At the state constitutional convention of 1890 attended by only one black delegate, Mississippi adopted a poll tax, increased residency requirements, and imposed a literacy and constitutional interpretation test in order to "legally" disenfranchise most blacks. Political debate now occurred almost entirely within one party—the Democratic party—because of the Republican party's traditional association with the protection of black rights.

Throughout this period and until 1950, the major political division among whites was between the Delta and the Hills. Aristocratic whites from the Mississippi River Delta region, which contained the large plantations and large numbers of blacks were more conservative on economic issues, opposed to prohibition, and allied with business interests in the more urban areas of the state (Gulf Coast cities, and the state capital of Jackson). White farmers from the northeast and eastern Hills region, often termed "rednecks" because of the red necks obtained from working in the sun, were poorer, Populist on economic issues, and more supportive of prohibition. Whites of both regions were unsupportive of black rights, though Delta whites were more paternalistic and restrained in their rhetoric than were Hill whites. An illustration of the position of blacks in Mississippi society during this period was provided by neo-Populist Governor James Vardaman, whose response to the question of adequate educational opportunities for blacks was: "Why squander money on his education when the only effect is to spoil a good field hand and make an insolent cook?" (Key, 1949, p. 230–246).

As the national government and the national Democratic party began to support civil rights and the national Republican party became more conservative after World War II, white Mississippians resisted changes in race relations and began to move away from the Democratic party. Mississippi supported the racially oriented presidential bids of States' Rightist Strom Thurmond in 1948, Republican Goldwater in 1964, and Independent George Wallace in 1968. Democrats continued to be elected governor and to other offices as they distanced themselves from the national Democratic party and resisted racial integration until the early 1970s. The racist rhetoric during campaigns of this period was so blatant that one governor even jokingly referred to the NAACP as standing for: "Niggers, Alligators, Apes, Coons, and Possoms" (Bass and DeVries, 1977, p. 194–202). As the state Democratic party (called "regular Democrats") continued to discriminate against blacks in the process of selecting delegates to attend the national convention, a coalition of blacks and liberal whites such as labor leaders (called "loyalists," due to their loyalty to the national Democratic party) was successful in unseating the regulars at the 1968 and 1972 national Democratic conventions.

MISSISSIPPI POLITICS IN RECENT YEARS

By the early 1970s white Mississippians had begun to accept the changes in race relations as permanent, and issues other than race became more salient as Mississippi politics began to nationalize and respond to the same forces affecting national politics. In 1972 Mississippi followed the nation and went for Nixon by a landslide, and Republi-

cans Thad Cochran and Trent Lott (the latter an administrative assistant of retiring conservative Democratic Congressman William Colmer)
were elected on Nixon's coattails to the more urban Fourth (Jackson)
and Fifth (Gulf Coast) Congressional Districts. With the support of
newly enfranchised blacks, Carter narrowly carried Mississippi and the
rest of the South in 1976, but in 1980 lost in another close election in
Mississippi to Reagan, who was subsequently reelected in a 1984 landslide (table 13.1).

In state elections Democratic candidates were usually successful at
forming biracial coalitions by appealing to blacks and working class
whites largely on economic issues. Elected as governor in 1971, William Waller began to appoint blacks to state boards and agencies. His
successor Cliff Finch won as a Populist candidate with heavy support
from blacks and working-class whites. During the campaign he demonstrated his sympathy for the working man by working at a different job
each week and carrying a lunchpail with his name on it, and during his
term he was successful at unifying the regular and loyalist Democrats
during the 1976 presidential delegate selection process. William Winter, elected in 1979, successfully enacted the 1982 Education Reform
Act, which improved public education and helped low- and middle-

Table 13.1
Recent Elections in Mississippi

Office	Democrat (%)	Republican (%)	Others (%)
President:			
1976 (Carter, Ford)	50	48	2
1980 (Carter, Reagan)	48	49	3
1984 (Mondale, Reagan)	38	62	0
Senate:			
1976 (Stennis)	100	0	0
1978 (Dantin, Cochran)	32	45	23
1982 (Stennis, Barbour)	64	36	0
1984 (Winter, Cochran)	39	61	0
Governor:			
1975 (Finch, Carmichael)	52	45	3
1979 (Winter, Carmichael)	61	39	0
1983 (Allain, Bramlett)	55	39	6

Note: In each case the name of the Democratic candidate is listed first, and the Republican second. In 1976 Democrat Stennis was unopposed for reelection.

income blacks and whites. His successor Bill Allain, a Populist elected with heavy black and working-class white support and with a campaign theme of having opposed utility price increases as state attorney general, continued to appoint blacks and women to important state offices. The Democrats have continued to dominate other state and local elections, and as late as 1986 only 8 of the legislature's 174 members were Republicans, as the Democratic party remained the home for officials whose ideologies ranged from the liberalism of blacks elected from black districts to conservative whites.

Republicans have had greater success in federal elections, partly because of the difficulty that Democrats have had in maintaining the unity of their ideologically and racially diverse coalition in more ideologically salient elections. In the 1978 Senate election occasioned by the retirement of former segregationist Democrat James Eastland, the Democratic vote was split between the white Democratic nominee Maurice Dantin and the black independent Charles Evers, permitting Republican Thad Cochran to be elected with 45 percent of the vote. (In 1984 Cochran was reelected despite a unified Democratic coalition by stressing incumbency and constituency service issues.) The selection of a black, state representative Robert Clark, as the Democratic nominee in the newly formed black majority Delta district in 1982 and his renomination in 1984 magnified racial and ideological differences between the candidates and permitted Republican Webb Franklin to narrowly win in this normally Democratic district. However, in 1986 the high unemployment in this agricultural and poor district led to the narrow victory of a black Democrat, Mike Espy, over Franklin. And by 1981 Democrats had regained the Fourth Congressional District with Wayne Dowdy, who formed a coalition of blacks with his support of the extension of the Voting Rights Act, and rural and working-class whites. The reelection of eighty-one-year-old Democratic Senator John Stennis in 1982 also demonstrated the renewed power of the majority Democratic party coalition based on black and moderate white support, as well as the power of incumbency.

CONTEMPORARY PARTY POLITICS
AND THE ROLE OF REAGAN

Republicans have made gains in Mississippi not only at the polls but also in voters' psychological identifications with the parties. A 1975 poll indicated that only 6% of Mississippi voters considered themselves Republicans, while 51% labeled themselves Democrats and the remainder were independent or unsure (Bass and DeVries, 1977, p. 216). A 1978 poll by Market Opinion Research demonstrated that 12% of Mississippians called themselves Republicans, while 57% labeled themselves Democrats with the remainder being independents (Eagle, 1986, p. 7). By 1981, Republicans constituted 18% of the population, as Democrats fell to 48%, and independents and the apolitical made up the remainder (table 13.2). The partisanship of the public has remained relatively stable since then with a brief dip in the numbers of Republicans in 1982 presumably because of the national economic recession and a modest rise in the numbers of Republicans since then.[1] Despite Republican gains, Mississippi today remains significantly more Democratic than Republican in partisanship, and somewhat more Democratic than the nation as a whole.[2]

A number of factors offer plausible explanations for Republican gains in party identification. One likely explanation is the phenomenon of secular realignment discussed by V. O. Key (1959), as it has taken

Table 13.2
Party Identification in Mississippi

Party	1981	1982	1984	1986
Democrat	48(42)	51(44)	44(36)	45(40)
Independent	30(31)	30(30)	36(34)	26(27)
Republican	18(27)	15(24)	17(28)	24(33)
Apolitical	4(0)	4(2)	3(2)	5(0)
	100%	100%	100%	100%
Strong Democrat	29	28	25	22
Weak Democrat	19	23	19	23
Independent Democrat	10	8	12	9
Independent	7	13	12	7
Independent Republican	13	9	12	10
Weak Republican	10	8	9	15
Strong Republican	8	7	8	9
Apolitical	4	4	3	5
	100%	100%	100%	100%

Note: Cell entries are the percentages of Mississippians in four years who fall in various partisan categories. Values in parentheses represent the entire nation. (Abramson, Aldrich, Rohde, 1986:211–13; Gallup Report, 1981, 1986).

Source: Mississippi data are from statewide polls conducted by Mississippi State University's Survey Research Unit.

decades for the New Deal political cleavages between the parties to replace the old Civil War concerns in Mississippi and for the Republicans to make gains among more conservative and higher socioeconomic status groups. A related explanation is that repeated behavioral defections from one's party (evidenced by Mississippi support for third-party and Republican presidential candidacies since 1948) can eventually cause changes in party identification as voters bring their attitudes into line with contemporary voting patterns (Howell, 1980). Such partisan change may be especially evident among the younger generation, which lacks the strong partisan ties associated with a tradition of party voting. These explanations and others are examined at greater length in the next section.

Another important explanation for Republican gains is quite probably the popularity of President Reagan. Except for the recession year of 1982, a majority of Mississippians have rated his job performance as excellent or good, and Reagan has clearly been more popular than the Republican party itself (table 13.3). Furthermore, there is a strong relationship between Mississippians' attitudes toward Reagan and their partisan identifications. Among those rating Reagan's performance as excellent, consistently more Mississippians have called themselves Republicans than Democrats. On the other hand, those rating Reagan's job performance as only fair or poor are heavily Democratic. When Reagan's popularity temporarily dipped in 1982, the fortunes of the Republican party in Mississippi also declined (table 13.2). It should also be noted that Republican gains and Democratic losses between 1984 and 1986 were most evident among those who felt that Reagan was doing an excellent job. While these findings are not definitive in determining the direction of causality, they certainly suggest that Reagan's popularity has helped a less popular Republican party in the state.

PARTY REALIGNMENT AMONG DEMOGRAPHIC GROUPS

Traditionally, Mississippi's one-party orientation was reflected in the absence of socioeconomic cleavages between the parties that emerged in the North during the Roosevelt New Deal era, as whites of all demographic groups were Democratic and blacks were denied the vote (Key, 1949; Ladd and Hadley, 1978). The rise of the Republican party in Mississippi leads one to examine the sources of rising Republicanism, as

Table 13.3
Reagan's Job Performance Rating (%)

Rating	1981	1982	1984	1986
Excellent	22	10	21	20
Good	30	29	33	35
Fair	29	34	22	27
Poor	19	27	24	18
Total	100%	100%	100%	100%
	(588)	(855)	(597)	(593)

Reagan's Job Performance Rating and Party Identification

Rating	Democrat				Republican				Independent			
	'81	'82	'84	'86	'81	'82	'84	'86	'81	'82	'84	'86
Excellent	23	23	24	18	37	40	38	53	40	37	38	29
Good	38	36	35	36	24	23	21	27	38	41	44	37
Fair	62	62	53	65	12	10	11	13	26	28	36	22
Poor	73	74	70	70	4	8	1	12	23	18	29	18

Note: In each year people were asked to "rate the job performance of President Reagan as excellent, good, fair, or poor."

In bottom of table percentages total 100% across the rows.

well as the question of whether the party system in Mississippi finally resembles the national party system rooted in New Deal political cleavages.

Party cleavages among Mississippians in the 1980s have come to resemble national patterns with respect to socioeconomic status and race. White Mississippians with higher incomes and college educations are significantly more Republican and less Democratic than are whites with less income and education (table 13.4). Blacks, regardless of socioeconomic status, are heavily Democratic in partisanship (Nie, Verba, Petrocik, 1979, p. 228).[3] These patterns were evident as early as 1981 and have persisted, though Republican gains among whites since 1981 are found in all socioeconomic status groups. Indeed, by 1986 whites overall were evenly split between the parties, though blacks remained heavily Democratic.

The Mississippi party system of the 1980s also resembles the national system with respect to the centrality of ideological cleavages, which

Table 13.4

The Correlates of Party Identification among White Mississippians

Group	Democratic ID					Republican ID					Independent ID				
	'81	'82	'84	'86	Avg.	'81	'82	'84	'86	Avg.	'81	'82	'84	'86	Avg.
Family Income:															
<10,000	53	56	49	48	52	14	11	22	22	17	33	33	29	30	31
$10–20,000	46	43	40	28	39	25	24	22	32	26	29	33	38	40	35
>20,000	26	34	23	28	28	30	24	26	39	30	44	42	51	33	42
Education:															
H.S. dropout	53	59	47	37	49	17	11	20	25	18	30	30	33	38	33
H.S. graduate	43	42	29	35	37	20	18	20	34	23	37	40	51	31	40
Some college	21	28	29	26	26	34	32	29	41	34	45	40	42	33	40
Ideology:															
Liberal	55	46	33	32	42	11	20	12	28	18	34	34	55	40	40
Moderate	41	49	33	34	39	21	12	23	28	21	38	39	44	38	40
Conservative	27	31	26	23	27	37	33	30	43	36	36	36	44	34	37
Age:															
18–30	32	30	26	24	28	25	34	31	40	33	43	36	43	36	39
31–60	41	44	32	31	37	23	16	19	36	24	36	40	49	33	39
61–99	49	59	51	50	52	21	14	18	20	18	30	27	31	30	30
State residence:															
0–15 years	23	33	24	21	25	25	24	27	36	28	52	43	49	43	47
Over 15 years	43	46	38	36	41	23	19	22	33	24	34	35	40	31	35

Sex:															
Male	37	38	29	28	33	23	21	19	37	25	40	41	52	35	42
Female	43	50	41	39	43	23	19	27	30	25	34	31	32	31	32
Race:															
White	40	44	34	33	38	23	20	23	34	25	37	36	43	33	37
Black	75	78	67	76	74	7	7	7	8	7	18	15	26	16	19

Note: Cell entries indicate the percentages of white Mississippians of various demographic groups who psychologically identify themselves as Democrats, Republicans, or independents. Values in the fifth, tenth, and fifteenth columns are averages of the four years. N sizes are omitted from the table to save space; they normally exceed 100, and always exceed 36.
The last row provides the partisanship of blacks.

emerged outside the South with the coming of the New Deal (Sundquist, 1973, p. 199). Among whites, self-identified conservatives are significantly more Republican and less Democratic than are liberals. Nevertheless, Republicans have made gains among all whites regardless of their ideological self-identifications (table 13.4). Once again, blacks are heavily Democratic regardless of ideology, though some realignment driven by ideological concerns may have occurred since 1981, as liberal blacks became more Democratic while conservative blacks became less Democratic.[4]

New generations have often played an important role in partisan realignment, helping a subordinate party to become the majority party. Andersen (1979), for example, found that new voters helped the Democratic party become the majority party in America during the 1930s. Studies suggest that the role of generational change in the contemporary South may have changed over the years. Converse (1963) found no generational differences among white southerners in partisan identifications in the 1950s, while studies of the 1960s and 1970s found that younger white southerners were more independent than their older counterparts (Beck, 1977; Norpoth and Rusk, 1982).

In Mississippi, the impact of generational forces was quite evident by the 1980s. The Republican party is nearly twice as strong among whites under thirty as among those over sixty, and it has made its greatest gains since 1981 among the younger and middle-aged groups. Indeed, by 1986 whites under sixty were more likely to be Republican than Democratic identifiers. The Democratic party remains dominant among whites over sixty, demonstrating the power of tradition among those whites who came of political age during the New Deal era. Some generational differences also exist among blacks, who are heavily Democratic regardless of age but among whom older blacks are especially Democratic and least Republican.[5] Generational change appears to be on the side of the Republican party in Mississippi, though the large numbers of blacks and poor whites may merely mean a future of intense partisan divisions rather than Republican domination.

In the early 1960s, Converse (1963) argued that migrants to the South were more Republican than were native southerners. Similar residential factors appear to play a role in Mississippi party politics, as whites who were relative newcomers to the state were slightly more Republican than Democratic, while long-time residents were significantly and consistently more Democratic than Republican.[6] No significant differences emerged among blacks, however.

Much has been written about the "gender gap" that has emerged nationally, as women by the 1980s were found to be more anti-Reagan, liberal, and Democratic than men (Poole and Zeigler, 1985). A similar gender gap exists among white Mississippians, as women throughout the 1980s were significantly more Democratic in identification than were men (table 13.4). Throughout the 1980s, Republicans made their greatest gains and Democrats suffered their greatest losses among white males, so that by 1986 white males were actually more likely to call themselves Republicans than Democrats. These findings suggest a different implication of the gender gap for the two parties—rather than Republicans being overly concerned about limited support among women; perhaps Democratic party leaders should be more concerned about their limited appeals to young, white males.[7]

In conclusion, the forces of nationalization have swept through Mississippi, and political cleavages in the 1980s mirror those that have existed nationally since the 1930s. The Republican party in Mississippi is strongest among conservatives and higher socioeconomic status groups that include whites and males, while the Democrats are strongest among liberals and lower socioeconomic status groups (including blacks and females). While the Republican party has made its greatest gains in the 1980s among young white males, it is unlikely that it will become the majority party in Mississippi in the foreseeable future because of the large numbers of blacks and disadvantaged whites in the state. A future of increasingly intense partisan competition is a more plausible scenario.

THE 1984 AND 1986 ELECTIONS AND PARTISAN CHANGE

It is instructive to examine the two most recent election years in Mississippi for further insight into the nature of partisan change in the state and likely future electoral developments involving the two parties.

By the mid-1980s, substantial partisan realignment had occurred among partisan activists. Nearly half of the Democratic delegates (48%) to the 1984 state party convention were black, compared to only 7% of Republican delegates.[8] Ideological differences between party activists were quite evident, as 53% of Democratic delegates called themselves liberals and only 9% conservative (38% were moderate), while 75% of Republican delegates to their state party convention called themselves conservative and only 1% liberal (24% were moderate). Democratic delegates were consistently more liberal than Republican delegates on a range of economic and social issues like health care, public works, food stamps, gun control, abortion, ERA, school prayer, affirmative action, and defense spending (Shaffer, 1986). While part of the Democratic liberalism may be accounted for by the permeability of the state party to the Reverend Jesse Jackson's campaign, it is likely that much of the ideological divergence between the two parties' activists reflects the realignment of the state parties to mirror national divisions.

The landslide victories of Republicans Reagan and Cochran in Mississippi in 1984 despite continued Democratic dominance in party identification suggest that some partisan dealignment is also occurring (Cover, 1977; Miller and Wattenberg, 1983). When asked why they voted as they did in the Senate election, two-thirds of the comments (68%) referred to the personal or performance attributes of the candidates, and fully 98% of those comments pertaining to Senator Cochran were favorable. The power of incumbency was quite evident, as voters cited Cochran's seniority, experience, and service to the state. Only 12% of voters mentioned issues, and most were favorable to the incumbent. Cochran's opponent, former Democratic Governor Winter, was advantaged on partisanship, as 76% of those who mentioned this factor favored him and only 24% favored Cochran, but only 10% of voters mentioned partisanship as a reason for their vote (Shaffer, 1986).

The 1986 elections entailing a Democratic gain in the U.S. House despite a Republican gain in party identification statewide demonstrate the strength of the majority Democratic party when economic issues are salient and the party remains united. As in the 1982 and 1984 election campaigns, Democratic party officials like Senator Stennis, Governor Allain, and the state party chairman campaigned for the black Democratic nominee for the Second Congressional District. Democrat Espy blamed Republican Franklin's support for Reagan administration policies for the poor economic conditions in the black majority and rural district, and enough whites stayed home or supported Espy to elect him as the first black congressman from Mississippi since Reconstruction. In order to be reelected Espy must overcome his race and suspected liberalism and unite the Democratic party by stressing his incumbency and economic issues.

The other House elections in the state demonstrated the power of incumbency and the heterogeneity of the state Democratic party. In the traditionally Democratic and rural First District, moderate Democrat Jamie Whitten, who chairs the powerful Appropriations Committee, was reelected with his usual 66% of the vote. In the more conservative and less Democratic Third District, conservative Democrat Sonny Montgomery was once again unopposed. Moderate Democrat Wayne Dowdy increased his reelection margin from 55% in 1984 to 72% in the marginal Fourth District by expanding his Populist coalition to include business groups attracted by his membership on the Energy and Commerce committee. Yet the Fourth District, which has a 42% black population, has been ideologically and racially polarized in other elections, and narrowly voted Republican in the last three presidential elections. Conservative Republican and House Minority Whip Trent Lott once again was easily reelected with 82% of the vote in the conservative Fifth District.

By 1986 some partisan realignment along policy lines had occurred among average white Mississippi citizens. White Democratic party identifiers were more liberal on many economic issues, being significantly more supportive of labor unions, national health insurance, and public works than were Republican identifiers. Yet partisan differences had not yet emerged on noneconomic issues involving women's rights, crime, moral, and civil rights issues. Blacks, regardless of party, were significantly more liberal than whites on a great range of economic and noneconomic issues (Shaffer, 1986). Economic issues can, therefore, unite Democrats of both races and provide electoral victories, while the salience of social or racial concerns can divide the party and permit Republican victories.

CONCLUSIONS

In recent years the party system in Mississippi has come to resemble the national patterns with a lower socioeconomic status and liberal Democratic party opposing a higher status and conservative Republican party. While the Republican party should continue to make long-term gains, the large numbers of blacks and lower SES whites should permit the state Democratic party to remain a very strong and competitive party. In any event, as the forces of dealignment affect the state as they have the nation, partisan considerations become less important to voters as incumbency and other candidate attributes become critical factors. Hence, it is likely that partisan and electoral competition in Mississippi will continue to intensify in the immediate future.

NOTES

1. I acknowledge with appreciation funding support from the MSU Social Science Research Center, the helpful comments of the editors and Douglas

Feig, and the graduate assistance work of Sheila Pickett Putnam and Susan E. Bapty.

Public opinion information from the 1980s was obtained from statewide telephone polls of adult Mississippi residents using random digit dialing and having approximately 75% response rates, conducted by the Mississippi State University Survey Research Unit. The dates and number of completed interviews are: October-November 1982 = 616; September 1982 = 894; April 1984 = 610; February 1986 = 611. All data are weighted by relevant demographic characteristics based on the 1980 census.

2. Party identification in the 1980s was measured by the traditional seven-point scale derived from a two-part question: "Generally speaking, do you consider yourself a Democrat, Republican, Independent, or what?" Those responding Democratic or Republican were asked: "Do you consider yourself a strong or not so strong Democrat/Republican?" Independents were asked: "Do you think of yourself as closer to the Democratic party or to the Republican party?" Some respondents were completely apolitical and answered Don't Know to both questions. All categories are provided in the bottom of table 13.2, while the top combines strong and weak partisans, and independent leaners with pure independents.

3. Socioeconomic differences in partisanship among Mississippi blacks are modest, and in the opposite direction to what is usually expected. Between 1981 and 1986, on the average 73% of black high-school dropouts were Democratic and 10% were Republican; 80% of blacks with some college were Democratic, and 1% were Republican. On the average, 71% of low-income blacks were Democratic and 8% were Republican; 77% of high-income blacks were Democratic and 4% were Republican. These modest differences suggest that Republicans may not make gains as blacks rise in socioeconomic status, as higher SES blacks may have a greater sense of consciousness and the relevance of Democratic partisan politics to the concerns of blacks than lower SES blacks.

4. Among self-identified black liberals, 89% were Democratic in 1986 compared to 68% in 1981. Democrats also gained among moderate blacks—from 70% to 76%—but lost among conservatives from 72% to 61% Democratic. Republicans made no gains among moderate and conservative blacks, but lost among liberals (2% of liberal blacks were Republican in 1986, compared to 5% in 1981).

5. In the 1980s, on the average 67% of blacks under thirty were Democratic and 9% were Republican; 86% of blacks over sixty were Democratic and 5% were Republican.

6. Our indicator of number of years lived in Mississippi is not strictly comparable to Converse's study, which included region of childhood. Our indicator measures the length of exposure to the historically very traditionalistic and Democratic political and social environment of Mississippi.

7. Among Mississippi blacks, men are somewhat more Independent than women. On average, 71% of men are Democratic, 5% are Republican, and 24% are independent; 77% of women are Democratic, 8% are Republican, and 15% are independent.

8. Written questionnaires were distributed to the delegates at the state party conventions. The Republican convention was held on April 14, 1984, and 203 delegates completed the surveys for a response rate of 44%. The Democratic convention was held on May 5, 1984, and 514 delegates completed surveys for a response rate of 30%. The demographic and candidate-preference makeup of those returning surveys was very similar to all delegates.

14

The Rise and Stall of Republican Ascendency in Louisiana Politics

Wayne Parent

The present state of the two-party system in Louisiana was summarized in a well-publicized comment by 1986 losing Republican Senate candidate Henson Moore, the six-term congressman from Baton Rouge. After suffering a more substantial defeat than his fellow Republicans in Alabama and Georgia, Mr. Moore commented that the only way a Republican candidate could win statewide in Louisiana was by having the good fortune to run against "a Democratic candidate unacceptable to the voters (Shuler and McMahon, 1986)." Mr. Moore had reason to be frustrated: he outspent the Democratic victor, Congressman John Breaux, two to one and was a consensus early favorite to capture a Louisiana Senate seat for the Republicans for the first time since Reconstruction. Although Mr. Moore may have overstated the case in the anguish of a bitter loss, his comment is not unsubstantiated. After all, Wright, Erikson, and McIver (1985) reported that Louisiana is the state with the most Democratic party identifiers in the United States. And, although Louisiana has a history of incredibly expensive and divisive campaigns, (the 1979 governor's race, for example, was the most expensive nonpresidential campaign of that time) winners in statewide elections in the last hundred years, and even the last twenty years, are almost always Democrats.

As table 14.1 illustrates, Republicans have made substantial gains in party registration over the last two decades, but the number of voters who choose to register as Republican remains less than one-fifth of Democratic registration. Gains in Republican party identification are more difficult to assess. An ABC-*Washington Post* Poll in late 1986 found only 26 percent of Louisianians identifying themselves as Republicans, while 59 percent identify themselves as Democrats and 14 percent as independents. A 1987 Roper Poll reinforces these figures: 62 percent of respondents identify themselves as Democrats, 22 percent as Republicans, and 12 percent volunteered that they were independents.

Table 14.1

Louisiana Voter Registration by Political Party, 1960–1987

Year	Total	Democratic	Republican	Other
1960	1,152,151	98.6	0.9	0.5
1964	1,201,785	98.1	1.5	0.4
1968	1,451,836	97.4	2.0	0.6
1972	1,780,288	95.3	2.9	1.6
1976	1,865,548	93.5	3.7	2.8
1980	2,015,402	86.6	7.4	6.0
1984	2,262,101	80.6	11.3	8.1
1987	2,139,861	78.1	12.8	6.9

Source: "Statement of Registered Voters: Report of the Secretary of State," Baton Rouge: State of Louisiana, 1960–1987. All are reported for the October 31, registration close, except 1987, when the report is from the March 31 statement.

The number of independents is probably understated in the Roper Poll because respondents had to volunteer "independent" as a category. Table 14.2 presents a summary of these results.

Clearly, Republican realignment is not occurring as dramatically or systematically as the recent successes of Republican presidential candidates Goldwater, Nixon, and Reagan might indicate. Even the election of a Republican governor in 1983 may have represented more an aberration than part of a trend. As table 14.3 clearly indicates, Louisiana's voters have recently taken to voting Republican for president and Democratic in statewide races. Although this phenomenon is not technically "ticket splitting" since most statewide races in Louisiana occur in odd-numbered years, it does suggest that some dealignment might be occur-

Table 14.2

Recent Measures of Party Identification in Louisiana

Poll	Democrat	Republican	Independent
Wright et al. Weighted CBS-*New York Times* 1974–1982	60.0%	13.2%	22.8%
ABC-*Washington Post* November 1986	59%	26%	14%
Roper Center February–March 1987	62.0%	22.3%	12.4%

Table 14.3

Popular Vote Percentage of Democratic and Republican Candidates in
Louisiana from 1976 to 1986

Year	Office	Democrat	Republican
1976	President	Carter, 51.7	Ford, 46.0
1979	Governor	Lambert, 49.7	Treen, 50.3
1980	Senate	(Democrat Long unopposed by Republican)	
1980	President	Carter, 45.8	Reagan, 51.2
1983	Governor	Edwards, 62.3	Treen, 37.7
1984	Senate	(Democrat Johnston unopposed by Republican)	
1984	President	Mondale, 38.6	Reagan, 61.4
1986	Senate	Breaux, 52.8	Moore, 47.2

ring. For a summary of Democratic and Republican strength in major
statewide elections since 1976, see table 14.3.

This chapter examines the current party system in Louisiana, where
Republicans have become a strong new force, but not a dominant one.
The thesis is that the period of Republican ascendancy peaked in the
1970s. Barry Goldwater's powerful message of racial conservativism
gave Republicans an opportunity to appeal to Louisianians who lost
touch with the national Democratic party during the Civil Rights
years. Although Richard Nixon and Gerald Ford sought to change racial conservativism as a national Republican issue, it allowed the Republican party to gain legitimacy. The other Republican messages of
fiscal conservativism and social conservativism (as contrasted with the
Populism of the Democrats) have become the lasting cross-cutting issues, and Republican strength depends largely on the appeal of those
messages. Now that Republicans have succeeded in becoming associated with these nonracial issues, the cleavages in Louisiana politics
after the civil rights movement have become remarkably similar to
those before the emergence of black political power. The Republican
politics of today can be fairly well understood as a successor to the
politics of the Reform faction of the Democratic party in the Huey
Long era of Democratic bifactionalism.

THE LEGACY OF LONG-ERA BIFACTIONALISM

Although the Whig-Democratic period from 1812 to the 1840s was the only time in Louisiana's history that the state had a competitive two-party system, Louisiana has had a political history of highly identifiable, predictable coalitions. The present coalitions are a logical outgrowth of factions formed in the early 1920s by Huey Long and transformed in the early 1960s by the Democratic and Republican national positions on civil rights and by the results of the civil rights movement itself.

Although Huey Long is often perceived as a Socialist or Populist, the Progressives actually set the stage for the Long era. Bifactionalism began in the 1920s when the Progressives first successfully confronted the Democratic elite in Louisiana by mounting a challenge within the Democratic party. The Progressives succeeded by discontinuing the practice of race baiting and focusing instead on economic grievances of the poor (Grosser, 1981). Huey Long saw the victory by Progressive gubernatorial candidate John M. Parker as an opportunity to create a strong cohesive winning coalition within the Democratic party made up of the newly enfranchised, less affluent members of the population. During this period, Louisianians became accustomed to a highly competitive political system where candidates could be clearly identified along factional lines. In this Democratic bifactional party system, blacks were generally excluded, as they were in the remainder of the Deep South. Among whites, the Longites were supported by the "have-nots" (those on the lower end of the socioeconomic scale) and the Anti-Longites, or Reform candidates, were supported by the "haves." Although there were strong cultural differences between the socially conservative Anglo-Saxon Protestants in north and central Louisiana and the socially liberal French, Spanish, and Creole Catholic cultures of south Louisiana (including New Orleans), the political system was defined primarily along economic, rather than cultural, lines.

In the late 1950s a tragic event occurred that signaled the end to the bifactional system and the beginning of a decade-long transition period of purely racial politics. Huey's brother, Governor Earl Long, was promoting a bill to prevent purging blacks from the voter rolls on the floor of the legislature in a mad speech "that had left small doubt that he had gone off his rocker" (Liebling, 1961: 16–17). He was sent to a sanitarium in Texas (although a few months later he returned to the governor's office). Although Earl Long was a segregationist, he was a friend of black voting rights and equal pay. His white supporters began deserting him because of relatively pro-black positions and ended the fifty years of Long coalition politics. Cross-cutting political polariza-

tion along racial, rather than economic lines, started a twelve-year
period characterized almost exclusively by race baiting.

THE EMERGENCE OF THE RACE ISSUE

In 1959 and again in 1963, statewide candidates won runoffs by pointing to their opponents' black support (Carleton, Howard, and Parker,
1975). Although New Orleans Mayor "Chep" Morrison, a "national
Democrat" (supporter of the civil rights movement) twice ran well as a
candidate for governor, segregationism was the winning political issue
in the statewide races of the 1960s. The position of blacks in Louisiana
politics, however, was stronger than the black position in other Deep
South states, which led to a fast end to the successful race-baiting politics of that decade. In 1960, before the Voting Rights Act, Louisiana's
statewide black registration rate (31.1%) was higher than that of the
other Deep South states with large black populations: the Mississippi
rate was 5 percent; the Alabama rate and South Carolina rates were 14
percent (*Statistical Abstract of the United States*, 1982–1983: p. 488).
The most comparable state in the Deep South was Georgia, with 29
percent black registration. The appeal to the race issue, however,
should not be understated. The pattern was fairly common in most
elections in Louisiana in districts where whites comprised a majority of
voters.

By 1971, however, black support no longer meant automatic defeat
for a statewide politician. Blacks have supported the winning candidate in three of four governors' races and the one competitive Senate
election since 1970. In 1987, blacks make up one-third of Louisiana's
population and one-fourth of its registered voters. Indeed, in 1987,
blacks are registered at almost exactly the same rate as whites (Grenier,
forthcoming). The black role in statewide politics is complemented by
a significant rise in more localized power. Black strength in Louisiana is
concentrated in New Orleans and in rural parishes along the Mississippi
River in north and central Louisiana. New Orleans has witnessed a
transformation in its political power structure with the election of a
black mayor in each of the last three elections and is likely to continue
this pattern in the foreseeable future. Louisiana's first black congressman of the modern era is also likely to be from New Orleans, representing majority black Second Congressional District. Presently, Democrat
Lindy Boggs has held the seat with the support of blacks, even though
she has received legitimate opposition from black candidates. Congresswoman Boggs is well received in the New Orleans black community

because of her fairly liberal voting record (Bogg's case is similar to Wyche Fowler's in Atlanta). A black will probably win the seat after the retirement of Ms. Boggs.

THE RISE OF THE REPUBLICANS

The growth of the Republican party in Louisiana began in the 1970s in the aftermath of the emergence of black political power. Republican attractiveness was in large part a result of black strength. The popularity of Republican presidential candidate Barry Goldwater and his opposition to the black agenda, especially as it was contrasted to the staunch pro-black agenda of the Democratic nominee, Lyndon Johnson, provided the Republicans an opportunity to capture segregationist sentiment and transform it into a political base. The national Republican party, however, quickly tempered its racial conservatism with a conscious and strong effort by Richard Nixon in 1968 and 1972 not to overtly appeal to racism. In the Reagan years, Republican social conservativism has emphasized moral and religious issues instead of race-related ones.

Perhaps more significantly, Republicans had the opportunity to tap another growing segment of the Louisiana population: the new middle class associated with the oil boom in the 1970s. These newly affluent Louisiana natives together with the professional and technical classes who moved into the state were fertile ground for the Republicans. They were comfortable with the Republican agenda of lower taxes and limited growth in social programs. Consequently, Republican support in Louisiana was galvanized in very predictable parts of the population, people who would accept the Republican credo.

Indeed, the dual message of social conservativism and fiscal conservativism was exactly the position taken by the white middle classes fleeing to the suburbs to escape high taxes and black political power. The suburbs in the high population growth areas, particularly around New Orleans and Baton Rouge, and to a lesser extent, around Lafayette and south toward the Gulf Coast, formed the heart of what might have been the beginning of a Republican realignment. In all statewide elections since 1970, these areas have provided the most intense Republican support. In 1983, for example, the only two parishes that incumbent Republican Governor Treen carried were suburban parishes north and west of New Orleans. If a realignment occurred in Louisiana, in the 1970s and 1980s, it occurred only here. Continued Republican strength in the state depends on acceptance in areas outside this suburban base, however.

THE VOLATILE COALITIONS: NORTH LOUISIANA PROTESTANTS AND CAJUNS

What emerged from the rubble of the race politics of the sixties were opportunities for both Republicans and Democrats. Candidates from both parties succeeded in creating identifiable factions in Louisiana politics. In the 1971 governor's race, Democratic Congressman Edwin Edwards seized the opportunity to create a majority black/labor/Catholic Democratic coalition. Despite strong segregationist rhetoric in Louisiana politics, a majority black-white Democratic coalition was sensible strategy to pursue. Edwards's 1971 winning coalition, first against a conservative north Louisiana Democrat (now U.S. Senator Bennett Johnston) and then against a Republican (the man who would succeed him, David Treen) set the framework for the present party system.

By the 1970s, four lasting identifiable political factions had clearly emerged in Louisiana. They are most easily defined geographically by their rough coterminous boundaries with Louisiana's eight congressional districts (see figure 14.1). The boundary similarity is primarily the result of the power of congressional incumbents during 1980 reapportionment: members of Congress successfully made their districts as homogenously representative of their coalitions as possible.

The first two coalitions, blacks and suburban Republicans, have been described. Blacks are concentrated in the Second Congressional District and scattered throughout the remainder of the state. The highest proportion of blacks in a congressional district outside New Orleans (36 percent) can be found in the Eighth District, which starts in Alexandria and makes its way down the industrial corridor between Baton Rouge and New Orleans. Suburban Republicans are concentrated most heavily in the First District around New Orleans and hold a majority in the Sixth Congressional District which includes most of Baton Rouge and its suburbs and extends eastward.

A third coalition consists of north Louisiana Protestant conservative Democrats. These voters are found in the Fourth and Fifth Congressional Districts of north Louisiana. This area includes Shreveport, which has a black and suburban population, but is characterized mainly by rural conservative Protestants. Although strong supporters of New Deal Populism in the national Democratic party, voting patterns indicate that many citizens are willing to vote Republican, certainly at the presidential level and often at the state level as well. The Republican appeal in the poorer, rural areas is a reflection of conservative stands on social and moral issues taken by national and state Republicans. The more urban and affluent north Louisiana Protestants (around Shreveport and Monroe) are even more likely to vote Republican. This is a reflection of the fiscal conservativism found in those populations. This north Louisiana Protestant coalition has been a fairly consistent fertile ground for Republicans as a logical outgrowth of the segregation period of the 1960s and the moral conservatism of the 1970s and 1980s.

South Louisiana poses a much more formidable obstacle to Republican growth. Three districts in South Louisiana, the Third, the Seventh, and the Eighth, in varying degrees, represent a Catholic, labor, "Cajun" culture. This is the part of Louisiana that has experienced rapid population growth in the last two decades and has been most affected by the rise and fall of oil prices in Louisiana. It is has also proven to be the most volatile area politically. These districts contain the smaller cities of Alexandria (culturally like north Louisiana), Lake Charles (with a strong union concentration), and Lafayette (the glamour and growth city of the oil boom). It is the people in the well-populated towns and communities outside these cities, however, that best demonstrate the political character of south Louisiana. These Democrats are more liberal socially than their Protestant counterparts in north Louisiana and are more likely to support labor issues. This is the part of Louisiana that was most reluctant to desert the Democratic party when John Kennedy placed the Democrats clearly in the civil rights camp. They form the necessary complement to blacks for any statewide Democratic majority.

Republicans have been somewhat successful in appealing to the more affluent Cajun Catholics affected by the oil boom, using the message of fiscal conservatism. Republicans must continue to make these efforts if Louisiana is to have a consistently competitive two-party system. An obvious problem to Republicans has been the decline in the oil industry and the shrinking middle class in south Louisiana. Republican inroads into Cajun south Louisiana is clearly the key to any realignment, or, short of that, continued Republican growth, in Louisiana.

THE REVITALIZATION OF THE DEMOCRATIC MAJORITY

Louisiana held an election for governor in 1983 and for the United

States Senate in 1986. These two most recent statewide elections provide fairly convincing evidence that the Democrats may no longer be the only party in Louisiana, but may consistently receive the winning majority in all but localized elections in the suburban areas, where Republicans are strongest. The other exception may be the presidential election process where, in 1984, Ronald Reagan defeated Democrat Walter Mondale with over 60 percent of the vote. Presidential politics warrant separate consideration, and will be discussed against the backdrop of state party politics.

In 1983, Edwin Edwards, who had forged the first post-civil rights black/white Democratic majority coalition in 1971, and repeated it in 1975, challenged incumbent Republican governor David Treen. The election was no contest: Edwards won with 62.3 percent of the vote. The magnitude of the victory was due to the mounting problems in the Louisiana economy and the perceived lack of leadership ability in the Treen administration. These short-term factors account for the landslide nature of the 1983 Democratic victory.

The nature of Edwards's support in 1983 in various parts of the state and within the major political cultures is much more revealing. Edwards gained support in the rural, less affluent parishes of north Louisiana, and lost some in parishes that became more affluent and experienced population growth in south Louisiana. This is a significant indication that Republicans are less and less able to rely on social conservativism alone in north Louisiana. With the decline of the race issue and as economic issues reemerge in north Louisiana, the Populist appeal of the Democratic party will become more attractive to that area of the state. The lines closely resemble those of Long-era bifactionalism, where Edwards appears to be consolidating the Longite power base of the less affluent. Notably, these growth areas are now experiencing retrenchment, and Republican chances for capturing new party identifiers appear to be slipping away.

In the 1986 Senate race between Republican Henson Moore and Democrat John Breaux, the patterns of party strength were almost identical. Indeed, there is an .83 correlation between parish votes for Edwards and for Breaux (Howard and Parent, forthcoming). Individual voting patterns revealed in ABC/*Washington Post* Exit Polls substantiate the importance of voting along economic class lines (see table 14.4). Voters whose incomes exceed $20,000 a year supported the Republican; those whose incomes are less than $20,000 supported the Democrat. As the Democratic party identifies itself again in the South in general and in Louisiana in particular with working class issues, and

Table 14.4
Demographic Correlates of Voting in the 1986 Senate Election

% of Sample	Characteristic	% Breaux Democrat	% Moore Republican
	Income:		
10	Under $5,000	82	17
12	$5,000 to $9000	72	28
19	$10,000 to $19,000	60	39
19	$20,000 to $29,000	44	55
16	$30,000 to $39,000	42	57
9	$40,000 to $49,000	41	59
16	over $50,000	33	67
	Religion:		
40	Protestant	42	58
37	Catholic	49	50
18	Other Christian	70	28
1	Jewish	71	29
2	Other Non-Christian	79	21
3	No Religion	59	41
	Sex:		
51	Male	50	50
49	Female	55	45
	Race:		
24	Black	91	9
75	White	39	61
	Age:		
11	18–24	65	35
9	25–29	47	51
28	30–39	54	45
22	40–49	51	49
15	50–59	49	52
16	60 +	46	53
	Education:		
13	Some HS or Less	71	29
35	HS Graduate	55	44
25	Some College	46	54
14	College Graduate	30	61
13	Postgraduate	48	52

Source: *ABC News Exit Poll*

as the race issue begins to wane, the chances for Republican majorities are slim.

THE NEW ELECTION SYSTEM AND
SPORADIC REPUBLICAN SUCCESS

One odd political development in the 1970s added to the prospects of Republican success in Louisiana. In 1975, despite howls of opposition from several major political and civic groups (and, perhaps most inconsequentially, from academics), Democratic Governor Edwin Edwards was able to convince the legislature to overwhelmingly pass a new election law that broke down at least one barrier to Republican growth. Under the previous closed-party primary with runoff law, many Louisianians registered Democratic in order to participate in the competitive Democratic primary. Under the new open election system, citizens register by party, but the elections are bipartisan. All candidates, regardless of party affiliation, participate in an "open election," and if no one receives a majority, the two top vote getters, regardless of party affiliation, meet in a runoff. This legal change allowed for more flexibility in party registration, since all voters can vote in every election. This freedom to register as a Republican, without concern over being unable to participate in a Democratic primary, led to Republican hopes of strong registration gains. Republican registration rose from 2.9 percent in 1972 to 12.8 percent in 1987 (see table 14.1). This reflects major relative gains, but fairly disappointing absolute gains for the Republican party.

Republicans have wisely used this system, however, to their advantages. The significant political result has been that these new election rules have, in effect, changed Louisiana from the dynamics of party-primary-with-runoff state (like the remainder of the South) to the dynamics of a party plurality system used outside the South. Under the open election system, Republicans have typically decided on a candidate before the election through a series of meetings or conventions. Democratic aspirants, on the other hand, all run in the open election. On two occasions in the past, this phenomenon has led to a Republican victory. The first occasion was the governor's race of 1979, when five legitimate Democratic contenders faced each other and a single Republican contender, Congressman David Treen. Treen led the field in this first major test of the open election system, with 21.8 percent. The other spot in the runoff went to Democratic Public Service Commissioner Louis Lambert, who had strong labor support, and who led the next Democratic contender by one-tenth of 1 percent of the vote. The remainder of the Democratic contenders were so opposed to Lambert that they all supported the Republican—the third-place finisher (Lieutenant Governor James Fitzmorris) even filed a voter fraud suit against Lambert. Republican Treen won the governorship by less than 10,000 votes out of 1,365,830 cast. Had Louisiana used the election system it replaced, where Lambert would have met another Democrat in a party primary runoff, a Democrat would almost certainly have been elected governor.

The open election system also worked to Republican advantage in the 1986 race to succeed Democrat Congresswoman Cathy Long, widow of Gillis Long. The Eighth District, 36 percent black and with a strong blue-collar population, has proven to be the most Democratic area in the state. Four Democrats and one Republican ran for the seat. The leader of the field was Faye Williams, a black Democrat; the second-place finisher was the Republican, Clyde Holloway. The other three Democrats were all white and were perceived as fitting the blue-collar Democrat mold more so than Ms. Williams. Although Ms. Williams ran a close race, the Republican won in this heavily Democratic district.

The fall 1987 governor's election fit this pattern until the last two weeks of the campaign. Four major Democratic contenders joined the serious Republican candidate in a hotly contested race. Throughout most of the six months prior to the election, Democratic incumbent Governor Edwin Edwards and Republican Congressman Robert Livingston appeared headed toward a runoff. A sagging economy and two trials for public bribery plagued Governor Edwards' candidacy; even though the courts finally acquitted Edwards, his popularity rating nose dived. In a runoff election with the besieged Democratic governor, the Republican challenger seemed likely to win. However, in the last two weeks of the campaign Democratic conservative Louisiana Congressman Buddy Roemer surged from fifth place to first, pushing Livingston out of the runoff. Roemer's certain victory led Edwards to pull out of the race. This time the Republicans were unable to take advantage of a runoff with an unpopular Democrat.

These three elections recall Senate candidate Moore's statement that opened this discussion: unless a Republican runs against an unacceptable Democrat, the Republican will probably lose. Under Louisiana's election system, Republicans have the chance to meet Democrats who are not acceptable to even a majority of Democrats. Therefore, Republicans will probably win some major offices in Louisiana. These wins should not be mistaken, however, for an underlying shift in the Republican direction.

THE NATIONALIZATION OF LOUISIANA POLITICS

Present trends certainly point toward continued Democratic success in Louisiana, with Republicans making strong strides only in localized areas. Republican success otherwise depends on the fortunate circumstance of having a very attractive candidate in a runoff against a Democratic candidate that is, in the haunting words of Henson Moore, "unacceptable." This situation is due in large part to some nationalization of the party process in Louisiana. Republicans in Louisiana are legitimately, for the first time, the party of the white-collar, affluent, suburban white; Democrats are the party of blue-collar voters, blacks and the less affluent. These patterns reflect voting patterns across the country. Significantly, the Republican legitimacy problem associated with the aftermath of the Civil War appears finally to have withered away. Republicans now constitute a strong force of opposition to Democratic hegemony in voting patterns and in state offices. This is clearly an indication that the state party system is becoming a more parallel reflection of the national party system (see Hadley, 1986, for an excellent discussion).

As the state party system more closely resembles the national system, and as the Democrats begin to show some revitalization under this new system, might we expect national Democratic candidates to begin to fare better in Louisiana than they have in the last few presidential elections? The answer depends on the direction of the national parties. If the Democrats return to an emphasis on their differences with Republicans on Populist issues, the party alignment in Louisiana will resemble the national party alignment. If however, foreign policy and social issues emerge as the cross-cutting issues, the Democrats will have trouble taking advantage of their grass-roots strength in Louisiana.

SUMMARY AND SOME CONCLUSIONS

The rise of the Republican party in Louisiana in the 1960s and 1970s resulted in a weak two-party system in the state, where the Republicans represent a dominant part of the two major factions in Louisiana. This new situation should not be described as a realignment; rather, it is a form of dealignment where party identification is one factor, but not a defining factor, in voting coalitions.

Louisiana has settled into a two-faction system that in many ways is as familiar as the old political alignments of the Long era. The names are different, but the issues are very similar. The Republican party has similar support and carries the banner of many old Reform candidate ideas; the Democratic coalition closely resembles the old Long coalition. Blacks are now included in the Democratic coalition; the Republicans are able to appeal to a sometimes wider range of people due to some socially conservative issues. Generally, however, voting patterns clearly indicate that politics in Louisiana is moving back to a system where the lines are clearly drawn and the players are identifiable. In the days of Long-era bifactionalism, the Long candidates had a solid base of those on the lower ends of the social-economic scale. As a result, the Long candidates usually won. The Reform candidates had a political base of the more affluent and would win only when they could convince part of the normal Long coalition that Longite officials had abused their power. Recent political trends make it appear that the Democrats and Republicans in Louisiana are in much the same situation today.

RECENT TRENDS

15

CREEPING REALIGNMENT IN THE SOUTH*

Charles S. Bullock III

While there is a consensus that the Solid South no longer exists, there is disagreement about what has replaced it. Campbell (1977) believed that there was a critical realignment among southern blacks who moved into the Democratic party in 1964 and a gradual realignment of whites to the Republican party (also see Carmines and Stimson, 1982; Sundquist, 1983; Stanley, Bianco, and Niemi, 1986). Beck (1977) concluded that while there had been a dealignment of southern whites from the Democratic party, as evidenced by growing numbers of independents, the modest increase in GOP identifiers refuted the notion of a realignment (also Stone, 1986). Ladd combines the two concepts, "dealignment, the weakening of voters' ties to the parties, seems better understood as a distinguishing feature of the present realignment than as an alternative to realignment" (1985: 4).

This chapter approaches realignment through electoral success rather than through attitudes tapped by surveys. Several reasons underlie the focus on office holding. First, the emphasis accorded party identification elsewhere is premised on the supposed permanence of party affect and its presumed linkage with voting behavior. While party identification is still a useful predictor of voting behavior, its utility has declined as party loyalties have weakened. Party-line voters in federal elections always constitute less than 80 percent of those having a party ID and, for some elections during the 1970s, the figure dipped below 70 percent (Ornstein et al., 1984: 59). Figures on split-ticket voting reveal that typically at least a third of the congressional districts chose one party's presidential candidate but elected the opposing party's U.S. House candidate (Ladd, 1985: 6; see also Stanley, 1987). In 1972 and 1984, more than 40 percent of the congressional districts displayed this schizophrenic reaction. With party identification less widespread and

*The author appreciates the helpful suggestions of Harold Stanley.

less fixed for individuals, it becomes less useful in determining voting behavior.

Second, the degree to which party identification is related to voting behavior varies across offices. For the 1980s, Stone (1986) reports a correlation coefficient between party identification and voting for president of .86 while the correlation between party and voting in House elections was .63. Only slightly smaller disparities exist in the South for earlier decades.

Third, changes in partisan fortunes may be more visible in data on office control than in attitudinal data. Changed voting behavior may be a harbinger of changes in attitudes. Voters who ultimately change parties may not acknowledge that their loyalties have shifted until after they have supported several candidates of their newfound party. Others vote for the candidates of one party while persisting to claim good standing in the opposition party.

Fourth, control of public office is critical to the maintenance of political parties and for the shaping of public policy. While partisan and regional patterns are not constant across time and issues, congressional Democrats and Republicans generally differ on social welfare, regulation of the economy, and civil rights issues (Sinclair, 1982; 1985). These disparities extend to the parties' southern wings (Bullock, 1981; 1985).

Fifth, a requirement that the Republican party be the choice of most southerners is too demanding as a threshold for realignment. If Republicans were consistently winning most of the public offices in the South, it would be hard to deny that they were the dominant party. Evidence of a realignment in the South, however, need not be premised on the GOP winning most offices or being the majority in terms of party identification. In the South, the Republican party could experience a 30- or 40-percentage point gain in the share of offices held, yet remain the minority. In other regions a gain of 40 percentage points would make the GOP dominant.

THEORY

It would be surprising if patterns of partisan control were constant across offices. When partisan fortunes are changing, it is likely that an emerging party will reap success earlier at one level than at others, with the emerging party enjoying initial successes at the top of the ticket.

Several factors may be operative here. First, the larger the constituency, the greater the potential for a heterogeneous population (Bond, 1983). The presence of diverse social and economic groups in a constituency provides the bases on which competing parties can seek to build winning coalitions. Bullock and Brady (1983) have shown that more heterogeneous states are more likely to be simultaneously represented by a Democratic and a Republican senator.

District size may facilitate the development of party competition in what had been a one-party area in a second way. The pool of potential candidates in larger districts is more likely to produce quality challengers. Third, larger districts are more likely to have enough members of the emerging party to make a candidacy competitive while smaller districts are more likely to be so overwhelmingly one-party that partisan competition is foreclosed. Fourth, the geographic size of the constituency is often related to the significance of the office. The enticement of an important statewide office can attract more credible candidates for the emerging party. For these reasons, the GOP has often found viable candidates for southern senatorial or gubernatorial contests while many state legislative seats go uncontested (Tidmarch, et al., 1986).

The proposition that district size is related to the likelihood of two-party competition leads to the hypothesis that GOP success will be most pronounced in statewide competition. We predict that Republican breakthroughs will be manifest earliest in winning presidential electors, gubernatorial offices and Senate seats. The least change is expected in state legislative seats, with U.S. House seats being in an intermediate position. District size may work differently at the state level. To the extent that there are interchamber differences, Democrats won larger shares of the vote in southern senates than houses during the 1970s (Tidmarch, et al., 1986).

Even among statewide contests there is variability. At times Republicans have had greater difficulty in winning governorships than Senate seats. One examination of the differences between GOP success at the state and federal levels explained that

> the Republicans have marched deeper into the South behind divisive national issues, such as the war in Vietnam and abortion, that set the Democratic Party's liberal northern wing against its southern conservative element. In state races, these issues don't obtain. And the overarching theme that Republicans have used for the past decade to define their identity in federal races—the appeal against big, intrusive government—doesn't work in these state

races, party leaders agree . . . Almost without exception, the GOP tries to present federal races as a crisply defined choice between a big-spending Democrat and a penny-pinching Republican. When state expenditures—for roads, schools, or economic develop-ment—are presented as an agent of progress, as they are in most of these southern states, the big spender argument becomes less rele-vant (Brownstein, 1986: 2230).

Weakening party ties and the advantages of incumbency provide ad-ditional reasons for expecting that party control will vary across offices. Use of the perquisites of office (see, e.g., Cover, 1977; Yiannakis, 1982; Mayhew, 1974; Fiorina, 1977), reliance on the media, and deteriorat-ing partisan ties among voters conspire to produce more personalized campaigns. Popular incumbents who have diligently maintained sup-port among their constituents may escape challenge by candidates of an emerging party long after it has made substantial headway in an area. Once the popular incumbent departs, there may be a change in party control. In recent years approximately 90 percent of the House (Orn-stein, et al., 1985) and state legislative (Grau, 1981; Rosenthal, 1981) incumbents who have sought additional terms have succeeded. These return rates exceed those for U.S. senators. This prompts the hypothesis that an emerging party will score earlier gains among senators than lower legislative offices (cf. Stanley, 1987). At the state level, there is little difference in incumbency reelection rates for the two chambers (Rosenthal, 1981: 24). Another hypothesis keyed to incumbency pre-dicts that southern Republicans can more rapidly achieve parity with the rest of the country when there is an upper limit on the length of an individual's service. The hypothesis, then, is that Republicans will fare better in presidential elections (length of service limited by the Twenty-Second Amendment) and governorships (all southern states except Ar-kansas limit a governor's service).

The wonders of legislative districting offer yet another potential ex-planation for differences in party control of various offices. A party that commands the loyalties of a majority of the electorate can win the presidential electors, Senate seats, and governor's office of a state. It may poll a majority of the votes cast for the U.S. House or state legisla-tive candidates, yet fail to capture the bulk of the seats because of the way in which its partisans are apportioned among districts. By crack-ing (i.e., dividing concentrations of Republicans so that they do not constitute a majority in any district despite there being a sufficient number that one or more districts would have GOP majorities under alternative plans) or packing (maximizing GOP presence in one or a few districts to prevent Republicans from winning additional districts), southern Democrats have retarded Republican advances in Congress and state legislatures.

DATA

Evidence of realignment will be sought in six types of elections: partisan shares of presidential electors, partisan shares of the seats in the U.S. House and Senate, in state legislative bodies and governorships. Data on presidential elections begin with 1944, the last year in which the South was solidly Democratic. House data begin with 1950 because Eisenhower's coattails in 1952 brought the first southern Republicans in modern times to Congress outside of two east Tennessee districts that had been electing Republicans since the Civil War. U.S. Senate, state legislative, and gubernatorial data begin with 1956. This pre-dates the elections of modern Republican senators and governors in the South. The success of the GOP in the South will be compared with its performance in the rest of the nation.

FINDINGS

President

In 1948, four Deep South states forsook the Democratic party to support South Carolina governor, Strom Thurmond, on the States Rights' ticket. Four years later Dwight Eisenhower became the first Republican presidential nominee to carry a southern state since the 1928 backlash against Catholic Al Smith. Eisenhower's Rim South states contained 44 percent of the region's electoral votes, certainly a respectable showing for the nominee of the party that had carried a total of six southern states in the preceding eighteen presidential elections. Nonetheless, Eisenhower's share of the South's electoral votes was 50 percentage points below that of the rest of the nation as figure 15.1 shows.

Since 1952, at least one southern state has supported the GOP in every presidential election, and the South has been more Republican than Democratic in its presidential voting behavior. In 1956, 1972, 1980, and 1984, a majority of the South's electors voted for the Republican nominee, and in 1968, Richard Nixon received a plurality. In three of the last four elections, southern support for the Republican

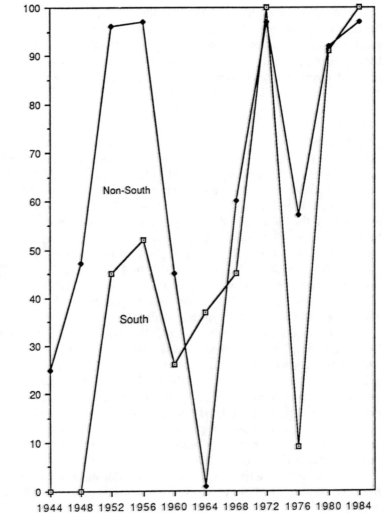

Figure 15.1
Republican share of presidential electors, South and non-South.

nominee has been almost identical to that of the rest of the nation. Even in the three-way 1968 race, Nixon's 45% of the South's electoral votes was only 15 points below that of the non-South. During the last twenty years, only in 1976, when there was an opportunity to vote for the first unquestionably southern candidate in more than a century, was the South more Democratic than the rest of the country.[1]

Senate

In 1961 John Tower (TX) became the first popularly elected Republican senator from the South. Through 1972, the trend line in figure 15.2 is gradually, but consistently, upward so that when Richard Nixon began his second term more than a quarter of the South's senators were Republicans. Republican strength in the Senate suffered in the South as elsewhere in the backwash of Watergate but made unprecedented gains in 1980. Figure 15.2 shows that the South was in the national mainstream in terms of Republican strength during the first half of the 1980s. With 45 to 50 percent of the seats, the GOP in the South was less than ten points below its strength in the non-South. The incidence of Republican seats in the South was almost identical with that in the Northeast and exceeded that in the Border states.

The 1986 elections were critical for GOP office control in the South. By narrow margins, Republicans lost the seats they had won in 1980 in Alabama, Georgia, and North Carolina. The Republican incumbent was also defeated in Florida, and the GOP failed to capture a seat in Louisiana. The proportion of Republicans among southern senators dropped to the pre-Reagan level and was little more than half the rate in the non-South. Nonetheless, the party demonstrated greater strength in its 1986 losses than at any time in the past, except for the close victories that it eked out in 1980.

Additional evidence that Republican senatorial successes are affected by forces similar to those at work outside the region comes from an analysis of the direction of election-to-election changes. Since 1966, the direction of the change in the South has been the same as that in the rest of the nation, except for 1972 and 1976. In 1972, Republicans gained seats in the South while losing strength elsewhere. Four years later, there was a one-seat net loss in the South while in the non-South there was a slight Republican gain. It remains to be seen whether the 1980–1984 or 1986 figures more accurately reflect GOP senatorial strength in the South. Should Republicans make net gains in the next two or three elections, then the party's southern strength should once again be similar to that nationwide.

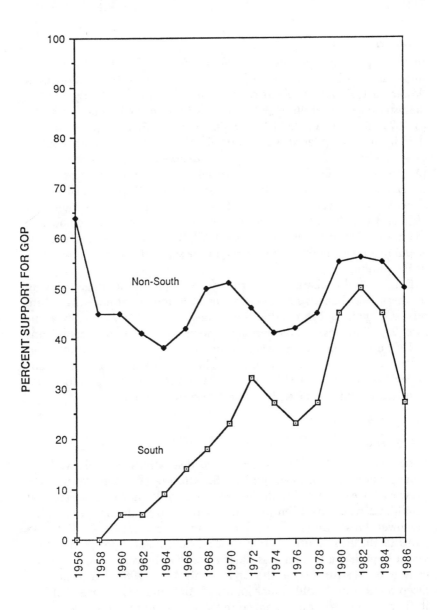

Figure 15.2
Republican share of Senate seats, South and non-South.

Governorships

Initial Republican successes in winning control of southern governorships came half a decade after Tower entered the Senate. Following a
slower start, Republicans moved more quickly and consistently into the
mainstream in controlling governorships than in holding Senate seats.
In 1974, Republicans held larger shares of the South's governorships
than in the remainder of the country. In 1972, 1980, and 1986, control
of the governors' mansions was almost identical in the two portions of
the country. While Republican governorships have occurred at about
the same rate in and out of the South since 1972, there were two years
in which there was a noticeable difference. As figure 15.3 shows, in
1982 and 1984 Republican governors were much more common outside
the South. Despite this gap, since 1978 changes in the incidence of
Republican governorships have been in the same direction in both parts
of the nation.

Earlier in this chapter, materials were quoted that suggested why
southern Republicans had done better at winning national than state
offices. Figure 15.3 shows that the proposition itself is not wholly accurate. The sharp rise in southern governorships held by the Republicans
in 1986 and the decline in Senate seats run counter to what Brownstein
(1986) sought to explain by distinguishing between the national concerns that influence presidential and senatorial elections and local development, which is often important in state elections.

U.S. House

Republican growth in southern House delegations has followed the
same general pattern as in the U.S. Senate. Marked increases in GOP
presence have coincided with the campaigns of Republican presidential
candidates who have been particularly popular in the South. The Eisenhower breakthrough opened the way for the initial GOP House
gains in the Rim South. While all Rim South states except Arkansas
sent a Republican to Congress during the Eisenhower years, it was the
congressional struggle over the Civil Rights Act of 1964 that turned the
Deep South into "Goldwater Country." Alabama, which was holding
its first elections after a prolonged redistricting imbroglio, sent a majority Republican delegation to the 89th Congress.[2]

The third presidential campaign to expand GOP enclaves in the
South was the Nixon landslide of 1972. With that election, the South
ceased to be the least Republican region, a position it relinquished to

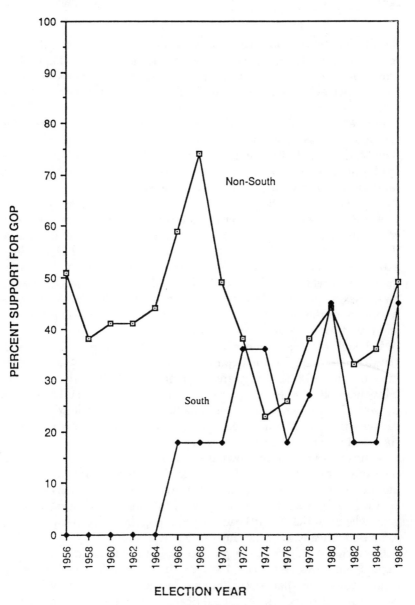

Figure 15.3
Republican share of governorships, South and non-South.

230   RECENT TRENDS

the Border states. That year also marked the first time since Reconstruction that all eleven southern states had at least one Republican
representative. The high water mark came with Reagan's sweep in
1984, which left Republicans holding 37 percent of the southern House
seats.

Figure 15.4 shows that during the sixteen elections since the
Eisenhower-based gains of 1952, the share of the southern seats held by
Republicans has declined only three times. The Watergate backlash of
1974 produced a 7-percentage-point drop in southern Republicans,
substantially below the 12-point-drop elsewhere.

The GOP also experienced a setback in 1982. Two factors seemingly
conspired to thwart Republicans in that year. Midterm losses were registered in Virginia, where Reagan's coattails had carried all but one of
the state's ten seats in 1980, and in North Carolina, whose House delegation may occupy the most competitive seats in the nation. The other
impediment was Democratic control of redistricting. The Democratic
majorities in the state legislatures drew districts so that Republicans
won none of the three new seats in Texas nor the new Tennessee seat,
and only two or the four new seats in Florida.

Although the proportion of southern House seats held by Republicans has never equaled the Republican share of northern seats, the two
lines in figure 15.4 obviously are converging. In the Ninety-ninth Congress, Republicans held 37 percent of the seats in the South and 43.6
percent of the other seats. While this has been the greatest similarity
between the regions, there has not been more than a 12-point difference during the last seven congresses.

As further evidence of growing similarity, the changes in the directions of the lines have been the same for both regions since 1976. During the Reagan era, an on-year and off-year oscillation occurs with the
South, like the rest of the country, sending more Republicans to Congress when the ticket was headed by the popular Reagan and retiring
some Republicans when the Reagan cue was absent.

Convergence has been the product of both gains in the South and
Republican losses elsewhere. Increases in the South have been suffi-
ciently consistent that a straight line provides a close fit. When the
percentage of seats held by Republicans in the South is regressed on
time, the r-square is .91 and the slope is .995 with a standard error of
.078. A regression line provides a good fit for the non-South, but is less
successful than in the South (r-square $= .54$, slope $= -.557$, and standard error $= .123$).

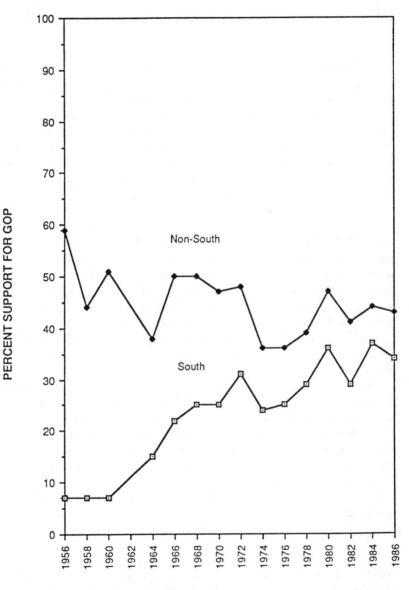

Figure 15.4
Republican share of U.S. House seats, South and non-South.

State Senate

As predicted, Republican acquisition of southern state senate seats has come more slowly than the advances in congressional delegations. In 1958, only four Rim South states (Florida, North Carolina, Tennessee, and Virginia) had any Republican senators and the first two states had one each. Increases came slowly until 1966 when, perhaps as a result of the weakening of partisan allegiance in some quarters and the recruitment of more and better candidates in the wake of the Goldwater candidacy, the number of Republicans more than doubled in one biennium. In 1967, 11 percent of the South's state senators were Republicans.

Gains over the last two decades have been modest as is obvious from figure 15.5. Two factors may account for the slow GOP growth in state senates. First, the backlash against Watergate pushed Republican representation below 10 percent. Second, by the mid-1970s, many ambitious Democrats had learned not simply the wisdom of but also the ways in which to win support among black voters. After a series of fits and starts, Republicans won 18 percent of the southern seats in 1986.

There has been less regional convergence in the control of state senate seats than for the positions previously discussed. Regional differences for this office through the mid-1980s are reminiscent of the pattern for other positions in earlier decades. Since 1972, the regional disparity has varied between 27 and 33 percentage points, a magnitude last observed in the U.S. House in 1967. Changes in the incidence of Republican Senate seats in the South have not paralleled changes in the rest of the country. Failure to track together distinguishes state senates from the patterns observed for gubernatorial, U.S. senatorial, and House seats and presidential electors. The nationalization of partisan politics visible for other positions has impacted less on state senates in the South.

State House

Republican growth in southern state houses has come more slowly than in either chamber of Congress but more rapidly than in state senates. As with other collegial bodies, Watergate reduced the Republican ranks with the ground lost not recovered until 1980. Reagan's showing in 1984 was associated with a four-point rise in GOP strength and, in 1986, GOP gains continued, rising to 24.3 percent. This increase—like that in state senates—ran counter to the trend in the rest of the nation, where the GOP experienced a net loss of four points.

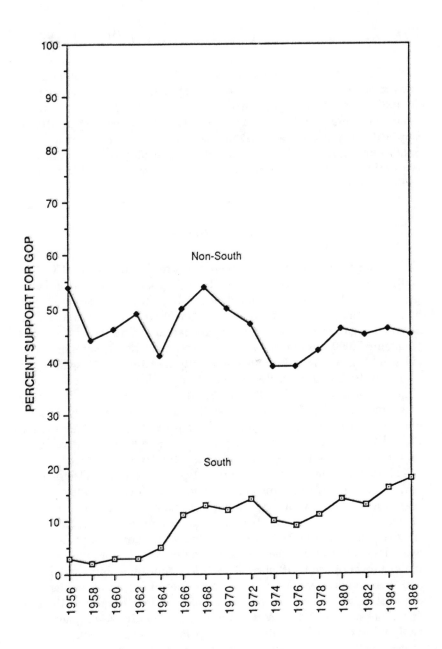

ELECTION YEAR

Figure 15.5
Republican share of state senators, South and non-South.

No chamber has yet been organized by the Republicans, although in 1969 they came within a single seat of capturing the Tennessee house. In 1987, Republicans constituted more than a third of the Florida, Tennessee, Texas, and Virginia houses. They were weakest in Mississippi (6% of the seats) and Arkansas (9%). As with state senates, the South remains heavily Democratic with a great disparity persisting between the percentage of seats held by Republicans there and in the rest of the county.

CONCLUSIONS

Despite occasional aberrations, such as Carter's success in 1976, the South, has now rejoined the union in the support it gives Republican presidential candidates. The incidence of Republican governors in the South is similar to that elsewhere and from 1980 to 1986, the southern Senate delegation was almost as Republican as the nation as a whole. Changing 7,000 votes in Alabama and fewer than 13,000 votes in Georgia would have maintained that similarity into the last Reagan biennium. In the U.S. House, Republican strength in the South is less than 10 percentage points below the non-South.

Among state legislatures, the South remains distinctively Democratic. Fewer than a quarter of the state representatives and less than a fifth of the senators are Republicans. GOP strength is comparable to that in congressional delegations fifteen to twenty years ago.

The 1986 Senate results are the most troubling exception to the pattern of greater successes and more convergence for statewide contests than district contests and generally more success in federal than state offices. Republican Senate defeats came despite heavy spending and frequent campaign visits by the president and other leading Republicans. The uniformity of the defeats are in line with the proposition that the members of the GOP class of 1980 were not blue-chip candidates, and their victories were the result of a series of fortuitous events, not the least of which was the popularity of President Reagan at the top of the ticket.[3] The 1986 losses in the South were also accompanied by GOP setbacks elsewhere, although the defeats were more concentrated in the South. This fluctuation suggests competitiveness more akin to the non-South than the one-party dominance for which the South was famous.

Table 15.1 compares GOP strength in the South since 1956 across the six types of offices discussed in this chapter. With the exception of Cart-

Table 15.1

Republican Strength (%) in the South, 1956–86

Office	1956	1958	1960	1962	1964	1966	1968	1970	1972	1974	1976	1978	1980	1982	1984	1986
Presidential Electors	52		26		37		45		100		9		91		100	
Senate	0	0	5*	5	9	14	18	23	32	27	23	27	45	50	45	27
Governor	0	0	0	0	0	18	18	18	36	36	18	27	45	18	18	45
U.S. House	7	7	7	10	15	22	25	25	31	24	25	29	36	29	37	34
State Senate	3	2	3	3	5	11	13	12	14	10	9	11	14	13	16	18
State House	4	2	4	5	7	12	13	13	17	12	12	14	18	18	22	24

*Reflects special election victory of John Tower (R-TX) in early 1961

er's presidential election, Republicans have done better in presidential elections than in any of the four sets of legislative offices. Republican strength in the U.S. Senate began later than in the U.S. House, was at a similar level to that in the House during the 1970s but has exceeded that of the House during the 1980s. The governorship was the last office won by Republicans and one marked by great variability; nonetheless, Republican control of governorships has approximated its congressional strength since 1966.

Except for Republicans doing less well in the lower than the upper chamber of state legislatures, GOP strength generally declines as the level of the office and the scope of the issues surrounding it lessen. Presidential elections that feature national and international issues have favored Republican candidates. A quarter to a half of the Senate elections, where national issues often play major roles and which generally have candidates well known to the electorate (Mann and Wolfinger, 1980; Hinckley, 1980), are won by Republicans. In southern House elections, an often unknown Republican is typically challenging a Democratic incumbent (Mann and Wolfinger, 1980). House contests that include a mélange of national and local issues are gradually, but increasingly, being won by Republicans. The GOP has done least well in state legislative contests, where local issues and local ties dominate and the influence of presidential coattails has been muted (cf. Campbell, 1986).

Two factors have delayed Republican growth. First, southern Democrats more readily abandoned racist appeals and courted black support than did southern Republicans. Southern Democrats in the U.S. House (Bullock, 1985) and in several state senates (Munro, 1987) have been more supportive of civil rights, redistributive, and social welfare stands than have southern Republicans. This allowed members of the party that erected the barricades that excluded black participation to benefit from a reinfranchised black electorate.

The second factor that resuscitated southern Democrats was the one-two punch of Watergate and the Carter candidacy. Following the 1976 elections, Republican ranks in the four sets of legislative chambers were reduced to the levels of six to ten years earlier. Not until the Reagan presidency did Republicans exceed the levels they had achieved in the 1972 election. Thus while Democratic overtures to blacks simply retarded Republican growth, the Watergate-Carter combination set the GOP back by perhaps as much as a decade.

It is premature to say that party competition in the South is identical with that in the rest of the nation. There is variation across offices and from election to election; nonetheless, the pattern is clear. Patterns of partisan office holding in the South are increasingly like those of the rest of the nation. Harold Stanley speculates that "If the trend continues, the voting loyalty of southern white Democrats to House candidates will soon be on a par with that toward Democratic presidential candidates" (1987). Data on office holding in this chapter point in the same direction as do the survey data Stanley relies on. Projections from past trends predict that southern Republican congressional successes may equal or even exceed those in the rest of the country. At some more distant point, the gap between GOP southern and nonsouthern state legislative seats may be eliminated.

NOTES

1. Lyndon Johnson came from Texas, leading some people to view him as a Westerner. Woodrow Wilson was born and reared in the South, but his political and vocational success came in New Jersey.

2. Alabama lost one seat following the 1960 census. The state legislature failed to redistrict the state, forcing the nine incumbents to run at large in the 1962 Democratic primary. The oldest member, Frank Boykin, ran ninth and, with the electorate having decided which incumbent to eliminate, the legislature produced eight districts in time for the 1964 elections.

3. Of the southern Republican freshman senators elected in 1980 only Paula Hawkins (FL) had prior office-holding experience. She had spent six years on her state's Public Utility Commission.

16

PARTISAN CHANGES IN THE SOUTH:

Making Sense of Scholarly Dissonance

Harold W. Stanley and David S. Castle

Watergate and the 1976 Carter candidacy set back earlier optimism about Republican increases in the South, but in the Reagan years southern Republicans have generally found brighter growth prospects. This chapter addresses two topics: how to account for strikingly different conclusions concerning southern partisan change and the implications of those different conclusions.

The search for signs of realignment in American party politics has generated a considerable body of scholarship and the transformation of southern party politics plays a prominent role therein. Yet previous research on southern partisan change supports starkly different conclusions:

1) the South has politically realigned (Bartley and Graham, 1975, pp. 196–197; Campbell, 1977a, p. 37 and 1977b, pp. 755–756; Hadley and Howell, 1980, pp. 147–148; Petrocik, 1987; Schreiber, 1971, p. 161; Seagull, 1975, p. 18; Wolfinger and Arseneau, 1978, p. 206; and Wolfinger and Hagen, 1985, pp. 8–9);
2) no southern realignment has occurred, Democratic dominance continues (Converse, 1966, p. 212 and 1972, pp. 310, 315–316; Prysby, 1980, p. 125; and Scammon and Barnes, 1985); and
3) the South has undergone dealignment (Beck, 1977, pp. 480, 484; and Gatlin, 1975, p. 50).

Support for each conclusion can be inferred from recent Republican gains in the South (figure 16.1). Republican victories, particularly at the presidential level, mark the death of the solidly Democratic South and suggest fundamental realignment. Yet these gains have occurred within a context of continued Democratic vitality. Except for gubernatorial results in 1980 and 1986 and congressional results for 1980–1984, Democrats have won over two-thirds of the elections below the presidential level. Even in 1986, the four Republican gains at the gubernatorial level were matched by four defeats in the U.S. Senate. The

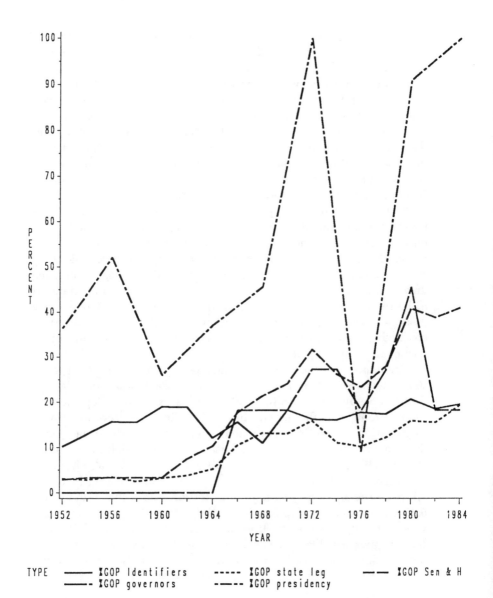

100 -

90 -

80 -

70 -

60 -

P
E
R 50 -
C
E
N
T 40 -

30 -

20 -

10 -

0 -

1952   1956   1960   1964   1968   1972   1976   1980   1984

YEAR

TYPE ———— %GOP Identifiers   ----- %GOP state leg   —— %GOP Sen & H
      —·— %GOP governors   —··— %GOP presidency

Only weak and strong identifiers are counted as partisans.

Sources: Bass and DeVries (1976:34–37), U.S. Bureau of the Census,
Statistical Abstract of the U.S.: 1987, and National Election studies data.

Figure 16.1
Republican gains in the South, 11-state South, 1952–1984.

gubernatorial gains of 1986 meant Republicans regained the level reached in 1980. Moreover, since greater Republican identification has not accompanied more frequent Republican victories, perhaps dealignment aptly describes southern partisan change.

These different research findings suggest that one hallmark of scientific research, cumulative knowledge, has not characterized the study of southern partisan change. Indeed, scholars disagree not only about the overall trends but also about the impact of the three distinct processes capable of producing shifts in southern partisanship. The processes are *conversion* (individual southerners switch partisan identification), *generational turnover* (youth, coming-of-age, replace the elderly, who have different partisan ties), or *migration* (those moving into or out of the South alter the partisan distribution). Researchers not only disagree about the impact of each process, they disagree further: are southern party coalitions more aligned along class lines, did white racial backlash cause the decline in Democratic strength, and does greater independence among southerners signify partisan neutrality or a "halfway house" to Republicanism. A brief overview of data management decisions precedes a consideration of definitions. An appraisal of conflicting conclusions about overall trends follows discussion of the particular disagreements mentioned.

Dissonance about southern partisan change is all the more surprising since most researchers have used the same data base—the National Election Study surveys (SRC/CPS). How can scholars using the same source produce conflicting conclusions? Hadley first drew attention to the question, suggesting data management decisions drive the conclusions apart (1981, p. 394). Scholars use different definitions of the "South" (10, 11, 13, or 16 states plus the District of Columbia); focus on different groups (native whites, migrant whites, whites, blacks, or all southerners); employ various indicators of change (partisan identifications, normal vote, split-ticket voting, party image, or aggregate vote); and study different time periods. Different factual findings, some supporting different conclusions, result in part from such data management decisions, but the varied conclusions also rest on matters of interpretation. Findings must be interpreted, and this leaves room for further disagreements.

REALIGNMENT AND DEALIGNMENT: DEFINITIONS

If scholars use dissimilar definitions of realignment or dealignment, different findings and conclusions come as no surprise.

To fix ideas, consider first the meaning of realignment. Realignment occurs when groups of individuals alter their attachment to a party. This alteration must endure for several elections. Initially Key defined a realignment as

> a category of elections in which voters are, at least from impressionistic evidence, unusually deeply concerned, in which the extent of electoral involvement is relatively quite high, and in which the decisive results of the voting reveal a sharp alteration of the pre-existing cleavage within the electorate. Moreover, and perhaps this is the truly differentiating characteristic of this sort of election, the realignment made manifest in the voting in such elections seems to persist for several succeeding elections. (1955, p. 4)

That description constitutes *critical* realignment. The recent South seems to fit these criteria: high salience elections with high turnout (Stanley, 1987) and sharply altered cleavages, perhaps persisting (Bartley and Graham, 1975, p. 196). (Persistence is more dubious given the force and extent of recent change.) Yet a valid question concerns the suddenness of recent partisan change. Some think critical realignment requires more abruptness than the South experienced. Key introduced a second concept relevant to these concerns, *secular* realignment "a movement of the members of a population category from party to party that extends over several presidential elections and appears to be independent of the peculiar factors influencing the vote at individual elections." (1959, p. 199)

Dealignment involves a durable weakening of individual partisan attachments, either a switch from identifying with parties to independence or a reduction in the connection between identifying with a party and voting for the party's candidates (Campbell and Trilling, 1980, p. 5).

Some scholars consider all three concepts, some focus on one or two, others modify the concepts.[1] Consider several examples.

Campbell, without directly considering dealignment prospects,[2] finds that southern whites underwent secular realignment; southern blacks, critical realignment (1977b, pp. 755–756).

Bartley and Graham find critical realignment, qualifying the finding by noting that more elections must pass before Key's central question of durability can be answered (1975, p. 196). Bartley and Graham discount little growth in Republican identifiers alongside great growth in independents, arguing that more affluent independents have tended to bolster Republican prospects by voting Republican (1975, p. 138)—an argument whose logic insists that dealignment occurs only when more voters fail to identify with a party and all segments of independents split their vote evenly (or fail to vote).

Seagull views realignment as "a durable change in the social bases of the vote" and finds that southern realignment has occurred (1975, p. 18).

Converse defines southern realignment as "a rapid shift of the South from a relatively one-party Democratic status to a one-party Republican one" (1966, p. 213). Beck contends that southern realignment requires "pronounced growth" in Republican partisan identification (1977, p. 480). Gatlin looks for "a rather wholesale conversion of southern whites of all social statuses from the Democratic to the Republican fold" (1975, p. 40). None finds realignment on the terms set forth, but they do find "convergence" (Converse, 1966, p. 220), "dealignment" (Beck, 1977, pp. 480, 484), or "disengagement" (Gatlin, 1975, p. 50).

Such differences in definitions and frames of reference facilitate differing overall conclusions. Differences in particular findings, to which we now turn, also have implications for the overall conclusions.

REALIGNMENT AND DEALIGNMENT: EXPLANATIONS

Conversion

How much of the southern partisan changes stems from the conversion of white Democratic identifiers to Republicanism? Beck (1977, p. 487), Converse (1972, p. 314), and Wolfinger and Arseneau (1978, p. 199) find little conversion; Campbell (1977a, p. 46) and Petrocik (1987) find significant conversion.

Both Converse and Campbell use the decline in the Democratic normal vote as the dependent variable. Converse claims that individual conversion accounts for no more than one-fifth (and probably much less) of the decline between 1952 and 1968 (1972, p. 314). Considering the decline in the normal vote between 1952 and 1972, Campbell notes the 10-point decline in expected normal vote among native southern white adults and claims, "the conclusion seems unavoidable that conversion has been responsible for more change than any of the other causes. . . ." (1977b, p. 749, 1977a, p. 46)

The time period studied accounts for some disagreement over the role of conversion in southern partisan change. Looking back from 1972 as Campbell did, one could note some partisan conversion among older native whites but, after four more years, much of the change had receded, suggesting apparent change as a result of short-term forces or sampling error (Wolfinger and Arseneau, 1978, p. 199, and Campbell, 1977b, p. 760).

Campbell's conclusions about conversion need qualification in two additional ways. First, he does not distinguish between the contributions to the declining Democratic normal vote made by greater independence and by limited growth in Republican identification (1977b, p. 749 n. 18). Should we consider switching from Democratic to independent "conversion" or "dealignment?" Campbell recognizes but does not analyze the fact that the declining Democratic normal vote may stem from some mixture of Democratic decline (in identification, turnout, or loyalty) and either Republican or independent growth (in identification, turnout or partisan voting patterns). If most of the Democratic decline stems from independent growth, not from gains in Republican identifiers, dealignment rather than conversion seems the most appropriate conclusion.[3] Second, Campbell's methods mean he includes as conversion the effects of the reduced rate at which recent generations mature into partisanship (Norpoth and Rusk, 1982, pp. 529–534). If southern youth have remained more independent as they aged than did their elders, these failures to become partisan showed up, inappropriately, as conversion in Campbell's calculations. Norpoth and Rusk's methodologically elegant analysis of dealignment in the U.S. electorate makes plausible the conjecture that Campbell's exceptional conclusions about conversion result in large part from this point.

Unquestionably, many southern blacks permanently switched from an apolitical orientation in the 1950s to Democratic identification in the 1960s. Counting this as conversion is invalid if conversion requires switching from one party to another. Campbell gives this subject the most extensive consideration and labels the switch "mobilization" (1979, pp. 274–275).

Most of the Democratic decline in white identifiers does not result from individuals switching to identify with the Republicans. Abandonment of party identification by many whites, not conversion, accounts for the Democratic decline. Party identification trends make clear the reluctance of native southern whites to change from Democratic to Republican identification. Voting Republican has become far more common, identifying as a Republican only slightly more so.

Generational Replacement

Researchers have produced three different conclusions regarding the partisanship of younger southern whites, a critical group if realignment arises from generational turnover. Petrocik (1987) and Wolfinger and his coauthors find this group is becoming more Republican: "the younger Southerners are leading the way toward two-party politics in the South" (Wolfinger and Arseneau, 1978, p. 197; cf. Wolfinger and Hagen, 1985, p. 11). Cassel (1977, p. 31) and Beck conclude the young are shifting toward independent identification: "those voters who entered the electorate in the postwar period were much more independent and much less Democratic by 1972 than their predecessors" (Beck, 1977, p. 485–486). Hadley and Howell (1980, p. 141) as well as Converse, contend the young do not differ significantly from older white southerners in partisan attitudes: "Over the years the younger southern white generation seems no more and no less Democratic than older generations." (Converse, 1966, p. 226)

In part, definitions of *young* and of *partisan* account for these differing views. Differences in classification produce different youth cohorts. Why suspect classification? Using comparable categories makes the differences disappear. Wolfinger and Arseneau define youth as those reaching voting age in 1964 or later. These native white youths were only 1 and 5 percentage points more Republican than older native whites in 1972 and 1976, but counting independents leaning Republican as partisans boosted that gap to 9 and 13 percentage points respectively (1974, p. 18 and 1978, p. 197). Beck, Cassel, and Converse, unlike Wolfinger and Arseneau, consider independents leaning Republican as independents. Later we return to the question of how to define partisanship. Consider age classifications. Combining Hadley and Howell's two younger cohorts yields a sample approximating Beck's postwar generation. This redefined cohort shows a marked increase in ticket splitting during the 1970s. No significant increase in straight-ticket Republican voting is evident; thus the increase in ticket splitting echoes Beck and Cassel's contention that younger southerners are moving toward political independence.

Migration

Recent migration patterns have altered the southern population. Between 1950 and 1970, almost 3 million blacks (a figure equaling one-third of the 1950 southern black population) migrated out of the 11-state South. In 1950 less than 9 percent of that region's population had been born outside the region, by 1970 over 18 percent had. Whites make up most of this shift (Bass and DeVries, 1976, pp. 22, 502).

Did these migration patterns produce political changes? Wolfinger and Hagen (1985, p. 10), Wolfinger and Arseneau (1978, p. 195), and Converse (1972, p. 314) find white migration into the South significantly changed southern partisanship. Campbell (1977b, p. 737); Nie, Verba, and Petrocik (1979, p. 221); Petrocik (1987); and Beck (1977, p. 481) come to the opposite conclusion, contending that migration patterns explain little partisan change. The impact of out-migration requires resolving the riddle of the partisanship of the out-migrants had they remained southerners and this proves difficult to disentangle. Had blacks remained rather than migrated during the 1950s and 1960s, far-reaching consequences may have resulted for the partisan trends of other southerners (Key, 1949, p. 672). Beck best finesses the difficulties and looks at the partisanship of southern out-migrants, migrants into the South and politically mobilizing blacks who remained in the South. The net effect of these three processes on the distribution of southern partisanship proves minimal (1977, pp. 480–484).

Restricting the analysis of migration to whites does not involve such offsetting patterns. Different time periods contribute to different findings concerning the political meaning of white in-migration patterns. Converse concludes that "a good four-fifths" of the decline in the white southern Democratic normal vote through the mid-1960s resulted from the high status, predominantly Republican in-migration (1972, pp. 314). Campbell notes in-migration effects were greatest during 1956–1960 but tapered off after 1960 such that in-migration "can explain only about one-quarter of the total change in (the expected Democratic vote) over the 20-year period from 1952 to 1972 . . ." (1977b, p. 737). Nie, Verba, and Petrocik make a comparable claim using partisan identification as the measure of change: "In overall effect, comparing the early 1950s with the 1970s, the decline in Democratic identification would have been almost as great (only 6 percent difference) if no newcomers had arrived." (1979, p. 221; cf. Petrocik, 1987)

Wolfinger and Arseneau provide different findings. Using 1952–1976 Survey Research Center data, they note the influx of in-migrants continues, the in-migrants remain predominantly white Republicans, and these in-migrants vote at a higher rate than native white southerners. By defining Republicans to include independents leaning Republican, Wolfinger and Arseneau find in-migrants have boosted the share of Republican identifiers among southern voters. Earlier, using a more limited time span and considering only weak and strong identifiers as Republicans, Wolfinger and Arseneau noted, "If we were to remove (migrants to the South) from the distribution of white southern party identification . . . , this (distribution) would look very much as it does now" (1974, p. 16). Why do these differences arise? The differing readings rest in part upon the definition of partisanship and the focus on voters rather than the adult population. The broader definition of Republican shows a 17-percentage-point rise in Republican identifiers among southern whites of voting age between 1952 and 1976; considering only weak and strong identifiers as Republican shows a smaller, 11-percentage-point rise (1978, p. 189). In 1972 and 1976, southern white voters have been about 5 percentage points more partisan than southern whites of voting age, so focusing on voters gives an even larger figure (21 percentage points) for Republican growth between 1952 and 1976. The broader definition of Republican and the concentration on white voters rather than the white voting-age population provides the foundations for finding a significant pro-Republican boost attributable to in-migration.

Class Polarization

Greater class polarization in southern partisan alignments, indicative of southern convergence with the rest of the nation, has been sighted by some, not by others. Many researchers anticipated the development of New Deal, class-based party coalitions in the South as upper status southerners found the Republican party appealing. Evidence of more class-based southern party coalitions can be found in Nie, Verba, and Petrocik (1979, pp. 221–222); Converse (1966, p. 222); Wolfinger and Arseneau (1978, p. 206); Hadley and Howell (1980, pp. 136–137); and DeVries and Bass (1978, p. 323). Strong (1971, pp. 254–255), Campbell (1977a, pp. 50–51), and Bartley and Graham (1975, pp. 137, 193–195) caution against this conclusion, while Gatlin (1975, p. 49) concludes that status polarization has not occurred.

The in-migration of upper-status, predominantly Republican whites, coupled with the black mobilization into Democratic identification and the relatively lower-class status of most southern blacks produces greater party polarization around class for the whole southern population as even Gatlin acknowledges. But, using correlation coefficients, Gatlin shows that most of the variation in southern partisanship is attributable to racial, not economic, cleavages. (One should question the use of the correlation coefficient, a sample-specific statistic, in such comparisons across samples—Achen, 1977).

Evidence reveals that all classes of native southern whites have shown Democratic decline, independent growth, and Republican gains, but upper-status southerners have registered the largest Democratic declines and the greatest Republican gains. For instance, native southern whites in households headed by a professional or managerial worker registered a 29-percentage-point Democratic drop and a 17-percentage-point Republican increase from the 1950s to 1976, but for similar respondents in households headed by a blue-collar worker, the comparable figures are 15 and 3 (Wolfinger and Arseneau, 1978, p. 205). Given the previously all-inclusive nature of the Democratic party in the South, any change other than toward more status polarization is difficult to imagine. Even so, southern status polarization still trails that in the nonsouth, where movement has been toward less status polarization.

White Racial Backlash

Researchers also disagree about the role of white backlash in bringing about Democratic decline. Lamis (1984), Sundquist (1983, pp. 403–404), Schreiber (1971, p. 161), and Phillips (1969, p. 205–212) suggest racial attitudes drove formerly Democratic whites to independence or the Republicans; Beck (1977, pp. 492–494), Campbell (1977b, p. 750), Wolfinger and Arseneau (1978, pp. 200–202), and Wolfinger and Hagen (1985, p. 12) contend white racial attitudes had little to do with Democratic decline.

Survey findings firmly support those researchers discounting racial backlash as the cause of Democratic decline. Researchers suggesting a sizable role to racial backlash rely on testable but untested assertions (Schreiber) or a small portion of the available evidence (Sundquist and Phillips). Beck as well as Wolfinger and Arseneau provide thorough analyses of the available survey data, finding racial backlash fails to explain the decline in Democratic identifiers. Survey data indicate race was not the sole concern of native whites. Racial issues were not the single force separating southern whites from the national Democratic party. Native white southerners showed increasing conservatism on all social welfare issues during the 1960s. Questions on government-guaranteed jobs and standards of living, government health insurance and medical care, and federal aid to education reveal sharp decreases in support among native whites during this period. The native white electorate was at odds with much of the Great Society. As Campbell notes, this broad ideological misfit rather than a preoccupation with race holds more promise as the reason the southern white population became less Democratic (1977b, pp. 748–754).

Independents

Researchers differ on the significance of partisan independence. Beck (1977, p. 484) and Gatlin (1975, p. 50) see southern independents as politically neutral, disengaged from the party system. Schreiber (1971, p. 161) as well as Bartley and Graham (1975, p. 138) speculate that independent identification may be a "halfway house" along the road to Republicanism, while Ladd and Hadley (1978, p. 144) directly dispute this. Wolfinger and Hagen (1985, p. 9) and Wolfinger and Arseneau (1978, p. 189) view most independents as "closet" partisans. Rather than equate partisan independence with partisan neutrality, Wolfinger and his coauthors show that southern independents who say they lean toward one party actually vote for that party more regularly than do weak partisan identifiers (1978, pp. 188–189; 1985, p. 9).

How should we characterize partisans? Individuals do not readily switch partisan identification. If independent leaners deserve inclusion with weak and strong partisans, they should have similar stability. Do they? If similarly stable, the inclusion of leaners with partisans seems reasonable; if less stable, grouping leaners together with partisans inflates the partisan figures with fickle, fair-weather "partisans." Do leaners vote as they do because of how they lean or do they lean as they do because of how they vote? (Shively, 1977; cf. Keith, et al., 1986)

Survey panel data offer the best insights to these questions. Findings from national respondents show that, over a four-year period, a smaller proportion of leaners in 1972 (39 percent) remain the same in 1976 than is the case for pure independents, weak partisans, or strong partisans (43, 52, and 58 percent, respectively) and that almost one-third of the leaners have moved by 1976 to identify with the party toward which they leaned in 1972 (Niemi, Katz and Newman, 1980, p. 640). Thus, leaners have been more fickle than weak or strong partisans and inflating partisan totals by including them makes the party identification measure more volatile.[4] If one out of every three leaners later goes over to identify with the party, the contribution this group makes to a party's strength soon shows up in the proportion of weak and strong identifiers.

Beck reports individual partisan changes across two-year panels during the 1950s and 1970s for the nation (1984). These results show leaners as the least stable of all the categories although the difference between leaners and partisans declined in the 1970s. These trends suggest leaners were not acting as partisans so much as partisans were acting more like independents, a suggestion indicative of dealignment rather than realignment.

The deeper disagreement this issue touches concerns the question of the proper measure of partisan change. Reliance on the normal vote or party identification provides a durable survey measure not easily changed. Reliance on the aggregate vote or voter choice from surveys makes the measure too reflective of short-term change.

Bartley and Graham reach a conclusion that illustrates the critical significance of independence and the importance of distinguishing between long-term and short-term change. After a masterful survey of recent southern electoral behavior, Bartley and Graham conclude critical realignment has occurred in the South.[5] To reach this conclusion they disregard the possibility of dealignment by minimizing the impact of growth among independents and by emphasizing that white independents have tended to vote Republican (1975, pp. 138–141). Yet the fact that someone votes Republican is less revealing than the relative strength of party as a motivating factor in the vote decision. Admittedly, the electoral prospects of a typical Republican candidate improve if the share of Democratic identifiers declines and the share of independents increases. But this means the significance of the party tie has declined among voters, making the realignment conclusions too strong and the dealignment conclusion more apt.

Scholars do agree that the rise of the southern independents has come disproportionately from the ranks of Democratic identifiers. However measured, more white southerners now exhibit independent political behavior. This implies Republican benefits, if not in the currency of party identification, then in enhanced electoral fortunes of Republican candidates. The past has not provided strong reason to think independent status is a halfway house to Republicanism. Perhaps "a strengthening of the Republican party in Dixie without an increase in Republican identifiers may be the permanent order of things." (Ladd and Hadley, 1978, p. 144).

TOWARD AN UNDERSTANDING OF SOUTHERN PARTISAN CHANGE: DIFFERENT BUT COMPLEMENTARY CONCLUSIONS?

The three major conclusions concerning southern partisan change could be reconciled if viewed as complementary rather than contradictory. Consider southern realignment in two dimensions (figure 16.2). One axis indicates the relative strength of the parties, a continuum

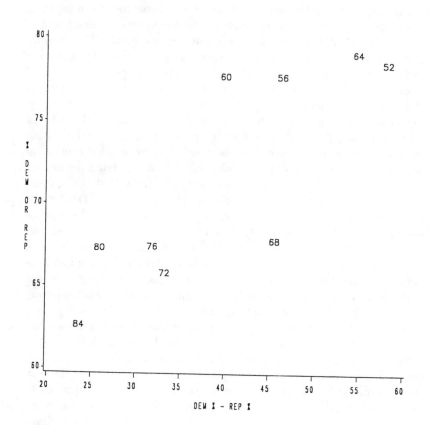

Only weak and strong identifiers are counted as partisans.
The vertical axis shows the percentage of the voting-age population identifying with either major party, the horizontal axis gives the relative partisan advantage (% Democratic identifiers – % Republican identifiers), and the plotted numbers indicate the presidential election year.

Figure 16.2
Change in recent southern partisanship, 11-state South, 1952–1984.

Source: Calculated by the authors from National Election Studies data.
Only weak and strong identifiers are counted as partisans.

from Democratic dominance to Republican dominance. Operationalize this as the percentage of Democratic identifiers minus the percentage of Republican identifiers. The other axis marks the level of individual attachments to parties, a continuum bounded by the extremes of total dealignment and total alignment. Operationalize this as the percentage of all individuals of voting age who claim Republican or Democratic identification. (Only a section of the two dimensions is presented in figure 16.2). For present purposes, concerns about alternative classifications and measurements need not detain us.

Scholarship on recent southern partisan realignment differs in part because of the importance scholars attribute to movement along or placement on the two axes. In 1952 the South occupied a position in the upper right of figure 16.2 but changes have shifted the region toward the lower left, movement resulting from dealignment as well as declining Democratic strength, but still leaving the Democrats in a dominant position relative to the Republicans. One can dwell on any of three conclusions—dealignment, Democratic decline, and relative Republican gain, or continuing Democratic dominance—without thereby ruling out the other conclusions. Beyond this, once scholars drop below the regional level to consider single states or groups such as blacks, young, elderly, native whites, or white migrants, the detection of several, differing, and partially offsetting changes can be expected. One can base conclusions on selected population groups without denying conclusions formed on the basis of a different set of groups. The same holds true for varying time periods and alternative definitions of the South. The resulting different conclusions need not be mutually destructive, exclusive alternatives. Instead, in any attempt to describe and explain change, different perspectives can yield differing results. The search for a single summary statement simplifies the complexity of southern partisan change.

Enlarging upon Seagull, we state that dealignment, critical realignment, and secular realignment "have all been manifest, sometimes simultaneously," in the recent South (1980, p. 76). The increased partisan independence of southern whites reflects dealignment; the shift of black partisan identification around 1964 indicates critical realignment; southern white partisanship provides evidence of secular realignment. And, while former Democratic dominance has been largely eroded, Democratic electoral victories below the presidential level reveal that Democrats still dominate. Southern Republicans have profited from the decreased importance of political parties in a still-Democratic region. But since partisanship means less, Republican consolidation is constrained and the significance of the Democratic decline lessened.

That scholars cannot agree on the nature and meaning of southern political change is due to differences in approach, definition, and classification. Differences in classification help lead to contradictory findings; differences in approach and definition of realignment help push scholars toward different conclusions.

The study of southern realignment has yet to show the cumulation of knowledge characteristic of science. Scholarly disagreement in charting and explaining change is understandable, beneficial in that it puzzles and challenges, regrettable in that it gives mixed readings about the same phenomenon. Riker has demonstrated that political science can indeed be cumulative (1982, p. 31). The American South provides fertile soil for the development of realignment theory; the study of southern realignment must not be left to columnists and historians.

NOTES

1. See Sundquist (1973, pp. 1-10), Campbell and Trilling (1980, pp. 3-10), and William Schneider (1982) for further discussions of realignment definitions.

2. Reliance on trends in the Democratic normal vote rather than in partisan identification typically works against reaching the dealignment conclusion. Researchers recognize but do not analyze the fact that the declining Democratic normal vote may stem from some mixture of Democratic decline (in identification, turnout, or loyalty) and either Republican or independent growth (in identification, turnout, or partisan voting patterns). The larger the independents bulk in the process, the smaller the Republicans, the more fitting the conclusion of dealignment.

3. Normal vote analysis offers advantages, particularly the strong insights into the mix of long-term and short-term forces. The strong, pro-Republican, short-term forces in the South since the 1950s (except for 1976) revealed by normal vote analysis help explain the gap between a greater Republican vote and the small number of Republican identifiers (Campbell, 1979, p. 273).

4. Beck reports individual partisan changes across two-year panels during the 1950s and 1970s for the nation (1984, p. 244). These results show leaners as the least stable of all the categories although the difference between leaners and partisans declined in the 1970s. These trends suggest leaners were not acting as partisans so much as partisans were acting more like independents, a suggestion indicative of dealignment rather than realignment.

5. They do qualify this realignment conclusion by noting that more elections must pass before Key's central question of durability can be answered (1975, p. 196).

Authors' Note: An earlier version of this chapter was presented at the Southern Political Science Association Convention in Atlanta, October 28-30, 1982.

17

STABILITY AND CHANGE IN PUBLIC EVALUATIONS OF THE AMERICAN PARTIES, 1952–84:

Nationwide and Regional Trends[1]

Lee Sigelman and Thomas M. Konda

Over the last three decades, Americans have looked with increasing disfavor upon their two major political parties, and as a consequence the American party system has been passing through a prolonged process of realignment. That, at least, is the conventional view, the most forceful statement of which is to be found in Nie, Verba, and Petrocik's (1976) *The Changing American Voter*.

Recently, this conventional view has been challenged. In *The Decline of American Political Parties, 1952–1980*, Martin Wattenberg (1984) argues that the American public has grown more apathetic toward the parties, not more alienated from them. "Once the central guiding forces in American electoral behavior," Wattenberg comments, "the parties are now perceived with almost complete indifference by a large proportion of the population" (1984, p. xv). Based on this interpretation of postwar trends in opinion toward the parties, Wattenberg holds out little hope for party resurgence through realignment.

The views articulated by Nie et al., on the one hand and Wattenberg on the other by no means exhaust the claims that have been made about where the parties currently stand with the American public and what their future prospects may be. Some observers who believe that the parties are moribund contend that the United States has been passing through a period of dealignment, not realignment (Broder, 1972; Crotty and Jacobson, 1980), with other institutions (such as the media and political action committees) usurping many traditional party functions. Others perceive signs of party renewal without realignment (Kayden and Mahe, 1985; Pomper, 1981), an optimistic reading that is out of step with both Nie, Verba, and Petrocik's interpretation and Wattenberg's reinterpretation.

We have recently taken a fresh look at the American party system's vital signs, analyzing new measures of public evaluations of the parties over time (Konda and Sigelman, 1987). Our purpose here is to help lay the groundwork for comparative state analyses of party realignment and dealignment in the South by summarizing our earlier nationwide findings concerning public evaluations of the parties and by presenting some new findings comparing party evaluations inside and outside the South.

NATIONWIDE TRENDS: A RECAPITULATION

Our analysis focuses, as did Nie, Verba, and Petrocik's and Wattenberg's, on a set of questions used in every one of the nine quadrennial American National Election Studies (ANES) conducted since 1952. In these surveys, respondents have been asked to name anything they like and anything they dislike about the Democratic and Republican parties. Five responses to each question have been recorded,[2] so a given respondent could register a total of anywhere between zero and twenty likes and dislikes. From these four likes-dislikes questions, which for convenience we label DL (Democratic likes), DD (Democratic dislikes), RL (Republican likes), and RD (Republican dislikes), we have constructed two separate measures of public evaluations of the parties. *Engagement* is the total number of likes and dislikes toward the two parties, divided by the number of respondents in a given ANES survey, i.e., the mean number of likes and dislikes per respondent:

Engagement = (DL + DD + RL + RD)/N

Since there are four likes and dislikes questions, with five responses allowed on each, the Engagement score potentially ranges from 0 (total disengagement) to 20 (total engagement). Even though it would be possible for someone to score 20 on this scale, a score of 7 or 8 is closer to the norm even for a highly engaged, partisan citizen. Accordingly, the mean Engagement score in a given year falls well short of 20.

We derived the other measures, *Positivity*, by dividing the number of positive responses (DL and RL) by the total number of responses. This yields the percentage of responses that are positive, which is multiplied by 100:

Positivity = 100 × (DL + RL)/(DL + RL + DD + RD)

The Positivity score ranges from 0 (when only dislikes are mentioned) to 100 (when only likes are mentioned), with 50 denoting a perfect balance of positive and negative comments.

Our analysis of data from the nine ANES presidential election-year surveys has been guided by two hypotheses, the first suggested by Wattenberg and the second by Nie et al.:

The Neutrality Hypothesis: Over the course of the 1952–1984 period, the mean Engagement score has declined toward the zero point.

The Negativity Hypothesis: Over the course of the 1952–1984 period, the Positivity score has declined toward the negative end of the scale.

In analyzing the nationwide 32-year Engagement and Positivity time lines, we observed, first, that there has been a long-term trend toward diminishing Engagement, consistent with the Wattenberg thesis of growing indifference toward the parties. However, the magnitude of this trend appeared to us to be more modest than Wattenberg had suggested: according to our reading, the erosion of Engagement has been somewhere in the neighborhood of 20% to 25%, well below Wattenberg's estimate of the extent to which indifference toward the parties has spread. Setting aside the reading for 1968 as a short-term aberration brought on by the tumultuous events of that year, we charted a decline in Engagement through the 1950s and mid-1960s, but no major movement in either direction since then. Examining Engagement toward each party separately, we detected the same pattern. That is, Engagement dropped noticeably for both parties prior to 1968, but since then there has been no perceptible trend. Moreover, with the exception of the 1960–1964 period, the two parties always moved in the same direction from survey to survey, suggesting that the growth of apathy was directed at the parties jointly rather than being targeted toward one or the other individually.

We also noted that the interparty differential in Engagement held fairly constant over the years. As Trilling (1976: 44) had previously observed, the Democratic party has always been the focus of more responses to the likes and dislikes questions, and by implication the more salient attitude object, than the Republican party. Even with the personality of Ronald Reagan dominating the 1980 and 1984 presidential elections, the Democrats' edge in citizen Engagement did not decrease. To be sure, the Democrats have fallen further from their 1952 baseline than the Republicans have, but in the absence of pre-1952 surveys it is impossible to determine how typical the 1952 Democratic baseline was. The only solid hint is the 1968 election, when the troubles that erupted at the Democratic national convention gave rise to a one-time reversal of the Engagement trend. This unusual circumstance generated an unusually large gap between the Democratic and Republican Engagement scores. In 1952, however, the difference between the two parties' means was even larger, suggesting that friction between the northern and southern wings of the Democratic party at that time may have generated a similar one-party anomaly. If 1952 is thus set aside as an aberrant case, it would seem that on a nationwide basis the interparty gap in Engagement has not narrowed over time.

While the 1952–1984 nationwide trend in Engagement with the two major parties can be described as erosion leading to a new low-level equilibrium, the Positivity time line has resembled a roller-coaster ride. The balance of positive and negative comments about the parties began slightly on the positive side, rose to its all-time heights in 1956 and 1960, and tailed off slightly in 1964. Then, between 1964 and 1968, Positivity declined precipitously, crossing the critical threshold from a basically positive assessment of the parties to a basically negative one. After some sliding for the next eight years, this drop was eventually reversed, with assessments reverting to the positive side of the ledger by 1980 and in 1984 returning to a level comparable to those of the 1950s.

More specifically, the mean number of positive comments about the parties fell from about two and a half in the early 1950s to about one and a half in the 1980s. Negative comments, on the other hand, have proven volatile, but without much long-term change. Accordingly, it has been the volatility of dislikes that has sent the Positivity time line on its roller-coaster course. Positive and negative comments about the parties declined together through 1964, producing a drop in Engagement while leaving Positivity basically unchanged. In 1968, however, dislikes shot up sharply, momentarily reversing the trend toward apathy but depressing the Positivity score. In 1972 the number of likes and dislikes fell off, and since then both have fluctuated without any clear pattern.

Unlike the more gradual, two-party decline in Engagement, the nationwide Positivity time line seems to have moved as a response to three separate events. Most important was the abrupt drop in Positivity suffered by the Democrats in 1968. Not only was this the steepest decline either party suffered over the entire 32-year period, and not only was it the only time the balance of opinion toward the Democrats has been negative, but it was also the only occasion on which the Democrats have suffered any loss of Positivity at all. Even so, this drop was so profound that all the other years of improvement have only raised the Democrats to the Positivity levels they enjoyed during the 1950s.

The major setback for the Republicans occurred in 1964, when the party's capture by its right wing caused a bottoming out of Positivity. Like the Democrats after 1968, the Republicans began to bounce back, but this recovery was interrupted by Watergate, bringing the party's national standing back almost to its 1964 low. Since 1976 the GOP's recovery has gotten back on track, and the Republicans are now edging back toward the positive side.

In sum, our analysis of nationwide trends in evaluations of the two major parties underlines the profound difference between apathy and negativity as problems besetting the American party system. Apathy seems to have beset the parties collectively, while negativity has afflicted them separately. With apathy, the parties' fortunes have risen and fallen together, with the single exception of 1960–1964. Exactly the opposite has been the rule for negativity: when one party has suffered a setback, the other has improved its standing. Thus Wattenberg's apathy and Nie, Verba, and Petrocik's, negativity, though unfolding over roughly the same period of time, have not been directly related. Apathy grew as a genuine trend, gradually increasing at the expense of both parties. It cannot be attributed to any sins of commission by either party, but seems genuinely to represent the diminishing importance of the parties to the public at large. Negativity, on the other hand, has moved in dramatic fits and starts, yielding, over the long term, little net change.

PARTY EVALUATIONS INSIDE AND OUTSIDE THE SOUTH

Although nationwide analyses can tell us a good deal about public evaluations of the Republican and Democratic parties, it is a simple fact of political life in the postwar United States that the geographic contours of the party system have been undergoing considerable change. The most conspicuous aspect of this transformation has, of course, been the advent of two-party competition in "the Solid South," which long served as the keystone of the national Democratic coalition. In 1952, 76% of all southerners considered themselves Democrats, with only 14% calling themselves independents and 10% Republicans. By 1984, however, the percentage of Democratic identifiers in the South had fallen all the way down to 40, while the percentages of independents and Republicans had risen to 35 and 25, respectively (Black and

Black, 1987: 237; see also Beck, 1977). A question naturally arises, then, as to whether the nationwide trends we have just described hold equally well when region is taken into account. To what extent have southerners' evaluations of the parties changed over the last thirty-two years? How do any such changes compare with what has been occurring in the rest of the country?

Engagement

The 32-year Engagement timeline, displayed separately for southerners and nonsoutherners in figure 17.1, reveals some overriding regional similarities, but also some significant points of differentiation, in the spread of apathy toward the parties. The national pattern described earlier—early erosion sliding into a low-level equilibrium, with an aberration in 1968—is evident in figure 17.1 for both southerners and nonsoutherners. However, in emphasizing that the two trend lines have followed a roughly parallel course, we should not lose sight of the fact that, throughout this period, levels of Engagement have, with the exception of 1968, been lower in the South than elsewhere. This gap may simply reflect a historically lower level of concern about electoral politics among southerners, but two other factors should also be borne in mind. First, the likes-dislikes responses that comprise our Engagement measure reflect, to some extent, differences in articulateness and information about politics (Smith, 1980). That being the case, the regional gap in Engagement levels may, among other things, be a function of the relatively lower levels of educational attainment found in the South. Second, the low Engagement of southerners may reflect greater apathy not toward the parties per se, but rather toward the Republican party, which for much of the period in question was not a major force in the political life of the South; more definitive evidence concerning the targeting of apathy among southerners can be glimpsed in figure 17.2, which we shall discuss presently.

A final noteworthy aspect of figure 17.1 is that over time the decline in Engagement has been somewhat steeper outside than inside the South. With the exceptions of 1952 and 1968, Engagement has followed a fairly flat course in the South, in contrast to the downward trend in the rest of the country. In other words, the once-pronounced regional differential in Engagement has narrowed over the years. It is tempting to attribute this closing of the gap to rising educational levels in the South and to the inroads the GOP has made there. However, we shall resist this temptation, since figure 17.1 reveals that Engagement

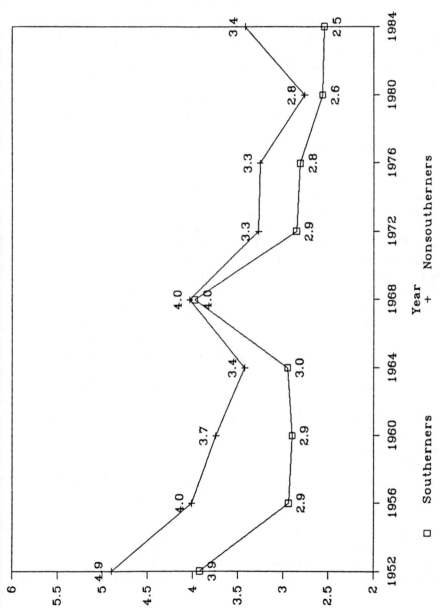

Figure 17.1
Engagement, 1952–1984.

levels have held fairly constant in the South. Education *has* spread in
the South, as has interparty competition, but the narrowing of the
Engagement gap has occurred because Engagement levels have declined outside the South. In that light, it makes the most sense to look
for the cause outside, not inside, the South. In our view, the best explanation for the narrowing of the regional gap is that Engagement was so
low in the South in the first place that it simply could not fall much
farther. Thus, it held more or less steady as the level in the rest of the
country dropped toward it.

These Engagement timelines are disaggregated in figure 17.2 according to target. By comparing the top and bottom halves of figure 17.2
we learn that what is true of the nation as a whole is true of each
region as well: the Democratic party has been the target of greater
public attention than the Republican party has received. This interparty differential in Engagement has been somewhat greater in the
South than elsewhere, reflecting, for the most part, widespread apathy
toward the Republican party in the South. For each party, the Engagement trend has run a course in the South roughly parallel to its course
in the rest of the nation. Still, for each party the South-nonsouth difference seems to have diminished somewhat in the 1970s and 1980s from
its level through the mid-1960s. Finally, by looking first at the top half
and then at the bottom half of figure 17.2, we also observe that
throughout the postwar era southerners have been less engaged than
nonsoutherners in each party, although this regional gap has been more
pronounced for the Republicans than for the Democrats.

While a long-term trend toward greater Republican Engagement in
the South might have been anticipated on the basis of Republican electoral gains in the South, figure 17.2 betrays no hint of any such tendency. Since the early 1950s the Republican Engagement line has been
essentially flat in the South; if it has sloped in any direction, it has been
very slightly downward. So while the Republican party has come a
long way toward winning the hearts of southerners, in the sense of
capturing their partisan allegiance, it does not seem to have made
equivalent progress in capturing their minds, in the sense of engaging
their attention. Nor, despite rallying from the New Deal era to win six
of the nine presidential elections since 1952, has the Republican party
received increasing attention outside the South. Indeed, the trend
among nonsoutherners has been in the direction of greater apathy toward the Republicans.

In sum, two facts concerning regional trends in Engagement stand
out above all the others. First, at a given point in time Engagement has

ENGAGEMENT TOWARD DEMOCRATS

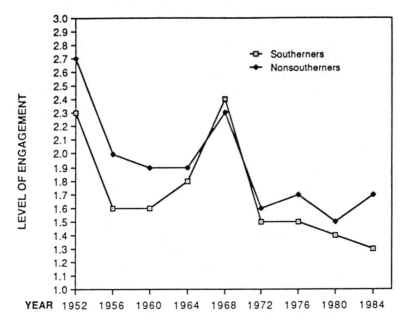

ENGAGEMENT TOWARD REPUBLICANS

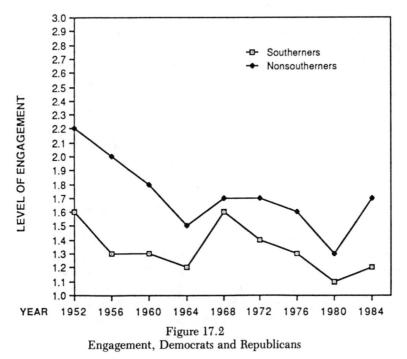

Figure 17.2
Engagement, Democrats and Republicans

been lower in the South than elsewhere. Second, over time Engagement levels have followed roughly the same path in the South as they have in the rest of the nation. To be sure, a narrowing of the regional differential in Engagement can be observed in figures 17.1 and 17.2, but this narrowing has occurred within the context of predominantly parallel trend lines.

Positivity

Of course, being engaged by the parties does not necessarily translate into being favorably disposed toward them. The 1968 election is a perfect case in point of the importance of maintaining the distinction between Engagement and Positivity. That year, as figure 17.1 indicates, the level of Engagement soared both inside and outside the South, but, as figure 17.3 reveals, the level of Positivity plummeted. It should thus occasion no great very surprise that the regional Positivity trends and differences are very different from the Engagement trends we have just been discussing.

Since 1952, Positivity toward the parties has risen and fallen in roughly parallel paths inside and outside the South. Both in the South and in the rest of the country. Positivity was relatively high through 1960. It fell between 1960 and 1964, and fell much more sharply between 1964 and 1968. Since then, the decline has been arrested, and the timeline eventually began to turn upward, to the point that in 1984 Positivity reached a point comparable to its level during the 1950s. On the other hand, an obvious point of regional differentiation is that while southerners have consistently been less engaged in the parties than nonsoutherners have, they have been more favorably oriented toward the parties than nonsoutherners. From 1952 through 1960, and again since 1976, we can see gaps in Positivity between southerners and those who reside elsewhere. During those years, southerners articulated more positive views of the parties than nonsoutherners did, though between 1964 and 1972 there was no perceptible regional gap.

Our understanding of these regional Positivity patterns is greatly enhanced by breaking them down according to the targeted party, Democratic or Republican, as in figure 17.4. In the top half of figure 17.4, we see that throughout the postwar period the Democratic party has consistently maintained a positive image in the South. From 1952 through 1964, positive comments about the Democrats outran negative comments by a ratio of roughly two to one. Since then, the Democrats' Positivity score has declined, but it has always remained well above 50, the score denoting an exact balance of positive and negative comments.

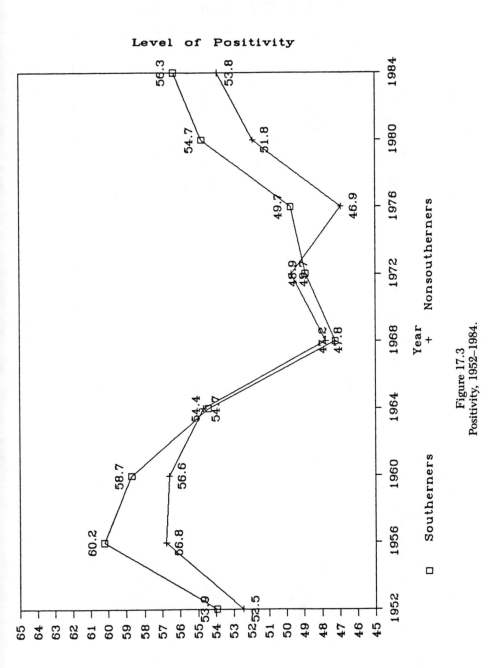

Figure 17.3
Positivity, 1952–1984.

POSITIVITY TOWARD DEMOCRATS

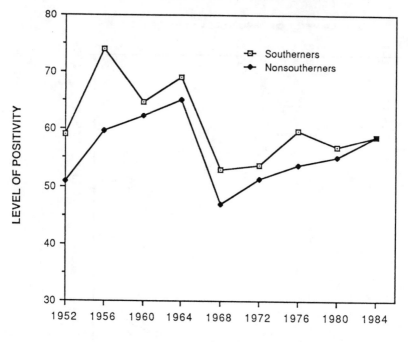

POSITIVITY TOWARD REPUBLICANS

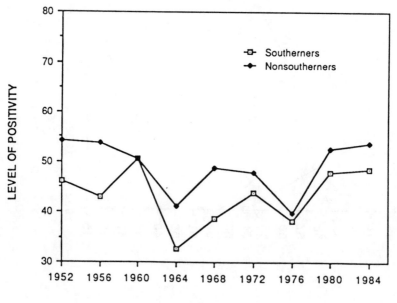

Figure 17.4
Positivity, Democrats and Republicans.

Outside the South, the Democratic Positivity timeline has moved in tandem with the southern trend, but it has remained below— sometimes by a large margin, sometimes by only a few points—the level of Democratic Positivity in the South. Having said that, we should also say that the regional disparity in Positivity toward the Democrats now shows signs of disappearing, the two trend lines having converged in the 1984 survey.

The regional trends in Positivity toward the Republican party tell an even more interesting tale. There has historically been a yawning regional gap in Positivity toward the Republican party, and—in sharp contrast to their tendency to be more positive than nonsoutherners to the Democratic party—it is southerners who have exhibited the lesser enthusiasm toward the GOP. Here again, the two trend lines have followed a reasonably parallel course, but until the 1970s there was typically considerable distance between the two lines. This distance narrowed in 1972, and then, in 1976, the two lines converged. In 1980, they crossed, where they remained in 1984. So, contrary to a long-standing tradition, Positivity toward the Republican party is now higher in the South than it is in the rest of the country. What cannot be known at this point is whether this reversal is wholly a byproduct of the Reagan phenomenon, and, therefore, whether it will outlive the Reagan presidency. It is worth noting, however, that since 1964, with only a momentary setback during the post-Watergate period, Positivity toward the Republicans has been on a steady upswing in the South, climbing more steeply there than in the rest of the country. The southern bull market for the Republican party is, then, more than two decades old, although it is only in recent years that the South's enthusiasm for the GOP has outrun that found outside the South.

A different way of describing the same trends is to compare the Democratic and Republican Positivity lines inside the South. Looking from the top to the bottom half of figure 17.4, we see that for most of the postwar period southerners have been much more positively disposed toward the Democrats than toward the Republicans. The two timelines have approached one another on only two occasions, but, significantly, these two occasions are the two most recent presidential elections. In 1980 and 1984, the Democrat-Republican Positivity gap in the South narrowed considerably, to only a few points. Thus, whereas the South has historically been hostile to the Republican party, in recent years the balance of Republican images has shifted to a favorable Republican image, and the Republican Positivity score is now approaching the traditionally high Democratic Positivity score.

CONCLUSION

What, then, can we conclude about American's evaluations of the parties, and more specifically about southerners' evaluations? In our view, neither the "neutrality" nor the "negativity" hypotheses provides a very adequate account of opinion trends since 1952. In terms of Engagement, the public seems to have settled into a low-level equilibrium: after what seems to have been a relatively steep decline during the 1950s and 1960s, Engagement has exhibited little further dynamism. With regard to Positivity, however, the situation is much more fluid. The growth of negativity appears to have run its course—supplanted, in both the South and the rest of the country, by increasingly positive views of each party. A key component of this trend has been the growth of favorable sentiments toward the GOP in the South, a development that has not been offset by any decline in Positivity toward the Democratic party.

Our reading of trends in public evaluations of the parties is thus much more optimistic than the prognoses of those whose interpretations center on either negativity or neutrality. We tend to see stability where others have perceived instability, and development (as in the advent of two-party competition in the South) where others have detected decay. In terms of party dealignment, realignment, and renewal, we find no evidence of growing public disenchantment with the parties, and some evidence that precisely the opposite has been occurring. The decline in Engagement appears to have been arrested, and Positivity toward each party is on the increase. Growing Positivity toward the Republican party in the South constitutes a reversal of the historical trend, pointing toward a regional realignment of party support. It bears reemphasis that Positivity toward the parties has historically been subject to abrupt, cyclical swings, a fact that makes long-term prognosis a very risky enterprise. For the foreseeable future, though, our analysis points toward a steady level of public concern about the parties and an increasing level of positive affect toward them, both inside and outside the South—not, we think, conditions consistent with a prognosis of party system decay.

NOTES

1. The data analyzed in this chapter come from the quadrennial American National Election Studies, 1952–1984, conducted by the Survey Research

Center/Center for Political Studies, University of Michigan, and made available by the Inter-University Consortium for Political and Social Research.

2. Except in 1972, when only three likes and dislikes were recorded. See Konda and Sigelman (1987) for our solution to this problem, which is also reflected in the figures presented here.

18

IDEOLOGY, ISSUES, AND REALIGNMENT AMONG SOUTHERN PARTY ACTIVISTS

Laurence W. Moreland, Robert P. Steed, and Tod A. Baker

Although much research and comment have addressed the question of the extent to which the mass public perceives politics in terms of ideology or issues (Goodman, 1980: 183–295; Campbell, Converse, Miller, and Stokes, 1960; Converse, 1964), there is less doubt that party leaders in competitive systems are more likely to be ideologically oriented and are more likely to take issue positions that distinctively identify the Republican and Democratic parties (McClosky, Hoffman, and O'Hara, 1960). While the evidence suggests that the mass electorate became more ideological in the 1960s and 1970s (Nie, Verba, and Petrocik, 1976; Miller and Levitin, 1976), the differences between party elites at all levels have continued to be greater than the differences between party identifiers in the general electorate (Soule and Clark, 1971). That these differences between party elites are important is a consequence of the fact that party elites sometimes choose party candidates (as at the national or presidential level), that they take issue positions through the adoption of platforms or resolutions (at almost all levels), and that they in general help to shape the image each party presents to the electorate. Eldersveld (1964, 180–181) has well summarized this last function:

> The party, in one sense, is what it believes—its attitudes and perspectives, at all echelons. And what the party leaders believe may certainly determine in large part the image it communicates to the public, and the success with which it mobilizes public support.

These interparty elite differences can occur only in systems that are, in some degree, two-party competitive. As a consequence, such differences have not been very useful in analyzing the politics of the South as much of the region was so thoroughly dominated by the Democratic party from the late nineteenth century up until relatively recently. Rather than reflecting interparty differences, the historic politics of the South was often characterized by fluid functions operating under the

all-encompassing umbrella of the Democratic party (Key, 1949). Ideologically, therefore, the Democratic party became the home of all
stripes of political opinion, and the shifting factions made voter choice
on the basis of issues or general ideology difficult if not impossible;
indeed, leaders of factions often themselves moved across the political
spectrum, moves facilitated by the fact that all candidates and all voters belonged to the same party (Key 1949, 142–147). As Key (1949: 146)
noted of South Carolina (and applicable to much of the rest of the pre-
1950 South as well),

> Uni-partisanship may make it possible for a politician to shift his
> general orientation with far less risk to personal political survival
> than under two-party conditions. Lack of party labels and of
> party lines means that there are no institutional obstacles to col-
> laboration with erstwhile enemies. Free and easy transfer of affec-
> tions, by both politician and follower, may be accomplished
> without treason to party.

In a few southern states one-party politics eventually evolved into a
bifactional system within the Democratic party, as in the case of Louisiana (Sindler, 1956: 281–286); political choice became somewhat eas-
ier in bifactional or multifactional systems but still lacked the clarity of
two-party choices. But in much of the South throughout the first five
decades of this century party systems continued to be best characterized as loose multifactional, even chaotic, systems to a large extent
based on personal and highly localized friends-and-neighbors followings. In such systems it was difficult even to tell the "ins" from the
"outs" and still more difficult to sort out issues and ideologies, even
where they existed.

But in the post-World War II era, the politics of the South changed
as a consequence of a variety of social, cultural, economic, and political influences that began to erode the one-party domination of the
Democratic party. A rapidly growing literature has repeatedly docu-
mented that the traditional descriptions of the region's politics have
been overcome by a variety of events and influences.[1] It is now beyond
dispute that the Democratic party in the South has lost its traditional
domination and that the Republican party has emerged as a significant
partisan organization capable of successfully challenging the Democrats at many levels.

The realignment literature reviewed in an earlier chapter suggests
that in rapidly changing party systems new issues should be emerging
which the old party system is unable to contain or exploit; opinions

may become so strongly held, as with race relations for example, that a single party can no longer provide an umbrella large enough to shelter all who may have joined a changing electorate (Sundquist, 1973, chapter 1). One consequence is that ideological polarization more clearly emerges as a manifestation of stress within the political system as the old arrangement breaks down; in more concrete terms, it would seen that those dissatisfied with the non-ideological or ideologically ambiguous stance of a fluid Democratic party might leave that party for a minority party with a clearer philosophical focus. The result is that both parties become more clearly ideologically defined; moreover, such ideological polarization occurs particularly with regard to political elites during periods of party realignment (Shannon, 1968: 175–176, 180–181; Sinclair, 1977, 940–953; Abramowitz, 1979).

The purpose of this chapter is to test the ideological element of political realignment as it relates to the South. As other studies have focused on the mass electorate, we shall examine the extent to which ideological polarization may have occurred between southern party elites. As Burnham (1970: 10) has observed, eras of "critical realignment" are marked, in part, "by ideological polarizations and issue-distances between the major parties which are exceptionally large by normal standards." In this chapter we test southern partisan activists for the kind of ideological clarity, even polarization, that typically marks eras of partisan realignment.

DATA

The data for this study were generated through the administration of an extensive questionnaire to delegates to the 1984 state party conventions held in twelve states (CSPAS, the Comparative State Party Activist Survey, codirected by the authors of this chapter). Of the twelve states, six were in the South: Arkansas, Louisiana, Mississippi, North Carolina, South Carolina, and Texas. With the exception of Louisiana, where only Democratic delegates were surveyed (no Republican convention was held in 1984), the data include both Democratic and Republican delegates in each state. Responses rates ranged from 35 percent to 75 percent. The total number of delegates surveyed in the six states was just over 5,000 (and n's, where they are not specifically given in the tables which follow, generally approach that figure).[2] While the six southern states included in the data do not provide exhaustive coverage of the South, they do provide useful geographical breadth as well as representation of both the Rim South and the Deep South. Finally, the delegates surveyed do not constitute a random sample of party activists across all levels or types of party activity, but they do represent those party activists among the most committed and the most active.

Table 18.1 reports summary background data on the delegates. As might be expected from other measures of political partisanship, women and blacks were more numerously represented among the Democratic delegates. Republican delegates tended to have higher incomes although a large proportion of Democrats had high levels of education (accounted for in large degree by the fact that 25 percent of the Democratic delegates reported their occupation as education or teaching). Republicans were also less likely to be natives of the South and more likely to identify with such status religions as Episcopalian and Presbyterian.

FINDINGS

The delegates attending the six state conventions were asked a series of questions pertaining to personal ideological orientation and to a number of contemporary political issues; specifically, they were asked to place themselves philosophically on a liberal-conservative continuum and to respond to a series of twenty-one specific issues.

Political Philosophy.

The first two columns of table 18.2 report data on the delegates' self-described political philosophy. Examination of the table indicates that, at least as defined by their activists, the two parties were clearly differentiated in terms of political philosophy with Republicans perceiving themselves essentially as a party of the right and Democrats seeing themselves, somewhat less monolithically, as a party of the left. The great bulk of Republicans (83%) described themselves as "conservative" or "extremely conservative"; when the additional 11% who described themselves as "slightly conservative" are added to that figure, the Republicans approached a significant degree of ideological unanimity, at least in the abstract. On the other hand, less than a fifth (18%) of the Democrats reported themselves to be any kind of conservative (with only 7% in the two most conservative cells). At the other end of the ideological spectrum, two-thirds of the Democrats described

Table 18.1
Background Characteristics of Delegates (%)

Characteristic	Democrats	Republicans
Gender:		
Female	51	43
Male	49	57
Totals	100	100
N =	2,924	1,901
Age:		
18–34	23	20
35–54	46	43
55 and over	31	37
Totals	100	100
N =	3,054	1,959
Race:		
White	70	97
Black	27	2
Other	3	1
Totals	100	100
N =	2,913	1,900
Region of Childhood*:		
South	81	64
Nonsouth	19	36
Totals	100	100
N =	3,068	1,968
Education:		
High school graduate or less	17	14
Some college	25	29
College graduate	18	26
Postgraduate	40	32
Totals	100	100
N =	2,912	1,889
Occupation:		
Professional	42	32
(Education)	(25)	(12)

* South consists of the eleven states of the Old Confederacy; nonsouth consists of all other states.

Table 18.1 *Continued*
Background Characteristics of Delegates (%)

Characteristic	Democrats	Republicans
Business/managerial/farmer/rancher	18	30
Housewife	6	13
Real estate/insurance/sales/clerical	8	10
Skilled/semi-skilled	8	3
Public/nonprofit official or employee	9	3
Student/unemployed	4	3
Other	6	6
Totals	101	100
$N =$	2,857	1,868
Income:		
0–$14,999	12	8
$15,000–24,999	21	16
$25,000–34,999	23	19
$35,000–44,999	18	19
$45,000–59,999	14	17
$60,000 +	13	21
Totals	101	100
$N =$	2,807	1,825
Religion:		
Baptist	35	29
Methodist	22	18
Presbyterian	7	13
Episcopalian	7	10
Catholic	11	7
Jewish	1	**
Other	18	23
Totals	100	100
$N =$	2,712	1,814

**less than 0.5 percent

Source: Data drawn from the Comparative State Party Activist Survey, 1984.

Table 18.2

Political Philosophy of Delegates by Party and History (%)

Political Philosophy	All Delegates		Delegates by Party History			
			Switched Parties		Did Not Switch	
	Dems	Repubs	Dems	Repubs	Dems	Repubs
Extremely liberal	10	*	9	1	10	*
Liberal	35	1	29	1	36	1
Slightly liberal	18	1	18	1	18	3
Middle of the road	18	4	18	4	18	3
Slightly conservative	11	11	15	12	11	11
Conservative	6	65	9	65	6	65
Extremely conservative	1	18	1	16	1	19
	99	100	99	100	100	102
N =	2,919	1,849	349	574	2,520	1,246

*less than 0.5 percent.

Source: Data drawn from the Comparative State Party Activist Survey, 1984.

themselves as some kind of liberal (63%); only 2% of the Republicans so regarded their ideological orientation. Clearly, these ideological patterns strongly support the existence of a southern party system with distinctive centers of gravity for each party.

Table 18.2 also supports a secondary point: southern Republicans were more heavily conservative than southern Democrats were heavily liberal. The Democratic delegates, although not evenly distributed across the liberal-conservative spectrum posed by the survey, were nevertheless much more widely distributed than the Republican delegates, who were concentrated in the two most conservative categories. Despite the erosion of Democratic strength in the electorate from its historic one-party dominance, the party elite still retains some ideological evidence of a broadly-based party.

Although data are not reported here on nonsouthern activists surveyed by the CSPAS, a comparison of the southern delegates with nonsouthern delegates offers some striking similarities: southern Democrats are almost completely congruent with their nonsouthern compatriots, and southern Republicans, while not quite so like their nonsouthern counterparts as the Democrats, are nevertheless not much different in terms of ideological self-placement. While southern Republicans are somewhat more conservative than nonsouthern Republicans, the southern party patterns are notably similar to the nonsouthern ones.

Issue Positions.
In addition to asking for a self-positioned political ideology, the delegates were asked, in effect, to operationalize their philosophies by responding to a series of twenty-one contemporary political issues, roughly falling into three areas: twelve social or "new politics" issues (such as the Equal Rights Amendment, affirmative action, abortion, gun control, and homosexuality), four economic issues (such as spending cuts, national health insurance, and tax increases to reduce the federal deficit), and five foreign policy/defense issues (such as increased defense spending, increased military presence in Latin America, a nuclear freeze, and arms control).

The responses on the issues reported in Table 18.3 give further evidence of the distinctive political outlooks of the delegates of each party. On fifteen of the twenty-one issues examined, a majority of southern Democrats were opposed by a majority of southern Republicans.[3] But in four instances, there was some agreement between the two sets of party delegates; and on the remaining two issues the Democrats evenly split.

Table 18.3
Issue Orientation by Party (%)

	Percent Approving	
Issue	Democrats	Republicans
Social issues:		
Equal Rights Amendment	85	16
Use of marijuana is morally wrong.	58	85
Homosexual behavior is morally wrong.	65	92
Governmental regulation to protect environment is excessive	28	74
Constitutional amendment to permit prayers, Bible-reading in the public schools.	44	88
Constitutional amendment to prohibit abortions	32	57
Affirmative action programs in jobs and higher education	78	15
Stricter legislation to control handguns	69	24
More rapid development of nuclear power	20	82
Reduce the number of persons getting food stamps	50	94
Increase taxes for public education.	85	26
Conservative Christian organizations such as Moral Majority	14	76
Economic issues:		
Government-sponsored national health insurance	75	10
Spending cuts to balance federal budget	59	92
Tax increase to reduce federal deficit	50	17
Public works to reduce unemployment	61	7
Military/defense issues:		
Increase U.S. military presence in Middle East	10	52

Table 18.1 *Continued*

Increase U.S. military presence in Latin America	13	78
More intensive negotiation on arms control	94	74
Nuclear freeze	92	47
Continued increase in defense spending	15	91

Source: Data drawn from the Comparative State Party Activist Survey, 1984.

Of the twelve social issues, a majority of southern Democrats opposed a majority of southern Republicans on nine of them. On two social issues—homosexual behavior and marijuana—there was a fair degree of agreement. While Republicans were solidly agreed that homosexual conduct and marijuana use are immoral (92% and 85%, respectively), the Democrats were not so unified: significantly smaller majorities (65% on homosexual behavior and 58% on marijuana use) of Democrats agreed on the immorality of these two types of behavior. On one social issue—reducing the number of people on food stamps— the Democrats were virtually evenly divided; Republicans overwhelmingly favored such action (94%). On support for, conservative Christian action organizations such as Moral Majority, the parties followed the general pattern by dividing decisively; such groups had only a 14% approval rate among Democrats as compared with 76% among Republicans.

On two of the four economic issues, the two groups of party delegates stood in opposing positions (on national health insurance and a public works program to reduce unemployment). But both groups agreed, although with a reduced margin for the Democrats, that spending should be cut in order to balance the federal budget. On the final economic issue—a tax increase to reduce the federal deficit—the Democrats split evenly (83% of the Republicans disapproved).

On one of the five foreign policy/defense issues—more intensive negotiation on nuclear arms control—majorities of the two elites agreed. Over nine out of ten southern Democrats (94%) perceived a need for such negotiation with more than seven out of ten southern Republicans so agreeing (74%). On the other four foreign policy/defense issues, however, majorities of the delegates stood opposed to each other. Even so, nearly half of the Republicans favored a nuclear freeze, and the Democrats overwhelmingly did so. The parties were more clearly differentiated on increased defense spending and on increased American military involvement in the Middle East and Latin America.

The responses described above can be roughly classified as conventionally conservative or liberal. On all but one of the twenty-one issues the majority responses for the Republican delegates were uniformly conservative. Strikingly, while the Democrats were not as consistent as the Republicans, their majority responses were liberal on sixteen of the twenty-one issues. Thus, in the South today highly consistent operational ideologies exist both for southern Democratic and southern Republican party activists. Where a majority of Democrats did join a majority of Republicans, they did so on just four issues, and these were not limited to a single type of controversy (instead they fell into all three areas under analysis); even here it is possible to make too much of this degree of congruency in that on specific issues on which majorities agreed as much as thirty-three percentage points still separated the two parties. In short, the two groups of delegates were generally polarized on all three sets of issues.

Although the nonsouthern data in the CSPAS are not formally reported in this study, it may still be worth noting in a final point of comparison that the nonsouthern Democrats and Republicans surveyed by the CSPAS reflected almost exactly the same general pattern described above for southern party activists, although in almost every case the nonsouthern Democrats were a bit more liberal than their southern counterparts, and nonsouthern Republicans were somewhat less conservative than southern members of their party (Moreland, Steed, and Baker, 1986). Only in the area of foreign policy did nonsouthern Republican activists veer away from the southern activists; in that category of issues, the nonsouthern Republicans favored a nuclear freeze but opposed an increased military presence in the Middle East, positions they did not share with the southern delegates. Nonsouthern Democrats generally followed the same pattern as southern Democrats, regardless of the type of issue.

Party Switching and Issue Orientation.
Each delegate was also surveyed on some basic questions as to party history, i.e., if he or she had ever switched parties, and, if so, what principal reason motivated that decision.

As might be expected for members of an emergent and growing party, southern Republican convention delegates were much more likely to have switched parties than southern Democratic delegates. Nearly a third (32%) of the Republicans reported a switch while only about a eighth (12%) of the Democrats so responded. When those delegates who switched were asked for the most important reason for switching, the responses are striking. For both groups, issue orientation ("the party to which I switched was much more likely to take the right stand on issues") was indicated as the most important reason; about three-fourths (76%) of the Republicans and over two-fifths (43%) of the Democrats indicated an issues-oriented switch. Less important for party switching was candidate appeal ("the party to which I switched had better, more appealing candidates"); only 11% of the Republicans but 28% of the Democrats switched for that reason. Other reasons were scattered and accounted for only very small percentages of the party-switchers.

The data reported above indicate that party switches in both directions contributed to greater ideological and issue homogeneity for each party. This finding is buttressed by the data in the last four columns of Table 18.2, which reports the ideological positions of southern party switchers. Former Democrats who became Republicans were almost as equally conservative as Republicans who had never been Democrats, and thus they were far more conservative than the party they left. Similarly, former Republicans who became Democrats, while not as liberal as the party they joined, were dramatically more liberal than the Republicans they left behind. Thus, the ideological clarity of both parties has been strengthened by those party activists who have changed their party identifications.

CONCLUSION

In this chapter we have described the issue and ideological orientations of one important type of partisan activist, southern party convention delegates. The evidence reported here suggests that each party has developed a clear ideological center of gravity, with the Republican party delegates almost uniformly following a conservative course and with the Democrats, somewhat less consistently, taking a generally liberal posture. This finding is supported both by the delegates' self-placement on a liberal-conservative continuum and by their responses on a series of contemporary political issues. On both sets of data, the Republicans were more closely clustered and more consistently conservative than the Democrats were liberal; the Democrats, while more widely distributed over the range of ideological positions and issue responses, nevertheless demonstrated considerable ideological cohesiveness.

Party switches contributed to the ideological and issue divergence of the two parties as both Democratic and Republican switchers cited a desire for a more hospitable issue environment as the main reason for changing parties, and, indeed, party switchers were ideologically generally quite different than the parties they left. What has been described as "party sorting" (Bowman, Hulbary, and Kelley, 1986) has become a part of the substantial changes that have characterized the southern party system in recent decades.

The literature on party realignment has postulated a number of indicators and their consequences relating to a party system undergoing dealignment and/or realignment. Data on one such indicator—an increasing ideological clarity between the two parties—demonstrates that, at least among party activists, such a political phenomenon has occurred in the South. Whether this development is called "convergence" (Converse, 1975) or "nationalization" (Beck and Lopatto, 1982; McKinney and Bourqe, 1971) or some other term is not as important as the finding that the southern party system now operates in important ways as a competitive one in ideological and issue terms. These data for party activists therefore help to confirm the realignment thesis for the southern party system.

These developments relating to southern party activists parallel similar changes occurring in the southern electorate. A group of recent studies analyzing the 1984 presidential vote in the South in the context of each state party system emphasized not only the growing competitiveness but also the increasing polarization of the parties in the electorate (Steed, Moreland, and Baker, 1985). Other research studies utilizing poll data and focusing on individual states have reached the same conclusion (e.g., Shaffer, 1986).

It was not so long ago that the Democrat party was characterized by fluid factions often both diverse and highly flexible in their ideological predispositions. But today activists in the two parties constitute remarkable clusters of opinion-holding, resulting in an increasing ideological sorting and clustering in the southern party system and representing still further evidence of partisan realignment in the South.

NOTES

1. For a citation and discussion of the recent literature on southern politics, see Baker, Steed, and Moreland, 1982; Steed, Moreland, and Baker, 1986; Havard, 1972: 731–740; Lamis, 1984: 237–304.

2. Within the six southern states in the survey, the response rates varied by state and by party as follows (n's are indicated in parentheses):

Arkansas: Republicans (262), 51%; Democrats (356), 60%.
Louisiana: Democrats (336), 45%.

Mississippi: Republicans (206), 35%; Democrats (514), 35%.

North Carolina: Republicans (327), 44%; Democrats (954), 62%.

South Carolina: Republicans (743), 75%; Democrats (526), 51%.

Texas: Republicans (430), 39%; Democrats (380), 35%.

In each state in the survey except Texas, questionnaires were administered to all delegates at their respective party conventions, and the response rate thus reflects the percentage of returns from the entire population; in Texas, because access to the conventions was not possible, the questionnaire was administered by mail to a random sample of delegates, and the response rate reflects the rate of return for the sample. The six nonsouthern states in the survey were Connecticut, Indiana, Maine, North Dakota, Oklahoma, and Utah.

3. For the purposes of Table 18.3 the questionnaire responses were collapsed from five categories ("strongly favor," "favor," "undecided," "oppose," and "strongly oppose") into two categories ("favor" and "oppose") so that the percentage reported is the proportion of those favoring or agreeing among those with an opinion on the issue (undecided responses have been excluded). A more detailed examination of the data based on the original five categories indicates that the two parties may be even more divergent on issues than a simple conservative-liberal comparison of model responses might suggest, even though that dimension standing alone indicates significant differences. The Democrats, although as a group notably much more liberal than the Republicans, were much less likely to be concentrated in a single response category. In other words, the Democrats were attitudinally considerably more heterogeneous. The Republicans, on the other hand, were much more likely to load up in one of the polar cells, that is, in the "strongly favor" or "strongly oppose" categories (which, in addition, is suggestive of a higher level of intensity of feeling among Republican delegates).

Moreover, grouping together the responses in the six states does not necessarily hide significant differences from state to state. For example, the ideology-issues pattern of South Carolina delegates (Moreland, 1985) closely resembles that of the delegates in the other five southern states.

CONCLUSION

19

FUTURE DIRECTIONS IN SOUTHERN POLITICS

Robert H. Swansbrough

By now both serious and casual readers are probably shaking their heads about the diversity of historical trends, political forces, and socioeconomic conditions underlying partisanship in the South. While no one argues that the Solid Democratic South still exists, questions about the degree of the erosion of the Democratic party's regional strength receive a different answer for each of the twelve southern states examined in this book. As Stanley and Castle stressed earlier, "The search for a single summary statement simplifies the complexity of southern partisan change."

SUNBELT POPULATION GROWTH AND PARTISAN SHIFTS

The nation's Sunbelt population explosion particularly wreaked havoc on Florida's and Texas's Democratic parties, as chapters 3 and 4 highlight. Parker concludes that dealignment in Florida, rather than realignment, best explains the erosion of the Democratic party's support. Republican presidential candidates carried Florida in seven of the last nine elections, with President Reagan's 1980 coattails helping to elect GOP Senator Paula Hawkins. In 1986 Floridians split their ballots to defeat Senator Hawkins while electing a Republican governor. Florida's Republican House members controlled slightly over one-third of the state's delegation in 1986. Although 57% of Floridians officially registered to vote as Democrats in 1986, compared with only 36% as Republicans, this represents a Democratic decline and slight Republican gain.

Florida's self-reported Republican party identification between 1980 and 1986 jumped to 38%, outnumbering the 32% of self-identified Democratic loyalists. This GOP increase occurred at the expense of Democratic identifiers, since the proportion of independents changed little. Although in-migration accounts for much of the growth of Florida's population, Parker finds that Republican identifiers rose among natives and long-term residents, as well as among immigrants. Similarly, the GOP gained support among all age cohorts, not simply young voters. While white voters primarily shifted their loyalty to the GOP, the data reveal no conservative upsurge within the Florida electorate; rather, the Republican party gained support from both conservatives and liberals. The analysis revealed that President Reagan's popularity and performance constituted an important period effect in bolstering recent GOP support. A weakening of Florida's partisan loyalties and ticket splitting thus signals an increasingly competitive party system subject to personal appeals and short-term factors.

Vedlitz, Dyer, and Hill discern a realignment to the GOP in Texas, escalated by what they colorfully describe as a ratcheting effect. Republican identification grew over many years, stimulated by attractive GOP presidential candidates, but afterwards declining to levels still above earlier Republican support. Since 1952 Texas cast its electoral votes for only two Democratic presidential candidates, favorite son Lyndon Johnson and fellow southerner Jimmy Carter in 1976. Republican Bill Clements won the governorship in 1978 and 1986, and the GOP replaced Republican Senator John Tower with former Democrat Phil Gramm in 1984. In twenty-two years the Republican House delegation rose from zero to almost one-third of the 27-member delegation in 1986.

While only about 10% to 12% of Texans called themselves Republicans in the early 1970s, the proportion increased by 1985 to virtual parity with the declining Democratic identifiers, although GOP identification slipped backwards in 1986. The tremendous immigration Texas experienced accounts for much of the increased Republican popularity, although the population influx slowed in recent years because of Texas's sagging oil industry. Furthermore, the Democratic tendencies of recent migrants may reverse the past pattern to the advantage of the besieged Democratic party. Demographically four-fifths of Texans now live in urban areas, with blacks and hispanics comprising 35% of the state's 1985 population. White conservatives and young voters especially find the GOP increasingly attractive.

The Republican party thus achieved significant standing and political clout in both Florida and Texas. GOP electoral victories increasingly extended to the gubernatorial, Senate, and congressional levels. Republican party identification climbed in the 1980s to achieve virtual parity with the Democrats. While in-migration boosted the share of the

GOP's electoral support in both states, Republican identifiers also rose among long-time residents and natives, younger voters, and whites. The national Republican party's conservative orientation and President Reagan's appeal also promoted the GOP advance. But dealignment in Florida, highlighted by 1986 ticket splitting and potential Texas Democratic coalitions of moderate whites, Hispanics and blacks underscore the fragility of GOP gains. The Republican party's continued growth thus confronts the tugs of traditional Democratic loyalties and economic conditions favoring Democratic candidates, creating a highly competitive partisan environment.

THE VOLATILE RIM SOUTH

The Civil War created regional pockets of Mountain Republicanism in Virginia, Tennessee, North Carolina, Kentucky, and Arkansas. Southwest Virginia, east Tennessee, western North Carolina, southeastern Kentucky, and Arkansas' Ozarks provided the historic GOP enclaves for the growth of more competitive party systems in these states. However, chapters 5–9 reveal the different pace and nature of changes in party competition in each of these Rim South states.

McGlennon describes Virginia as one of the most competitive southern party systems, resulting from a dramatic realignment to the GOP banner. Virginia voters elected three successive Republican governors, sent two Republicans to the Senate since 1973, and chose a 1980 congressional delegation in which the GOP held nine of ten House seats. Virginia stands out as the only southern state Jimmy Carter failed to capture in 1976.

Republican identification rose in nine years from a two to one partisan disadvantage to a 1985 GOP edge of 31% to 28% over Democratic identifiers, with independents encompassing 41% of Virginia's voters. Rapid population growth through migration, Democratic factionalism, and a strong GOP state party organization contributed to these remarkable Republican gains. The GOP won the support of many young voters and benefited from President Reagan's popularity; but, when the president's popularity fell during the 1982 recession, the GOP lost favor. The Democrats rallied after they began nominating more moderate statewide candidates in party conventions, rather than selecting nominees through divisive primaries. Democratic candidates swept the top three state offices in both 1981 and 1985 and won half of the House seats in 1986.

Swansbrough and Brodsky find that Tennessee Democrats regained their traditional dominant position in 1986, although the competitiveness of statewide races and party identification trends underscore the vitality of the state's two-party system. The zenith of Republican success came earlier in Tennessee than in other southern states. In 1970 the GOP won the governorship, controlled both U.S. Senate seats, commanded a majority of the House delegation, and held 46 of the General Assembly's 99 seats. Senator Albert Gore, Jr.'s 1984 victory, upon the retirement of Republican Majority Leader Howard Baker, gave the Democrats control of Tennessee's two Senate seats. The 1986 election placed Democrat Ned McWherter in the governor's mansion, maintained the Democrats' six to three congressional majority and kept the Democrats in solid control of the General Assembly.

Surveys show that between 1981 and 1985 Democratic identifiers declined 10% to 32%, while Republican supporters rose 4% to 29%. Although Republicans clearly benefited from Tennessee's realignment, dealignment to independent identification represents a stronger force; independents (39%) outnumbered both Democrats and Republicans in a 1985 survey. Substantial ticket splitting also reflects the diminished importance of party identification in Republican East Tennessee as well as Democratic West and Middle Tennessee. Many whites, young voters, and conservatives shifted to the GOP banner, but it remains unclear whether this partisan movement represents merely a short-term response to President Ronald Reagan's popularity and the new image of the GOP as the party of prosperity.

North Carolina also experienced dealignment, with some realignment to the Republican party, according to Fleer, Lowery, and Prysby. Republican nominees won four of North Carolina presidential elections between 1968 and 1984. GOP candidates captured the governor's mansion in 1972 and 1984, benefiting from Democratic divisions, presidential coattails, and sharply contested Senate races. Jesse Helms won a U.S. Senate seat for the GOP in 1972, joined by fellow Republican John East in 1980; the GOP held both of North Carolina's Senate seats until 1986. In 1985 the North Carolina congressional delegation contained six Democrats and five Republicans; two years later the Democrats enjoyed an eight to three seat advantage.

But although Republican identification grew to 30% in 1986, Democratic identifiers still comprised a majority of the North Carolina voters. The almost doubling of registered black voters between 1968 and 1986 particularly helped the Democratic party. Despite these GOP gains, the authors' examination of defectors, ticket splitters and party switchers revealed substantial voter dealignment. In terms of party identification, though, the number of independents failed to rise above one-fifth of the state's voters in two decades. Short-term forces, such as President Reagan's popularity and the upbeat state of the economy, favored North Carolina's Republican party in the early 1980s. The appeal of Senator Jesse Helms among conservative Democratic "Jessecrats" and the swing vote of the young, Piedmont professionals contribute to much of the recent volatility of the Tar Heel electorate and the reduced utility of party identification to predict voting behavior.

Jewell and Roeder see little recent evidence of either partisan realignment or dealignment in Kentucky, even though Republican candidates fared well in Kentucky's presidential elections since 1956, captured U.S. Senate seats, and periodically occupied the governor's mansion. Between 1979 and 1986 the party identification percentages for Democrats, independents, and Republicans varied little, with Democrats maintaining the loyalties of a majority of Kentuckians.

Even President Reagan's landslide 1984 victory failed to noticeably bolster the GOP's share of partisan identifiers. Party registration data from 1980 to 1986 reveal the same flat pattern, with Republicans staying at 29% and registered Democrats hovering at 68%. Jewell and Roeder attribute some of the Democratic party's dominance to Kentucky's closed primaries, particularly the hotly contested Democratic primaries. Swing independent voters account for much of the difference in party identification, voter registration, and electoral behavior. Also contrary to many other southern states, young voters prefer independent status over Republican identification. And despite the so-called Reagan Revolution, the general electorate increasingly expresses a moderate ideological stance.

Blair and Savage's assessment of recent Arkansas political developments somewhat approximates the picture in Kentucky. While they find modest realignment to the Republican party, the Democrats continue to dominate the state's politics. The Republican party fares poorly below the presidential electoral level. Democrats maintain control over Arkansas' U.S. Senate seats, despite serious Republican challenges, and the GOP will have held the governor's chair only six years between 1967 and the end of Governor Clinton's term in 1991. The Republican party occupies only 10% of the state legislature's seats.

In spite of President Reagan's popularity and his 1980 and 1984 victories in Arkansas, the Democrats averaged in the early 1980s a 53% party identification, a substantial edge over the GOP's 22% of identifiers. The out-migration of blacks and an influx of Republican-oriented retirees failed to undermine the Democratic party's strength. Blair and Savage find the Arkansas electorate favoring more progressive candidates, with white voters not expressing rigid conservative views. Instead, Arkansas' tradition of independence leads voters to cast ballots for attractive Republican candidates without abandoning their Democratic affiliation.

The Republican party clearly achieved serious grass roots strength in Virginia and established a full ballot alternative to the Democratic party in Tennessee and North Carolina. The GOP bolstered its electoral appeal in these three Rim South states well beyond their historic regional strongholds by building upon the appeal of Republican presidential candidates, offering attractive gubernatorial and congressional candidates, emphasizing conservative issues and taking advantages of Democratic factionalism. President Reagan's popularity also contributed heavily to the GOP's improved fortunes in these three states.

But although considerable realignment to the Republican party occurred in Virginia, Tennessee, and North Carolina, electoral and survey data also suggest the presence of dealignment, mitigating some of the advantages to GOP candidates. The Democratic sweep of Virginia's 1985 statewide races, ticket splitting in Tennessee and North Carolina and the 1986 return of many Democratic defectors to their historic partisan allegiance reflect this powerful countertrend. The Republican party failed to achieve a commanding electoral position below the presidential level in Kentucky or Arkansas. The Democrats offer progressive candidates to maintain control over most elective offices and the partisan loyalties of a majority of Kentucky and Arkansas voters.

GOP INROADS IN THE DEEP SOUTH

While the Republican party has scored some victories in the Deep South in recent years, chapters 10–14 point out how the GOP still faces strong white Democratic loyalties and a large bloc of solidly Democratic black voters. Cotter and Stovall's analysis of Alabama finds some evidence of realignment to the GOP, stimulated considerably by President Reagan's popularity. Republican presidential nominees failed to carry Alabama only once since 1960, but fared much worse in other statewide elections, largely because of George Wallace's influence. GOP candidates managed to capture an Alabama Senate seat in 1980 for the first time since Reconstruction, losing it six years later, and won the governor's mansion in 1986 for the first time this century, primarily because of a Democratic nomination dispute.

Surveys between 1981 and 1986 disclose considerable fluctuations in the party identification of Alabamians, with Democratic identifiers declining to 46% and Republican supporters growing to 40% by 1986. Younger voters moved toward the GOP and whites favored the Republican party over the Democrats by a slight margin. The relatively small number of independent identifiers remained fairly stable as Alabamians expressed partisan preferences and generally voted accordingly, undermining the dealignment argument. Neither economic status nor ideology appear as major explanations for Alabama's realignment. Instead, the data reveal how President Reagan's popularity and performance ratings directly influenced the fluctuations in Republican party identification, reflecting a short-term impact on Alabama's partisanship trend.

Graham views the weakening of Democratic loyalty among South Carolina's voters and the rise in the number of independents as a sign of dealignment. Although Republican presidential nominees won South Carolina's electoral votes in all but one election since 1960, they only narrowly won the 1974 and 1986 governors' races. Former Democrat and Dixiecrat Strom Thurmond served in the U.S. Senate two terms before switching parties in 1964, easily winning reelection as a Republican since then.

Graham finds that almost one-half of South Carolina's voters don't identify with either party; independents represent a clear plurality over white Democratic and Republican identifiers. Furthermore, among white voters, Republicans outnumber Democratic identifiers in the South Carolina electorate. Over half of South Carolina's citizens presently reside in urban areas, with voters from metropolitan counties more favorably inclined toward GOP presidential and gubernatorial candidates. But the Democratic party also confronts defections in rural counties, largely because of white opposition to more liberal national Democratic presidential candidates.

Binford, while pinpointing the GOP's strength in the rapidly growing suburban Atlanta counties, concludes that dealignment most accurately describes Georgia's evolving partisan scene. Republican candidates succeed best at the presidential level, with only native-son Jimmy Carter winning (twice) Georgia's Electoral College votes for the

Democratic party over the last twenty-six years. Mack Mattingly became Georgia's first Republican U.S. Senator since Reconstruction in 1980, but narrowly lost his reelection bid in 1986. Georgia voters regularly return to their traditional partisanship to cast ballots for the Democratic gubernatorial candidates, although the GOP does better in local suburban races and sends 2 out of 10 members to the House of Representatives.

A 1987 poll found the Georgia Democratic party enjoying a 2 to 1 advantage over the Republican party with 51% of the respondents calling themselves Democrats. Population in-migration to the greater Atlanta area, where much of the state's economic growth has occurred, bolsters Republican electoral chances, although the concentration of GOP supporters hinders statewide organization and support. Blacks move from rural counties to urban areas or leave the state, aggregating one-third of Georgia's blacks in two Atlanta counties. Binford's electoral analysis of Georgia's counties found the Democrats benefiting from a more broadly based political stability across the state.

Shaffer concludes that Mississippi's realignment to the GOP signals increasing party competition, but with some dealignment due to the power of incumbency or the personal attractiveness of candidates. Responding largely to racial issues, Mississippi voters supported States' Rights presidential candidate Strom Thurmond in 1948, Barry Goldwater in 1964, and American Independent George Wallace in 1968, not supporting a Democrat until or since Jimmy Carter's 1976 White House race. A Democratic racial split in the 1978 Senate election gave Republican Thad Cochran a plurality win, a seat which he retained in 1984. But Democratic biracial coalitions, focusing on economic issues, keep Democrats in the governor's mansion; Republicans managed to win only 5% of Mississippi's state legislative seats.

A 1975 poll revealed Republicans comprised only 6% of Mississippi's voters, but the proportion of GOP identifiers climbed to 24% by 1986 as Democrats dipped to 45%. The 1982 national economic recession and President Reagan's fluctuating popularity directly impacted upon Republican partisan identification. Republican support grew in recent years among younger Mississippi whites. Although the GOP enhanced its identifiers among all whites regardless of their ideology, conservatives particularly moved into the Republican camp.

Parent argues that although Louisiana's Republican partisan identification and registration increased since the 1960s, the state actually dealigned and reestablished the two-faction system that existed in the precivil-rights Huey Long era. The Democratic party resembles the older Long populist coalition of less advantaged whites and blacks, while the GOP represents the more affluent and conservative groups that traditionally backed the Reform candidates. Parent feels that the GOP presidential victories of Goldwater, Nixon, and Reagan, as well as the 1979 election of a Republican governor, fail to signal realignment in Louisiana.

Extreme race-baiting politics subsided in the face of Louisiana's sizeable and politically active black population, which in 1987 encompassed one-fourth of Louisiana's population and one-third of its registered voters. Barry Goldwater's presidential bid and his opposition to the 1964 Civil Rights Act helped legitimize the Republican party. The GOP's calls for social and fiscal conservativism increasingly win adherents in the suburbs, especially areas expanding from Louisiana's 1970s oil boom. Any Louisiana realignment occurred primarily in these suburban areas, rather than statewide. The GOP's opportunities emerge less from partisan realignment than the 1975 establishment of an open election system, which allows all candidates to participate in an open election with a runoff among the two top vote getters, regardless of party. However, the Republican party's registration climbed from 2.9% to 12.8% in 1987, despite the demise of the formerly critical Democratic primary with its important runoff election. In 1986 Democratic identifiers enjoyed more than a two to one advantage over Republican identifiers. The decline of the race issue gives the Democratic party's economic populism considerable appeal among lower income whites and blacks, the pivotal groups that brought the Long coalition many victories.

The Republican party apparently failed to deeply penetrate the Democratic bastion of the Deep South by the 1980s. The civil rights issue and more conservative Republican presidential candidates garned Democratic defections, but these partisans often resumed their rational voting patterns to cast ballots for other Democratic candidates. The GOP won new identifiers among whites, especially more conservative and younger white voters, but not in sufficient numbers to signal a major realignment to the Republican party. President Reagan's popularity provided a short-term boost for the GOP, but Democratic white and black coalitions focusing on economic issues threaten to torpedo the Reagan phenomena's impact on Deep South party attachments.

ASSESSING REGIONAL TRENDS

Chapters 15–18 provide overviews of various aspects of the changing nature of southern party politics. Observers have long noted the growing support received by the GOP's presidential candidates in the South. Bullock emphasizes that in the past twenty years the South voted more Democratic than the rest of the country only in 1976, when the region's native son Jimmy Carter ran for the White House. Bullock's analysis of electoral trends in the South also underscores the Republican party's increasing success in statewide races. By the early 1980s the South held 45% to 50% of the Republican party's seats in the U.S. Senate. The Republican party held more southern governorships than in the rest of the country by 1974, but the general tendency has been for the success or failure of GOP gubernatorial fortunes in the South to parallel the party's trends in state house races in the non-South.

Nationwide issues, such as Watergate and the 1982 recession, adversely affected the success of GOP House candidates. The recent victories of GOP congressional candidates appear closely related to the strength of President Reagan's coattails. Reagan's 1984 landslide helped the Republican party win 37% of the South's House seats. The GOP fares less well in the region's state legislative races. In 1986 the Republican party controlled only 18% of the South's state senate seats and 24% of the state house seats. National issues and presidential coattails apparently offer little assistance to Republicans in state legislative elections. Local issues, incumbency, and traditional Democratic loyalties minimize Republican advances.

Bullock foresees continued Republican party successes in presidential, Senate, gubernatorial, and House elections, with only modest Republican inroads on the Democratic party's dominance in the region's state legislatures. But as he notes, control of state houses facilitates electoral advantage through the gerrymandering of legislative districts, and these will be redrawn after the 1990 census. Bullock feels the question of whether significant numbers of southern voters have realigned to identify themselves as Republicans or dealigned to become independents pales in relation to the central fact that substantially more southern voters now cast their ballots for GOP candidates. He concludes that the sizeable growth in the number of Republican office holders reflects a realignment in the South, creating a truly competitive two-party system.

Chapters 16–18 utilize survey data to explore the nature of the South's political landscape. Stanley and Castle explain that conflicting interpretations of the direction and scope of southern partisan change often stem from different methodological approaches, operational definitions, and data classifications. They reject the argument that white

Democratic identifiers have converted to Republicanism. They find that many southern whites have abandoned the Democratic party to vote for Republican candidates without shifting their partisan loyalties. They explore different definitions of "young" and "partisan" and conclude that young white southerners are moving toward political independence, rather than embracing the Democratic traditions of their elders or becoming Republicans. While agreeing that the rise in southern independents occurs at the Democratic party's expense, they reject the argument that independent identification represents a way station toward the Republican party.

Southern migration patterns, whether focusing on the adult population or simply voters, reveal a 17% to 21% increase respectively in Republican identifiers among southern whites between 1952 and 1976. Stanley and Castle attribute some of the this growth in the proportion of Republican identifiers in the South to both the in-migration of whites and the exodus of almost 3 million blacks between 1950 and 1970. Class cleavages also influence partisanship as the GOP increased its identifiers primarily among upper-status white southerners, although gains also occurred among other socioeconomic groups. They argue that racial backlash alone didn't cause the Democratic party's decline; since the 1960s native white southerners have also opposed the national Democratic party's liberal position on a broad range of social welfare issues, and this disagreement contributed to a decline in Democratic loyalty.

Stanley and Castle find dealignment, critical realignment, and secular realignment all present in the contemporary South. But they caution that the increase in southern white independents, the mobilization of black voters, and the boost in GOP identifiers must be assessed in relation to the Democratic party's continued strength below the presidential level. Bullock also flagged the GOP's steady but much slower inroads in capturing lesser southern elective offices, particularly state legislative seats. Therefore, while the Republican party benefits from the Democrat's partisan decline, the weakened importance of partisanship generally reduces the positive effect on the GOP's fortunes.

In their chapter, Sigelman and Konda assert that in surveys southerners express positive images of both the Democratic and Republican parties, a historical change in public attitudes that benefits the GOP in the region. Nevertheless, the South's traditional Democratic allegiance has maintained Positivity scores toward the Democrats well above an exact balance of positive and negative comments. They optimistically conclude that the development of party competition throughout the South has thus enhanced the vitality of the region's party system.

Southern Democratic and Republican activists will play an important role in charting the direction their respective parties take through
the region's shifting political waters. Moreland, Steed, and Baker's
study of party elites in six southern and six nonsouthern states found
realignment among southern party activists. Almost one-third of the
Republican state convention delegates from the South reported switching parties, compared with 12% of the Democratic delegates. Ideology
and issues appear to play a major role in accounting for party shifts
among activists.

They found that 83% of the Republican party delegates described
themselves as conservative, with GOP activists expressing solidly conservative views on most issues. While two-thirds of the Democratic delegates identified themselves in general as liberals, the Democrats
sampled represented a broader spectrum of views on ideology and issues. Many Republican activists switched parties because of their conservative positions on issues. The authors concluded that both parties
increasingly represent an issue and ideological homogeneity, with
southern Republican activists expressing conservative views on issues
and Democrats voicing a more moderate to liberal stance.

These last chapters portray a southern political party system clearly
straying from its Democratic roots. The electoral and attitudinal data
raise doubts that the Solid Democratic South can rise again. While no
one contests the steady advances of the Republican party at the polls,
southerners still appear hesitant to fully shift their partisan loyalties
to the GOP. While the Republican party's image and candidates attract favorable attention, the trend seems to embody a weakening of
Democratic support through either ticket splitting or dealignment to
independence, rather than a full conversion to Republican self-
identification. But whether candidates pragmatically blur these partisan ideological and issue distinctions in order to build a winning
electoral coalition poses a more important question. As Lamis (1984:
p. 6) warns about regional generalizations, "the election-by-election
state-level analyses offer a sober realization that the overall interpretation is but a collection of the colorful and often chaotic actions of
individuals struggling for political ascendency amid forces not always
clearly understood by contemporary observers."

THE SOUTH AND THEORIES OF PARTISAN CHANGE

The picture of southern politics that emerges from the state and regional chapters leads to one inescapable conclusion, that a complete

understanding of partisan transformation will escape those seeking single explanations for or summary descriptions of changes in the party preferences held by the electorate. Indeed, the variations in the extent and the causes of partisan change in each of the southern states suggest the need for a catholic approach to the study of partisan change.

The data indicate the electorates in some states have experienced either secular or critical realignment, variously fueled by migration, generational replacement, or conversion. In some areas, such as Tennessee and Virginia, these realignments resulted in electorates where Republican identifiers outnumber Democrats. In other states the GOP benefited from changes in the composition of party coalitions, but the Democrats maintained their party identification advantage over the Republicans. Other states have undergone dealignments characterized by increased proportions of independent voters, heightened levels of split-ticket voting and the diminished importance of party identification as a cue guiding electoral decisions. Some southern states have experienced both realignment and dealignment.

The chapters also make clear the need to consider additional explanatory factors in any examination of partisan change. These include such institutional arrangements as party registration and the processes of candidate selection. The failure of Kentucky's Republican party to make significant electoral inroads appears related to the closed primary system, with hotly contested Democratic party primaries maintaining voter interest and registration in the Democratic camp. In contrast, the 1975 abandonment of Louisiana's Democratic primary with a runoff, in favor of an open election, with runoffs among the two top candidates regardless of party, undermines the Democrats' natural partisan advantage in that state.

Virginia's Democratic party turned to a convention system to nominate more electable candidates, restoring their political fortunes through the victories of the three top Democratic state officials in 1981 and 1985. In contrast, Alabama's Democratic nomination machinations lost the governorship to the GOP for the first time this century by alienating the Democratic party's traditional supporters. As the Republican party continues to gain adherents in the region, the Democratic leaders will probably turn toward those nomination procedures that unite their supporters and maximize their political appeal to the general electorate. Democratic factionalism only elects more southern Republican office holders. Black and Black (1987) observed how most southern governorships have already been "insulated" from the effect of Republican wins by the Democratic legislatures through scheduling gubernatorial contests in non-presidential years.

THE 1986 ELECTION: A PEEK AT THE POST-REAGAN ERA?

The erosion of the Democratic party's dominance in the South through Republican presidential victories increasingly influenced other races. Figure 19.1 displays the GOP's presidential success in each southern state between 1976 and 1984. The state-by-state analyses particularly point out the importance of President Reagan's 1980 and 1984 victories and his high popularity ratings on the political fortunes of Republican candidates and GOP identifiers in many southern states. The absence of President Reagan at the top of the Republican ballot in the 1982 off-year elections possibly lost the GOP electoral support and partisan identifiers, although President Reagan's popularity waned that year. The 1982 "Reaganomics" recession cost many workers their jobs, breathing new life into traditional Democratic issues.

In 1986 President Reagan's high popularity persisted from his 1984 landslide, and the perceived robust economy fueled GOP election hopes. In order to keep Republican control of the Senate, President Reagan stumped vigorously, and the GOP outspent the Democrats in a carefully orchestrated campaign to reelect some of the southern senators swept into office with Reagan's 1980 victory. Nevertheless, President Reagan's personal prestige failed to rub off on the region's 1986 Republican senatorial candidates. While the GOP Senate incumbents made strong showings, the Democratic party's nominees defeated Alabama's Jeremiah Denton, Florida's Paula Hawkins, Georgia's Mack Mattingly, North Carolina's James Broyhill, and won the open Louisiana seat with Democrat John Breaux (figure 19.2). The southern Republican gubernatorial candidates fared better with the victories of Alabama's Guy Hunt, Florida's Bob Martinez, South Carolina's Carroll Campbell, and Texas' Bill Clements, although Democrat Ned McWherter recaptured the Tennessee governor's mansion after the eight-year occupancy of Republican Lamar Alexander (figures 19.3 and 19.4).

The chapters indicate that the 1986 electoral weaknesses of individual Republican Senate or gubernatorial candidates in the South, combined with the salience of local issues, undercut President Reagan's partisan appeals. The economic problems of farmers and the textile industry also hurt the GOP at the polls. Furthermore, the high incidence of ticket splitting suggests the reduced reliability of party identification as the major voting cue. North Carolina's new Democratic Senator Terry Sanford's ability to attract defecting "Jessecrat" low-income whites back to the Democratic party brought about his surprise victory. The Democrats also recaptured two of North Carolina's House

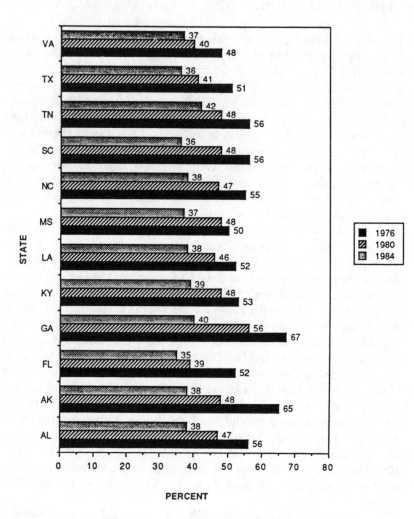

Figure 19.1
Votes for Democratic presidential candidates, 1976–1984.

Source: *American Votes, 1984* and *Congressional Quarterly*, November 8, 1986

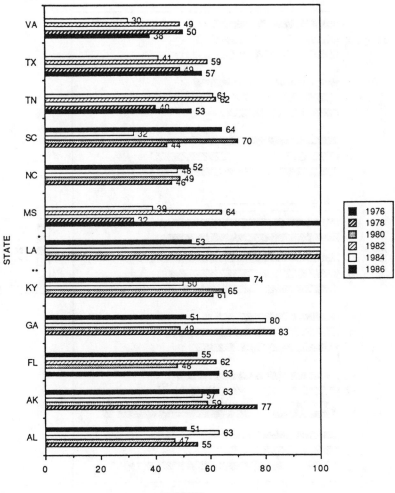

Figure 19.2
Votes for Democratic Senate candidates, 1976–1986.

Source: *American Votes, 1984* and *Congressional Quarterly*, November 8, 1986.

*No runoff General Election in 1978, 1980, and 1984
**The Democratic candidate lost.

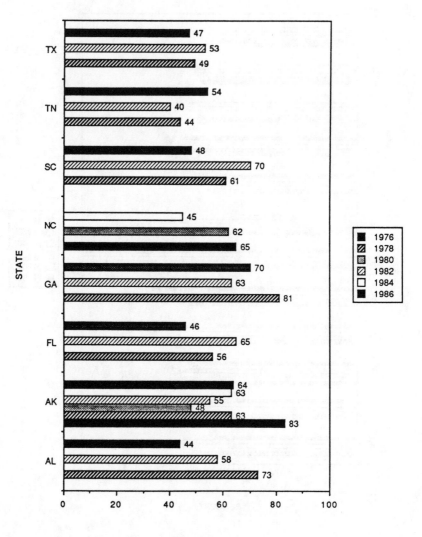

Figure 19.3
Votes for Democratic governor candidates, 1976–1986.

Source: *American Votes, 1984* and *Congressional Quarterly,* November 8, 1986.

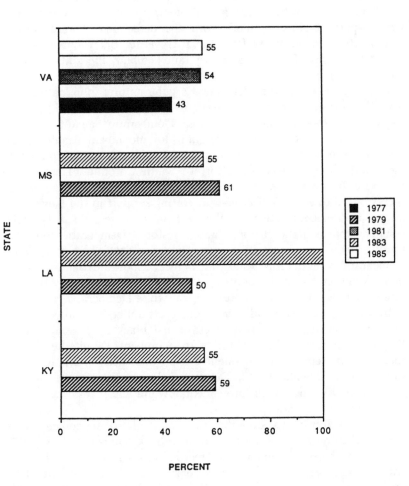

Figure 19.4
Votes for Democratic governor candidates, 1977–1985.

Source: *American Votes, 1984* and *Congressional Quarterly*, November 8, 1986.

*No runoff General Election in 1983
**The Democratic candidate lost.

seats. Floridians split their ballots to elect Senator Bob Graham over the incumbent Paula Hawkins and place Republican Bob Martinez in the governor's mansion, despite the fact that GOP identifiers outnumbered Democrats. Only about one-third of Texas voters cast straight-party ballots in 1986, with the defections of conservative Democrats contributing to Republican Governor Bill Clements's success. Nevertheless, Clements's victory failed to buoy the ranks of GOP party identifiers.

In Alabama a confusing Democratic gubernatorial nomination angered Democrats, encouraging many to split their ballots to vote for Republican Governor Guy Hunt and Democratic Senator Richard Shelby. President Reagan's campaigning for incumbent Senator Jeremiah Denton failed to reelect him or increase the number of GOP identifiers. The unsuccessful effort of South Carolina's Democratic Governor Richard Riley to handpick his protégé Mike Daniel as his successor led to charges of cronyism, costing support in the metropolitan areas. Democratic Senator Wyche Fowler's upset win in Georgia resulted from a higher turnout and a restored Democratic coalition uniting behind a consensus Democratic candidate. The progressive Democrat Fowler cut into Mack Mattingly's support in Atlanta's suburban "doughnut" ring of counties, won the black center of Atlanta's electoral doughnut, and recaptured rural white Democratic votes.

In Mississippi, white and black Democrats united around economic issues to elect Mike Espy as the state's first black congressman since Reconstruction, defeating a Republican incumbent. Despite being outspent by his Republican opponent two to one, Senator Breaux kept Louisiana's U.S. Senate Seat in Democratic hands. Voting generally fell along economic lines, with lower-income white and blacks supporting the Democratic nominee.

The 1986 election outcome thus presents a fascinating collage, with positive features for each party. But as Bullock points out, the GOP's share of southern U.S. Senate seats receded to levels of the pre-Reagan era. Furthermore, Ronald Reagan's weakness as a lame-duck president unable to extend his popular coattails to Republican senatorial candidates floundering in the electoral stream undermined his political clout in Washington, encouraging both Democrats and Republicans to challenge or ignore his White House leadership.

An ABC News Exit Poll after the 1986 General Election highlights the party identification advantage Democrats generally enjoy in the southern states. Since the ABC News Exit Poll failed to oversample in Mississippi and Virginia, figure 19.5 includes survey data obtained

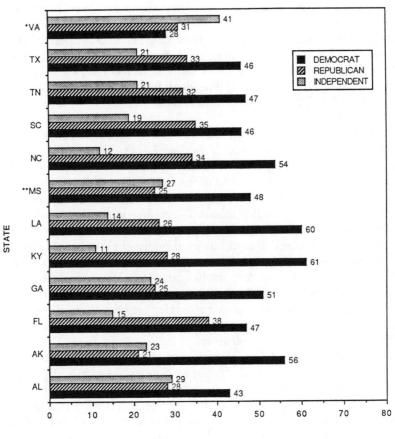

Figure 19.5
Southern party identification by state, 1986.*

Source: 1986 ABC News Exit Poll. Mississippi and Virginia were not oversampled by
ABC News. Data excludes "Something Else" and "Not Applicable" responses.

*Virginia survey data gathered October 1985 by Media General Research Unit,
Richmond, Virginia

**Mississippi survey data gathered February 1986 by Mississippi State University Survey
Research Unit

nearest to the November 1986 election from those two state chapters. Kentucky (61%), Louisiana (60%), Arkansas (56%), North Carolina (54%), and Georgia (51%) manifest the strongest Democratic party identification. The Democrats' partisan advantage over Republican identifiers ranges from 35% in Arkansas to 9% in Florida; Republican identifiers lead Democratics only in Virginia. Independents slightly outnumber Republicans in Alabama, Arkansas, and Mississippi, while Virginia's independents lead both GOP and Democratic identifiers. As already noted, the absence of President Reagan's name on the 1986 ballot hurt the GOP's party identification as well as the weaker Republican candidates.

The Iran-Contra arms scandal and the subsequent congressional hearings only further diminish President Reagan's mystique and the partisan muscle he may flex on behalf of the Republican party's 1988 presidential nominee and the rest of the GOP ticket. This represents the flip side of what Petrocik (1987) calls the "performance realignment" created by Reagan and Republican-directed economic prosperity. Although the GOP tallied significant gains in party identification, President Reagan's personal appeal attracted many of these new identifiers to the Republican party. But the recently minted Republicans may defect in tandem with the drop in Reagan's popularity sparked by the Iran-Contra revelations. The Republican party additionally confronts the challenge of intraparty power struggles between its moderate and conservative factions, such as in Virginia and North Carolina, to set the GOP's course in the post-Reagan era.

The strategy behind the formation of the Democratic Leadership Council and the creation of the Super Tuesday (March 8, 1988) primary in most southern states sought to promote the nomination of a moderate or conservative Democratic presidential candidate attractive to white southern voters. Southern Democratic party leaders know too well the adverse electoral impact of an unpopular presidential nominee on other Democratic candidates in their state. Even the region's favorite son Jimmy Carter received only 46% of the 1976 votes cast by white southerners. President Reagan's 1980 and 1984 coattails especially increased the proportion of white Republican identifiers in the South.

The results of the 1986 election demonstrate the validity of this Democratic party concern. Despite the party's 1986 Senate victories, the Democratic winner failed to win a majority of white votes cast in Alabama (37%), Georgia (46%), Louisiana (39%), and North Carolina (44%), according to an ABC News election day survey (*Public Opinion*, January/February 1987: 31). These new southern senators won mainly through the overwhelming support blacks gave to the Democratic party's nominees. Furthermore, the 1986 Democratic gubernatorial candidates received less than a majority of the white vote in Alabama (27%), Florida (46%), South Carolina (35%), and Texas (45%).

While some of the white southern votes for Republican candidates developed from migration, particularly in Florida and Texas, native white southerners provide the backbone of the realignment to the Republican party (Petrocik, 1987). But the earlier chapters point out that the white Democratic exodus often combines elements of both realignment and dealignment, thus making the often volatile white southerner a key target for both parties in planning their 1988 strategies. Clearly many southern white voters find it more acceptable than in the past to cast their ballots for Republican Senate and gubernatorial candidates, even if they retain their Democratic partisan identity. Likewise, new Republican identifiers may split their ticket, become independents, or even defect back to the Democratic party as the rosy hue of the first six years of the Reagan administration fades. Local issues, appealing candidates, and well-organized party efforts attract weak partisans and the increasingly pivotal independent voters to either party's standard.

Black and Black (1987) concluded that the movement of middle-class southern whites toward the GOP has virtually ensured future Republican success in presidential races in the region. "In the contemporary South the presidency has become the Republicans' office to lose rather than the Democrats' office to win." They acknowledge, however, that short-term factors such as charismatic Democratic candidates or Republican economic or foreign policy failures could lead to Democratic presidential electoral victories in the South. This study also acknowledges Republican southern gains at the presidential level but the editors, underscoring the region's diversity, feel the situation is more fluid than portrayed by the Blacks.

The skill of Democratic leaders in forging what Lamis (1984) calls "night-and-day" coalitions between increasingly mobilized southern blacks and moderate whites on economic issues seems crucial for the Democrats to succeed in an increasingly competitive electoral arena. Presidential candidate Jesse Jackson emphasized to a June 23, 1987, Democratic forum on the southern Super Tuesday primary, "The party has a progressive wing and a conservative wing, but it takes two wings to fly." A number of southern Democratic state parties and office holders already follow this flight plan for electoral success in the New South.

This study makes clear that general statements about southern politics too often ignore the local impact of national issues and candidates, as well as the institutions, issues, and personalities peculiar to each state. The region's Democratic and Republican parties face many challenges and opportunities in the days ahead. The critical role the South will play in the 1988 presidential election has already drawn national attention to the region's increasingly competitive partisan environment. Southern Democrats can no longer count on traditional voting patterns. Republicans will have to chart trails without Ronald Reagan to lead them. It's a politically exciting time in Dixie.

REFERENCES

REFERENCES

BOOKS OR CHAPTERS IN BOOKS

Abramowitz, Alan. 1980. Voting in the Democratic Primary: The 1977 Virginia Gubernatorial Race. In Robert Steed, Laurence Moreland, and Tod Baker, eds., *Party Politics in the South*. New York: Praeger.

Abramowitz, Alan, John McGlennon, and Ronald Rapoport. 1981. *Party Activists in Virginia: A Study of Delegates to the 1978 Senatorial Nominating Conventions*. Charlottesville: Institute of Government, University of Virginia.

Abramson, Paul R., John H. Aldrich, and David W. Rohde. 1986. *Change and Continuity in the 1984 Elections*. Washington, DC: CQ Press.

Anderson, Kristi. 1979. Generation, Partisan Shift, and Realignment: A Glance Back to the New Deal. In Nie, Verba, Petrocik, eds., *The Changing American Voter*. Cambridge: Harvard University Press.

———. 1979. *The Creation of a Democratic Majority, 1928–1936*. Chicago: University of Chicago Press.

Arkansas Votes, 1972. 1973. Conway, AR: Institute of Politics, Hendrix College.

Baer, Michael, Philip Roeder, and Lee Sigelman. 1984. Public Opinion in Kentucky. In Joel Goldstein, ed., *Kentucky Politics*. Bloomington, IN: Tichenor Publishing.

Bain, Chester. 1972. South Carolina: Partisan Prelude. In William C. Havard, *The Changing Politics of the South*. Baton Rouge: Louisiana State University Press.

Baker, Tod A., Robert P. Steed, and Laurence W. Moreland. 1982. Southern Distinctiveness and the Emergence of Party Competition. In Laurence W. Moreland, Tod A. Baker, and Robert P. Steed, eds., *Contemporary Southern Political Attitudes and Behavior*. New York: Praeger.

Banner, James M., Jr. 1974. The Problem of South Carolina. In Stanley Elkins and Eric McKitrick, eds., *The Hofstader aegis: A Memorial*. New York: Knopf.

Bartley, Numan. 1970. *From Thurmond to Wallace: Political Trends in Georgia.* Baltimore, MD: Johns Hopkins Press.

Bartley, Numan, and Hugh D. Graham. 1975. *Southern Politics and the Second Reconstruction.* Baltimore: Johns Hopkins University Press.

Bass, Jack, and Walter DeVries. 1977. *The Transformation of Southern Politics.* New York: New American Library, Basic Books.

Beck, Paul Allen. 1984a. The Dealignment Era in America. In Paul Allen Beck, Russell Dalton, and Scott Flanagan, eds., *Electoral Change in Industrial Democracies.* Princeton, NJ: Princeton University Press.

———. 1984b. The Electoral Cycle and Patterns of American Politics. In Richard G. Niemi and Herbert F. Weisberg, eds., *Controversies in Voting Behavior.* 2d Edition. Washington, DC: CQ Press.

Beck, Paul Allen, and Paul Lopatto. 1981. The End of Southern Distinctiveness. In Laurence W. Moreland, Tod A. Baker, and Robert P. Steed, eds., *Contemporary Southern Political Attitudes.* New York: Praeger.

Bernd, Joseph. 1972. Georgia: Static and Dynamic. In William Havard, ed., *Changing Politics of the South.* Baton Rouge, LA: Louisiana State University Press.

Bettersworth, John K. 1959. *Mississippi: A. History,* Austin, TX: The Steck Company.

Bibby, John, et al. 1983. Parties in State Politics. In Virginia Gray, Herbert Jacob, and Kenneth Vines, eds., *Politics in the American States,* 4th ed. Boston: Little, Brown.

Black, Earl. 1976. *Southern Governors and Civil Rights: Racial Segregation as a Campaign Issue in the Second Reconstruction.* Cambridge, MA: Harvard University Press.

Black, Earl, and Merle Black. 1987. *Politics and Society in the South.* Cambridge, MA: Harvard University Press.

Blair, Diane D. (forthcoming). *Arkansas Politics.* Lincoln: University of Nebraska Press.

Blair, Diane D. 1986. Arkansas. In *The 1984 Presidential Election in the South.* Robert P. Steed, Laurence W. Moreland, and Tod A. Baker, eds. New York: Praeger.

Blanchard, Paul. 1984. Political Parties and Elections. In Joel Goldstein, ed., *Kentucky Politics.* Bloomington, IN: Tichenor Publishing.

Broder, David. 1972. *The Party's Over: The Failure of Politics in America.* New York: Harper & Row.

Burnham, Walter Dean. 1970. *Critical Elections and the Mainsprings of American Politics.* New York: W. W. Norton.

Campbell, Angus. 1966. A Classification of the Presidential Elections. In Angus Campbell, Philip E. Converse, Warren E. Miller, and Donald E. Stokes, eds., *Controversies in Voting Behavior*. 2d Edition. Washington, DC.: CQ Press.

Campbell, Angus, Philip E. Converse, Warren E. Miller, and Donald F. Stokes. 1960. *The American Voter*. New York: John Wiley & Sons.

Campbell, Bruce A. 1979. *The American Electorate: Attitudes and Action*. New York: Holt, Rinehart, Winston.

Campbell, Bruce A., and Richard J. Trilling. 1980. *Realignment in American Politics*. Austin: University of Texas Press.

Carleton, Mark T., Perry H. Howard, and Joseph B. Parker, eds. 1975. *Readings in Louisiana Politics*. Baton Rouge: Claitor's Publishing Division.

Carlson, Jody. 1981. *George C. Wallace and the Politics of Powerlessness*. New Brunswick, NJ: Transaction.

Carmines, Edward G., Steven H. Renten, and James A. Stimson. 1984. Events and Alignments: The Party Image Link. In Richard G. Niemi and Herbert F. Weisberg, eds., *Controversies in Voting Behaviors*. 2d Edition. Washington, D.C.: CQ Press.

Cauthen, John K. 1965. *Speaker Blatt—His Challenges Were Greater*. Columbia, SC: R. L. Bryan Company.

Clark, Thomas D. 1960. *A History of Kentucky*. Lexington, KY: John Bradford Press.

Clubb, Jerome M., William H. Flanigan, and Nancy H. Zingale. 1980. *Partisan Realignment. Voters, Parties and Government in American History*. Beverly Hills: Sage.

Colburn, David, and Richard Sher. 1984. Florida's Politics in the Twentieth Century. In Manning J. Dauer, ed., *Florida's Politics and Government*. Gainesville: University Presses of Florida.

Converse, Philip E. 1963. On the Possibility of Major Political Realignment in the South. In A. P. Sindler, ed., *Change in the Contemporary South*. Durham, NC: Duke University Press.

―――. 1964. The Nature of Belief Systems in Mass Publics. In David Apter, ed., *Ideology and Discontent*. New York: Free Press.

―――. 1966. On the Possibility of Major Political Realignment in the South. In Angus Campbell, Philip E. Converse, Warren E. Miller, and Donald F. Stokes eds., *Elections and the Political Order*. New York: John Wiley & Sons.

―――. 1972. Change in the American Electorate. In Angus Campbell and Philip E. Converse, eds., *The Human Meaning of Social Change*. New York: Russell Sage.

―――. 1975. On the Possibility of Major Political Realignment in the South. In Darryl Paulson, ed., *Contemporary Southern Politics*. Washington, DC: College and University Press.

Crotty, William J., and Gary C. Jacobson. 1980. *American Parties in Decline.* Boston: Little, Brown.

Dalton, Russell J., Paul Allen Beck, and Scott C. Flanagan. 1984. Electoral Change in Advanced Industrial Democracies. In Russell J. Dalton, Scott C. Flanagan, and Paul Allen Beck, eds., *Electoral Change in Advanced Industrial Democracies: Realignment or Dealignment.* Princeton, NJ: Princeton University Press.

Darcy, R., Susan Welch, and Janet Clar. 1987. *Women, Elections, and Representation.* White Plains, NY: Longman.

Dauer, Manning J. 1972. Florida: The Different State. In William C. Harvard, ed., *The Changing Politics of the South.* Baton Rouge: Louisiana State University Press.

DeVries, Walter, and V. Lance Tarrance. 1972. *The Ticket-Splitter: A New Force in American Politics:* Grand Rapids, MI: William G. Eerdmans Publishing Company.

DeVries, Walter, and Jack Bass. 1978. Cross Pressures in the White South. In S. M. Lipset, ed., *Emerging Coalitions in American Politics:* San Francisco: Institute for Contemporary Studies.

Edgar, Walter B. 1984. *History of Santee-Cooper, 1934–1984.* Columbia, SC: R. L. Bryan Company.

Eisenberg, Ralph. 1971. *Virginia Votes 1924–1968.* Charlottesville: Institute of Government, University of Virginia.

Eldersveld, Samuel J. 1964. *Political Parties.* Chicago: Rand McNally.

Fiorina, Morris P. 1977. *Congress: Keystone of the Washington Establishment.* New Haven: Yale University Press.

————. 1981. *Retrospective Voting in American National Elections.* New Haven, CT: Yale University Press.

Fleer, Jack D. 1968. *North Carolina Politics: An Introduction.* Chapel Hill, NC: University of North Carolina Press.

————. 1986. North Carolina. In Robert P. Steed, Laurence W. Moreland, and Tod A. Baker, eds. *The 1984 Presidential Election in the South: Patterns of Southern Party Politics.* New York: Praeger Publishers.

Fowler, Donald L. 1966. *Presidential Voting in South Carolina, 1948–1964.* Columbia: University of South Carolina Bureau of Governmental Research and Service.

Freeman, J. Leiper. 1980. *Political Change in Tennessee, 1948–1978: Party Politics Trickles Down.* Knoxville: Bureau of Public Administration, University of Tennessee.

Ginsberg, Benjamin, and Martin Shefter. 1985. A Critical Realignment? The

New Politics, the Reconstituted Right, and the Election of 1984. In Michael Nelson, ed., *The Elections of 1984*. Washington, DC: CQ Press.

Goodman, William. 1980. *The Party System in America*. Englewood Cliffs, NJ: Prentice-Hall.

Greene, Lee S., David H. Grubbs, and Victor C. Hobday. 1975. *Government in Tennessee*, 3d ed. Knoxville: University of Tennessee Press.

Grenier, Charles. Forthcoming. Black Political Mobilization in Louisiana Revisited. In Mark T. Carleton, Perry H. Howard, and Joseph B. Parker, eds., *Readings in Louisiana Politics*, 2d ed. Baton Rouge: Claitor's Publishing Division.

Grosser, Paul. 1981. Political Parties. In James E. Bolnwe, ed. *Louisiana Politics: Festival in a Labyrinth*. Baton Rouge: Louisiana State University Press.

Hackney, Sheldon. 1969. *Populism to Progressivism in Alabama*. Princeton: Princeton University Press.

Hadley, Charles D., and Susan E. Howell. 1980. The Southern Split Ticket Voter, 1952–1976: Republican Conversion or Democratic Decline. In Robert Steed, Larry Moreland, Tod Baker, eds., *Party Politics in the South*. New York: Praeger.

Hadley, Charles. 1986. Louisiana. In Robert P. Steed, Laurence W. Moreland, and Tod A. Baker, eds., *The 1984 Presidential Election in the South: Patterns of Southern Party Politics*. New York: Praeger.

Havard, William C., ed. 1972. *The Changing Politics of the South*. Baton Rouge: Louisiana State University Press.

Hopkins, Anne H., William Lyons, and Steve Metcalf. 1986. Tennessee. In Robert P. Steed, Laurence W. Moreland, and Tod A. Baker, eds., *The 1984 Presidential Election in the South: Patterns of Southern Party Politics*. New York: Praeger Publishers.

Jacob, Herbert, and Kenneth N. Vines. 1976. *Politics in the American States: A Comparative Analysis*. 3d Edition. Boston: Little, Brown.

Jewell, Malcolm E., and Everett W. Cunningham. 1968. *Kentucky Politics*. Lexington, KY: University of Kentucky Press.

Jewell, Malcolm, and David Olson. 1982. *American State Political Parties and Elections*, rev. ed. Homewood, IL: Dorsey Press.

Kayden, Xandra, and Eddie Mahe, Jr. 1985. *The Party Goes On*. New York: Basic Books.

Key, V. O., Jr. 1949. *Southern Politics*. New York: Vintage Books.

————. 1966. *The Responsible Electorate: Rationality in Presidential Voting, 1936–1960*. Cambridge: Belknap Press of Harvard University Press.

Kiewiet, D. Roderick. 1963. *Macroeconomics and Micropolitics*. Chicago: University of Chicago Press.

Kirwan, Albert D. 1964. *Revolt of the Rednecks—Mississippi Politics: 1876–1925.* Lexington, KY: University of Kentucky Press.

Kleppner, Paul, Walter Dean Burnham, Ronald P. Formisano, Samuel P. Hays, Richard Jensen, and William G. Shade. 1981. *The Evolution of American Electoral Systems.* Westport, CT: Greenwood Press.

Krane, Dale, and Tip Allen. 1980. Factional Durability in Mississippi's Gubernatorial Elections, 1927–1975. In Robert P. Steed, Laurence W. Moreland, and Tod A. Baker, ed., *Party Politics in the South.* New York: Praeger.

Ladd, Everett Carll, and Charles D. Hadley. 1978. *Transformations of the American Party System: Political Coalitions from the New Deal to the 1970s,* 2d ed. New York: W. W. Norton & Company

Lamis, Alexander P. 1984. *The Two Party South.* New York: Oxford University Press.

Lander, Ernest M., Jr. 1970. *A History of South Carolina 1865–1960.* 2d ed. Columbia: University of South Carolina Press.

Landry, David M., and Joseph B. Parker. 1976. *Mississippi Government and Politics in Transition.* Dubuque, IA: Kendall-Hunt Company.

Liebling, A. J. 1961. *The Earl of Louisiana.* Baton Rouge: Louisiana State University Press.

Lilie, Stuart A., and William S. Maddox. 1981. An Alternative Analysis of Mass Brief Systems: Liberal, Conservative, Populist, and Libertarian. In *Policy Analysis.* Washington, DC: Cato Institute.

Loewen, James W., and Charles Sallis. 1974. *Mississippi: Conflict and Change.* New York: Pantheon, Random House.

Maddox, William S., and Stuart A. Lilie. 1984. *Beyond Liberal and Conservative: Reassessing the Political Spectrum.* Washington, DC: Cato Institute.

Mayhew, David R. 1974. *The Electoral Connection.* New Haven: Yale University Press.

McLemore, Richard A. 1973. *A History of Mississippi,* 2 volumes. Hattiesburg, MS: University and College Press of Mississippi.

Miller, Arthur H. 1987. Public Opinion and Regional Political Realignment. In R. Simmons, P. Galderisi, J. Francis, and R. Benedict eds., *Politics in the Intermountain West: Forerunner to Realignment?* Boulder, CO.: Westview Press.

―――. 1986b. Partisan Cognitions in Transition. In Richard P. Lau and David O. Sears, eds., *Political Cognition.* Hillsdale, NJ: Lawrence Erblaum Associates.

Miller, Warren E., and Teresa E. Levitin. 1976. *Leadership and Change: Presidential Elections from 1952 to 1976.* Cambridge, MA: Winthrop Publishers.

Mueller, John E. 1973. *War, Presidents and Public Opinion*. New York: John Wiley.

Murdock, S. H., and S. Hwang. 1986. *The Slowdown in Texas Population Growth: Post-1980 Population Change in Texas Counties*. Austin: Texas State Data Center.

Nie, Norman H., Sidney Verba, and John R. Petrocik. 1976. *The Changing American Voter*. Cambridge, MA: Harvrd University Press.

Ornstein, Norman J., Thomas E. Mann, Michael J. Malbin, Allen Schick, and John F. Bibby. 1984. *Vital Statistics on Congress, 1984-1985*. Washington, DC: American Enterprise Institute.

Perry, Howard, and Wayne Parent. Forthcoming. The 1983 Edwards Victory. In Mark T. Carleton, Perry H. Howard, and Joseph B. Parker, eds., *Readings in Louisiana Politics*, 2d ed. Baton Rouge: Claitor's Publishing Division.

Phillips, Kevin P. 1969. *The Emerging Republican Majority*. New Rochelle: Arlington.

Pierce, Neal, and Jerry Hagstrom. 1983. South Carolina: Fossil No More in *The Book of America: Inside Fifty States Today*. New York: W. W. Norton.

Pomper, Gerald M., ed. 1981. *Party Renewal in America*. New York: Praeger.

Poole, Keith T., and L. Harmon Zeigler. 1985. *Women, Public Opinion, and Politics*. New York: Longman.

Prenshaw, Peggy W., and Jessy O. McKee. 1979. *Sense of Place: Mississippi*. Jackson, MS: University Press of Mississippi.

Prysby, Charles L. 1980. Electoral Behavior in the U.S. South: Recent and Emerging Trends. In Robert P. Steed, Laurence W. Moreland, Tod A. Baker, eds., *Party Politics in the South*. New York: Praeger.

Rapoport, Ronald, Alan Abramowitz, and John McGlennon, eds. 1986. *The Life of the Parties*. Lexington, KY: University of Kentucky Press.

Rosenthal, Alan. 1981. *Legislative Life*, New York: Harper & Row.

Sabato, Larry. 1976. *Virginia Votes, 1969-1974*. Charlottesville: Institute of Government, University of Virginia.

———. 1979. *Virginia Votes, 1975-1978*. Charlottesville: Institute of Government, University of Virginia.

———. 1983. *Virginia Votes, 1979-1982*. Charlottesville: Institute of Government, University of Virginia.

Seagull, Louis M. 1975. *Southern Republicanism*. New York: John Wiley.

Shannon, Jasper B., and Ruth McQuown. 1950. Presidential Politics in Kentucky, 1824-1948. Lexington: Bureau of Government Research, University of Kentucky.

Shannon, W. Wayne. 1968. *Party, Constituency and Congressional Voting: A Study of Legislative Behavior in the United States House of Representatives.* Baton Rouge: Louisiana State University Press.

Shively, W. Philips. 1980. The Nature of Party Identification: A Review of Recent Developments. In John C. Pierce and John L. Sullivan, eds., *The Electorate Reconsidered.* Beverly Hills: Sage.

Sinclair, Barbara. 1982. *Congressional Realignment, 1925–1978.* Austin: University of Texas.

———. 1985. Agenda, Policy, and Alignment Change from Coolidge to Reagan. In Lawrence C. Dodd and Bruce I. Oppenheimer, eds., *Congress Reconsidered*, 3d ed. Washington, DC: CQ Press.

Sindler, Allan P. 1956. *Huey Long's Louisiana.* Baltimore: Johns Hopkins University Press.

Skrabanek, R. L., S. H. Murdock and P. K. Guseman. 1985. *The Population of Texas: An Overview of Texas Population Change, 1970–1980.* Austin: Texas Data Center.

Snider, William D. 1985. *Helms & Hunt: The North Carolina Senate Race, 1984.* Chapel Hill: University of North Carolina Press.

Stanley, Harold W. 1986. The 1984 Presidential Election in the South: Race and Realignment. In Robert P. Steed, Lawrence W. Moreland, Tod A. Baker, eds., *The 1984 Presidential Election in the South: Patterns of Southern Party Politics.* New York: Praeger.

———.1987. *Voter Mobilization and the Politics of Race: The South and Universal Suffrage, 1952–1984.* New York: Praeger.

Steed, Robert P., Laurence W. Moreland, and Tod A. Baker, eds. 1985. *The 1984 Presidential Election in the South: Patterns of Southern Party Politics.* New York: Praeger.

Stern, Mark. 1984. Florida's Elections. In Manning J. Dauer, ed., *Florida's Politics and Government.* Gainesville: University Presses of FLorida.

Stone, Walter J. 1986. Regional Variation in Partisan Change: Realignment in the Mountain West. In Randy T. Simmons, ed. *The Politics of Realignment.* Boulder, CO: Westview.

Strong, Donald S. 1972. Alabama Tradition and Alienation. In William C. Havard, ed., *The Changing Politics of the South.* Baton Rouge: Louisiana State University Press.

Sundquist, James L. 1973. *Dynamics of the Party System.* Washington, DC: Brokings Institution.

———. 1983. *Dynamics of the Party System: Alignment and Realignment of Political Parties in the United States.* 2d edition. Washington: Brookings.

Swansbrough, Robert H. 1985. *Political Change in Tennessee.* Knoxville, TN: Bureau of Public Administration, The University of Tennessee.

Trilling, Richard J. 1976. *Party Image and Electoral Behavior.* New York: John Wiley & Sons.

Tyer, Charlie B. 1980. *Public Attitudes on Government, Taxes and the Quality of Community Services.* Columbia: University of South Carolina Bureau of Governmental Research and Service.

Wattenberg, Martin P. 1984. *The Decline of American Political Parties, 1952–1980.* Cambridge, MA: Harvard University Press.

Wattenberg, Martin P. and Arthur H. Miller. 1981. Decay in Regional Party Coalitions: 1952–1980. In Seymour Martin Lipset, ed., *Party Coalitions in the 1980s.* San Francisco: Institute for Contemporary Studies.

Wolfinger, Raymond, and Robert B. Arseneau. 1978. Partisan Change in the South, 1952–1976. In Louis Maisel, Joseph Cooper, eds., *Political Parties: Development and Decay.* Beverly Hills: Sage.

Workman, William D., Jr. 1963. *The Bishop from Barnwell: The Political Life and Times of Senator Edgar A. Brown.* Columbia, SC: W. D. Workman, Jr.

OTHER

ABC News Poll. *1984: Yearend Wrapup.* New York: ABC News.

A Report on Public Attitudes toward Arkansas Louisiana Gas Company. 1983. Little Rock: Precision Research, Inc.

Bailey, Kenneth D. 1986. The Bailey Poll for Arkansas. Report #8619. Tulsa, OK: KDB Research Associates.

Blair, Diane D., and Robert L. Savage. 1981. The 1980 Elections at the State Level, Arkansas. *Comparative State Politics Newsletter,* 2: 12–13.

Eagle: Mississippi Republican Party. 1986. Poll Confirms GOP Is Closing in on Democrats. *Eagle,* December: 7.

Harris, Louis, and Associates. 1971. Priorities for Progress in South Carolina. Mimeographed Report (October).

Kielhorn, Thomas G. 1973. Party Development and Partisan Change: An Analysis of Changing Patterns of Mass Supports for the Parties in Arkansas. Unpublished Ph.D. dissertation, University of Illinois.

Munro, Mary. 1987. *The Influence of Black Constituents on Legislative Decision Making.* Unpublished dissertation, University of Georgia.

Shuler, Marsha, and Bill McMahon. November 5, 1986. Breaux for Finance Post. *State Times.*

Texas State Data Center Newsletter, Summer/Fall, 1986.

Toner, Robin. 1986. Splintering of Once-Solid South Poses New Problems for Democratic Party. *New York Times*, October 16, p. 16-Y.

Voth, Donald E. 1984. Impact of Migration on Arkansas. Lecture presented for Center for Arkansas and Regional Studies, University of Arkansas, Fayetteville.

Walker, Tom. 1987. Study Finds Few of New Jobs in Georgia Go to Rural Areas. *Atlanta Constitution*, January 8, p. 1-B.

GOVERNMENT DOCUMENTS

Bullock, Bob, Texas Comptroller of Public Accounts, October 1986, *Fiscal Notes*.

Ladd, Everett Carl. 1985. Alignment and Realignment: Where Are All the Voters Going? *The Ladd Report* No. 3. New York: W. W. Norton.

Ranchino, Jim. 1972. *Faubus to Bumpers: Arkansas Votes, 1960–1970*. Arkadelphia: Action Research.

South Carolina Election Commission. *Annual Report*, various years.

South Carolina *Statistical Abstract*. 1985. Columbia: Division of Research and Statistical Services, State Budget and Control Board.

JOURNAL ARTICLES

Achen, Christopher H. 1977. Measuring Representation: Perils of the Correlation Coefficient. *American Journal of Political Science* 21:805–815.

Beck, Paul Allen. 1977. Partisan Dealignment of the Postwar South. *American Political Science Review* 71:477–496.

———. 1979. The Electoral Cycle and Patterns of American Politics. *British Journal of Political Science* 9:129–156.

———. 1982. Realignment Begins? The Republican Surge in Florida. *American Politics Quarterly* 10:421–438.

Black, Earl, and Merle Black. 1973a. The Demographic Basis of Wallace Support in Alabama. *American Politics Quarterly* 1:279–304.

———. 1973b. The Wallace Vote in Alabama: A Multiple Regression Analysis. *Journal of Politics* 35:730–736.

Bond, Jon R. 1983. The Influence of Constituency Diversity on Electoral Competition in Voting for Congress, 1974–1978. *Legislative Studies Quarterly* 8:201–217.

Brady, David W. 1985. A Reevaluation of Realignments in American Politics: Evidence from the House of Representatives. *American Political Science Review* 79:28–45.

Brownstein, Ronald. 1986. Still No Breakthrough. *National Journal* 18:2228–2232.

Bullock, Charles S. III. 1981. Congressional Voting and the Mobilization of a Black Electorate in the South. *Journal of Politics* 43:662–682.

———. 1985. Congressional Roll Call Voting in a Two-Party South. *Social Science Quarterly* 66:789–804.

———. and David W. Brady. 1983. Party, Constituency and Roll Call Voting in the U.S. Senate. *Legislative Studies Quarterly* 8:29–44.

Burnham, Walter Dean. 1964. The Alabama Senatorial Election of 1962. Return of Inter-Party Competition. *Journal of Politics* 26:798–829.

———. 1969. The End of American Party Politics. *Transaction* 7:12–22.

Campbell, Angus, and Warren E. Miller. 1957. The Motivational Basis of Straight and Split Ticket Voting. *American Political Science Review* 51:293–312.

Campbell, Bruce A. 1977a. Change in the Southern Electorate. *American Journal of Political Science*, 21:37–64.

———. 1977b. Patterns of Change in the Partisan Loyalties of Native Southerners, 1952–1972. *Journal of Politics* 39:730–763.

Campbell, James E. 1986. Presidential Coattails and Midterm Losses in State Legislative Elections. *American Political Science Review* 80:45–64.

Carmines, Edward G. and James A. Stimson. 1981. Issue Evolution, Population Replacement, and Normal Partisan Change. *American Political Science Review* 75:107–118.

———. 1982. Racial Issues and the Structure of Mass Belief Systems. *Journal of Politics* 44:2–20.

Carmines, Edward G., John P. McIves, and James A. Stimson. 1987. Unrealized Partisanship. A Theory of Dealignment. *Journal of Politics* 49:376–400.

Cassel, Carol A. 1977. Cohort Analysis of Party Identification among Southern Whites: 1952–1972. *Public Opinion Quarterly* 41:28–33.

Claggett, William. 1981. Partisan Acquisition versus Partisan Intensity: Life Cycle, Generation, and Period Effects, 1952–1976. *American Journal of Political Science*, 25:193–214.

Clarke, Harold D. and Marianne C. Stewart. 1984. Dealignment of Degree: Partisan Change in Britain, 1974–1983. *Journal of Politics* 46:689–718.

Cover, Albert D. 1977. One Good Term Deserves Another: The Advantage of Incumbency in Congressional Elections. *American Journal of Political Science* 21:523–542.

Craig, Stephen C. 1985. Partisanship, Independence, and No Preference: Another Look at the Measurement of Party Identification. *American Journal of Political Science* 29:274–290.

Dalton, Russell J. 1984. Cognitive Mobilization and Partisan Dealignment in Advanced Industrial Democracies. *Journal of Politics* 46:264–284.

Dobson, Douglas, and Douglas St. Angelo. 1975. Party Identification and the Floating Vote: Some Dynamics. *American Political Science Review* 69:481–490.

Epstein, Laurily K. 1985. The Changing Structure of Party Identification. *PS* 18:48–52.

Erikson, Robert S., and Kent L. Tedin. 1981. The 1928–36 Partisan Realignment: The Case for the Conversion Hypothesis. *American Political Science Review* 75:951–962.

Feigert, Frank B. 1979. Illusions of Ticket-Splitting. *American Politics Quarterly* 7: 470–488.

Finkel, Steven E., and Howard A. Scarrow. 1985. Party Identification and Party Enrollment: The Difference and the Consequence. *Journal of Politics* 47:620–642.

Franklin, Charles H., and John E. Jackson. 1983. The Dynamics of Party Identification. *American Political Science Review* 77:957–973.

Gatlin, Douglas S. 1975. Party Identification, Status, and Race in the South: 1952–1974. *Public Opinion Quarterly* 39:39–51.

Gibson, James L. et al. 1985. Whither the Local Parties? *American Journal of Political Science* 29:139–160.

Hadley, Charles D. 1981. Survey Research and Southern Politics: The Implications of Data Management. *Public Opinion Quarterly* 45:393–401.

———. 1985. Dual Partisan Identification in the South. *Journal of Politics* 47:254–268.

Hart, Peter, and Richard Wirthlin. 1985. Moving Right Along: Campaign '84's Lessons for 1988. *Public Opinion* 7:8–ff.

Hinckley, Barbara. 1980. House Reelections and Senate Defeats: The Role of the Challenger. *British Journal of Political Science* 10:441–460.

Howell, Susan E. 1980. The Behavioral Component of Changing Partisanship. *American Politics Quarterly* 8:270–302.

———. 1981. Short Term Forces and Changing Partisanship. *Political Behavior* 1:163–180.

Jennings, M. Kent, and Richard G. Niemi. 1966. Party Identification at Multiple Levels of Government. *American Journal of Sociology* 72:86–101.

Keith, Bruce E., David B. Magleby, Candice J. Nelson, Elizabeth Orr, Mark C. Westlye, and Raymond E. Wolfinger. 1986. The Partisan Affinities of Independent "Leaners". *British Journal of Political Science* 16:155–184.

Key, V. O., Jr. 1955. A Theory of Critical Elections. *Journal of Politics* 17:3–18.

―――. 1959. Secular Realignment and the Party System. *Journal of Politics* 21:198–210.

Konda, Thomas M., and Lee Sigelman. 1987. Public Evaluation of the American Parties, 1952–1984. *Journal of Politics*, (in press.)

Ladd, Everett Carll. 1985. As the Realignment Turns: A Drama in Many Acts. *Public Opinion* 7:2–7.

Lipset, Seymour M. 1985. The Elections, the Economy, and Public Opinion: 1984. *PS*, 18:28–38.

Mann, Thomas E., and Raymond E. Wolfinger. 1980. Candidates and Parties in Congressional Elections. *American Political Science Review* 74:617–632.

Margolis, Diane R. 1979. The Invisible Hands: Sex Roles and the Division of Labor in Two Local Political Parties. *Social Problems* 26:314–324.

Markus, Gregory B., and Philip E. Converse. 1979. A Dynamic Simultaneous Equation Model of Electoral Choice. *American Political Science Review*. 73:1055–1070.

McClosky, Herbert, Paul J. Hoffman, and Rosemary O'Hara. 1960 Issue Conflict and Consensus among Party Leaders and Followers. *American Political Science Review* 54:406–427.

McGrath, Wilma E., and John W. Soule. 1974. Rocking the Cradle or Rocking the Boat: Women at the 1972 Democratic National Convention. *Social Science Quarterly* 55:141–150.

McKinney, John C., and Linda Brookover Bourge. 1971. The Changing South: National Incorporation of a Region. *American Sociological Review* 36:399–412.

Miller, Arthur H., and Martin P. Wattenberg. 1983. Measuring Party Identification: Independent or No Partisan Preference? *American Journal of Political Science* 27:106–121.

Miller, Arthur H. 1986a. Realigning Forces in the United States Elections of 1984. *Electoral Studies* 5:3–18.

Niemi, Richard G., Richard S. Katz, and David Newman. 1980. Reconstructing Past Partisanship: The Failure of the Party Identification Recall Questions. *American Journal of Political Science* 24:633–651.

Norpoth, Helmut, and Jerrold Rusk. 1982. Partisan Dealignment in the American Electorate: Itemizing the Deductions since 1964. *American Political Science Review* 76: 522–537.

Page, Benjamin I., and Calvin C. Jones. 1979. Reciprocal Effects of Policy Preferences, Party Loyalties and the Vote. *American Political Science Review* 73:1071–1090.

Perkins, Jerry, and Randall Guynes. 1976. Partisanship in National and State Politics. *Public Opinion Quarterly* 40:376–378.

Petrocik, John R. 1987. Realignment: New Party Coalitions and the Nationalization of the South. *Journal of Politics* 49:347–375.

Rabinowitz, George, and Stuart McDonald. 1986. The Power of the States in the U.S. Presidential Elections: *American Political Science Review* 80:65–88.

Riker, William. 1982. The Two-Party System and Duverger's Law: An Essay on the History of Political Science. *American Political Science Review* 76:753–766.

Savage, Robert L., and Richard J. Gallagher. 1977. Politicocultural Regions in a Southern State: An Empirical Typology of Arkansas Counties. *Publius* 7:91–105.

Savage, Robert L., and Diane D. Blair. 1984. Regionalism and Political Opinion in Arkansas: An Exploratory Survey. *Arkansas Political Science Journal* 5:59–85.

Scammon, Richard, and James A. Barnes. 1985. Republican Prospects: Southern Discomfort. *Public Opinion* October/November: 14–17.

Schneider, William. 1982. Realignment: The Eternal Question. *PS* 15:449–457.

Schreiber, E. M. 1971. "Where the Ducks Are": Southern Strategy versus Fourth Party. *Public Opinion Quarterly* 35:157–167.

Shively, W. Phillips. 1982. The Electoral Impact of Party Loyalists and the 'Floating Vote': A New Measure and a New Perspective. *Journal of Politics* 44:679–691.

Sinclair, Barbara D. 1977. Party Relignment and the Transformation of the Political Agenda: The House of Representatives, 1925–1938. *American Political Science Review*, 71:940–953.

Smith, Eric. R.A.N. The Levels of Conceptualization: False Measures of Ideological Sophistication. *American Political Science Review* 74:685–696.

Soule, John W., and James W. Clarke. 1971. Issue Conflict and Consensus: A Comparative Study of Democratic and Republican Delegates to the 1968 National Conventions. *Journal of Politics* 33:72–91.

Stanley, Harold. 1987. Southern Partisan Changes: Dealignment, Realignment or Both? *Journal of Politics*, (forthcoming).

Stanley, Harold, William T. Bianco, and Richard G. Niemi. 1986. Partisanship and Group Support over Time: A Multivariate Analysis. *American Political Science Review* 80:969–976.

Strong, Donald S. 1971. Further Reflections on Southern Politics. *Journal of Politics* 33:239–256.

Swansbrough, Robert H., and David M. Brodsky. 1987. Partisan Realignment and Dealignment in Tennessee. *Southeastern Political Review* 15:89–110.

Tidmarch, Charles M., Edward Lonergan, and John Sciortine. 1986. Interparty Competition in the U.S. States: Legislative Elections, 1970–1978: *Legislative Studies Quarterly*, 11:353–374.

Weisberg, Herbert F. 1980. A Multidimensional Conceptualization of Party Identification. *Political Behavior* 2:33–60.

Wirthlin, Richard, and John White. 1987. From Political Poverty to Parity: The Restoration of the Republican Party? *Public Opinion* 9:18, 19, 58–60.

Wolfinger, Raymond, and Michael G. Hagen. 1985. Republican Prospects: Southern Comfort. *Public Opinion* 8:8–13.

Wright, Gerald C., Robert S. Erikson, and John P. McIver. 1985. Measuring State Partisanship and Ideology with Survey Data. *Journal of Politics* 47:469–489.

Yiannakis, Diana Evans. 1982. House Members' Communication Styles: Newsletters and Press Releases. *Journal of Politics* 44:1049–1071.

UNPUBLISHED PAPERS DELIVERED AT MEETINGS

Abramowitz, Alan I. Ideological Realignment and the Nationalization of Southern Politics: A Study of Party Activists and Candidates in a Southern State. Paper presented at the annual meeting of the Southern Political Science Association.

Binford, Michael. 1986. Partisan Stability and Floating Voters in the Southern Electorate. Paper presented at The Citadel Symposium on Southern Politics, Charleston, SC.

Bowman, Lewis, William E. Hulbary, and Anne E. Kelley. 1986. Party Sorting at the Grassroots. Paper presented at the fifth Citadel Symposium on Southern Politics, Charleston, SC.

Boyd, Richard W. 1985. Electoral Change and the Floating Voter: The Reagan Elections. Paper presented at the annual meeting of the American Political Science Association, New Orleans, LA.

Carmines, Edward, and Harold Stanley. 1986. Ideological Realignment in the Contemporary South. Paper presented at The Citadel Symposium on Southern Politics, Charleston, SC.

Cotter, Patrick R. 1983. George Wallace and the Changing Politics of Alabama. Paper presented at the annual meeting of the Southern Political Science Association, Birmingham, AL.

———. 1985. Split Ticket Voting in the 1984 Election: Presidential and Senate voting in Alabama. Paper presented at the annual meeting of the Southern Political Science Association, Birmingham, AL.

Craig, Stephen C., and Michael D. Martinez. 1986. Not A Dime's Worth of Difference: Perceived Choice and Partisanship in the United States, 1964–1984. Paper presented at the Annual Meeting of the American Political Science Association, Washington, DC.

Davis, Shannon. 1987. Age and Stability of Partisan Identification. Paper presented at the Annual Meeting of the Arkansas Political Science Association, North Little Rock, AR.

Feigert, Frank. 1983. Electoral Shifts in the American States. Paper presented at the annual meeting of the Southern Political Science Association, Birmingham, AL.

Franklin, Charles H. 1986. Party Identification and Party Realignment. Paper presented at the Annual Meeting of the Political Science Association, Washington, DC.

Grau, Craig H. 1981. The Neglected World of State Legislative Elections. Paper presented at the annual meeting of the Midwest Political Science Association, Cincinnati, OH.

Jackson, John S. III. 1986. The Southernization of National Politics. Plenary address at the Annual Meeting of the Arkansas Political Science Association, North Little Rock, AR.

Maggiotto, Michael A., and Samuel A. Haggar. 1986. Toward a Synthetic Understanding of Partisan Realignment. Paper presented at the Annual Meeting of the American Political Science Association, Washington, DC.

Maggiotto, Michael A., and Gary D. Wekkin. 1987. Global Concepts and Segmented Partisans: The Disjunction of Theory and Reality. Paper presented at the Annual Meeting of the Southwestern Political Science Association, Dallas, TX.

Moreland, Laurence W., Robert P. Steed, and Tod A. Baker. 1986. Party Activists in the South: Ideology, Issues, and Realignment. Paper presented at the fifth Citadel Symposium on Southern Politics, Charleston, SC.

Norpoth, Helmut, and Barbara G. Farah. 1986. Trends in Partisan Realignment, 1976–1986: A Decade of Waiting. Paper presented at the Annual Meeting of the American Political Science Association, Washington, DC.

Savage, Robert L., and Diane D. Blair. 1982. Ideological Orientations and State Issue Responses: Are They Related? Paper presented at the Annual Meeting of the Southern Political Science Association, Atlanta, GA.

Shaffer, Stephen D. 1986a. Partisan Realignment in the South: The Case of Mississippi. Paper presented at the annual meting of the Southern Political Science Association, Atlanta, GA.

————. 1986b. The Nationalization of Mississippi Politics. Paper presented at the fifth Citadel Symposium on Southern Politics, Charleston, SC.

Shively, W. Phillips. 1977. Information Costs and the Partisan Life Cycle. Paper presented at the American Political Science Association Convention, Washington, DC.

Stanley, Harold. 1985. Southern Partisan Changes: Dealignment or Realignment? Paper presented at Annual Meeting of Southern Political Science Association, Nashville, TN.

Stanley, Harold W. 1986. Southern Partisan Cleavages: Dealignment, Realignment or Both? Revised version of Paper presented at the Annual Meeting of the Southern Political Science Association, Atlanta, GA.

Steed, Robert P., Tod A. Baker, and Laurence W. Moreland. 1986. Whither Southern Culture? Looking for the South in the Second Reconstruction. Paper presented at the joint annual meetings of the Popular Culture Association and the American Culture Association, Atlanta, GA.

CONTRIBUTORS

CONTRIBUTORS

EDITORS

David M. Brodsky, University of Chattanooga Foundation Professor of Political Science, the University of Tennessee at Chattanooga; Editorial Board member, *Journal of Applied Gerontology*; public opinion consultant, Chattanooga Area Regional Transportation Authority, the State Credit Union Share Insurance Corporation, the Tennessee Credit Union League, the Hamilton County (Tennessee) Sheriff's Department. Papers and publications include: "Ticket Splitting in Tennessee" (1986, with Robert H. Swansbrough) "Political Realignment in Tennessee" (1985, with Robert H. Swansbrough), "The Impact of Presidential Popularity and Performance on an Incumbent Member of Congress" (1984, with Robert H. Swansbrough).

Robert H. Swansbrough, Professor and Head, Department of Political Science, the University of Tennessee at Chattanooga; American Political Science Association Congressional Fellow; Administrative Assistant to Congresswoman Marilyn Lloyd; Partner, Southern Opinion Associates. Papers and publications include: *Political Change in Tennessee* (1985), "The Tennessee Voter," in *The Volunteer State: Readings in Tennessee Politics* (1985), "Ticket Splitting in Tennessee" (1986, with David M. Brodsky), "Political Realignment in Tennessee" (1985, with David M. Brodsky).

CONTRIBUTORS

Tod A. Baker, Professor of Political Science, The Citadel; Codirector, Citadel Symposium on Southern Politics. Papers and publications include: Coeditor and contributor, *The 1984 Presidential Election in the South: Mass and Elite Perspectives* (1983); *Contemporary Southern Political Attitudes and Behavior* (1982); *Party Politics in the South* (1980). "Migration and Politics: A Comparative Analysis of State Party Elites," in Alan Abramowitz, John McGlennon, and Ronald Rapoport (eds.), *The Life of the Parties: Activists in Presidential Politics* (forthcoming).

326

Michael B. Binford, Associate Professor of Political Science, Georgia State University. Papers and publications include: "The Political Science Education of Campaign Professionals," (1985); "Semi-projective Methods, Political Attitudes and Political Reasoning," (1984).

Diane D. Blair, Associate Professor of Political Science, University of Arkansas. Publications and papers include: "Arkansas," in *The 1984 Presidential Election in the South* (eds), Robert P. Steed, Laurence W. Moreland, and Tod A. Baker (1986); "Dimensions of Responsiveness to Women's Policies in the American States" (1984, with Robert Savage).

Charles S. Bullock III, Richard B. Russell Professor of Political Science, University of Georgia; President, Southern Political Science Association (1986, 1987); Editorial Board Member, *Social Science Quarterly, Journal of Politics, American Journal of Political Science, Policy Studies Journal*. Publications and papers include: "Runoff Elections in Georgia" (1985, with Loch Johnson), "Partisan Defections and Senate Incumbent Elections" (1985, with Michael J. Scicchitano) in *Studies of Congress*, Glenn R. Parker (ed.); "Congressional Voting and the Mobilization of a Black Electorate in the South," (1981).

David S. Castle, Assistant Professor of Political Science, Lamar University. Papers and publications include: "Goldwaters' Presidential Candidacy and Political Realignment" (forthcoming); "When Politicians Switch Parties—Conscience or Calculation?" (1985, with Patrick J. Fett); and "Partisan Realignment in the South: Making Sense of Scholarly Dissonance," (1981, with Harold W. Stanley).

Patrick R. Cotter, Associate Professor of Political Science, University of Alabama; Codirector Capstone Poll; Chair, Executive Council, National Network of State Polls. Papers and publications include: "The Decline of Partisanship: A Test of Four Explanations" (1986); "Split Ticket Voting in the 1984 Election: Presidential and Senate Voting in Alabama" (1985); "The Changing Structure of Southern Political Participation: Matthews and Prothro Twenty Years Later" (1983 with Jeffery Cohen and Philip Coulter).

James A. Dyer, Associate Professor, Department of Political Science and Public Policy Resources Laboratory, Texas A&M University. Papers and publications include: *An Introduction to Political Science Methods* (with Robert Bernstein), 1984; "Bureaucratic Response to Citizen Contacts: Neighborhood Demand and Bureaucratic Reaction in Dallas" (1984 with Arnold Vedlitz); "The Partisan Transformation of Texas," (1985).

Jack D. Fleer, Chairman and Professor, Department of Politics, Wake Forest University. Papers and publications include: *North Carolina Politics; An Introduction* (1968); "The Transformation of North Carolina Politics," in *The 1984 Presidential Election in the South: Patterns of Southern Party Politics* (1986).

Cole Blease Graham, Jr., Associate Professor, Department of Government and International Studies, University of South Carolina; Senior Research Fellow, Institute for Southern Studies, University of South Carolina. Publications include articles in *Administrative Science Quarterly, Southeastern Political Review,* and *State and Local Government Review.*

David B. Hill, Vice President, Tarrance and Associates, formerly Director of *The Texas Poll,* a quarterly statewide telephone survey of 1,000 Texas adults. Papers and publications include: *Trends in American Electoral Behavior* (1980, 1983, with Norman Luttbeg); "The Partisan Transformation of Texas" (1985, with J. A. Dyer, A. Vedlitz, and S. N. White).

Malcolm E. Jewell, Professor and former Chairman, Department of Political Science, University of Kentucky; President, Southern Political Science Association (1980–81); Coeditor, *Legislative Studies Quarterly* (1983 to date); Editorial Board member, *Journal of Politics* (1983 to date). Papers and publications include: *American State Political Parties* (1978, 1982, coauthor); "The Neglected World of State Politics" (1982); "The 1978 Elections and American State Party Systems" (1979).

Thomas M. Konda, Assistant Professor of Political Science, State University of New York at Plattsburgh; Papers and publications include: "Trends in Evaluations of the American Parties, 1952–1984" (with Lee Sigelman).

Roger C. Lowery, Associate Professor of Political Science, University of North Carolina at Wilmington. Publications include; "Asking the 'Born-Again' Question" (1987), and "A Note about Identifying Christians and 'Born-Again' Christians" (1984).

John J. McGlennon, Associate Professor of Government, College of William and Mary. Coprincipal investigator, "Collaborative Research on Presidential Activists in 1984: Precinct Caucus Attenders Before and After the Convention," funded by the National Science Foundation (1983–1986). Papers and publications include: *The Life of the Parties: A Study of Presidential Activists* (coauthor); "Voting in the Democratic Primary: The 1977 Virginia Gubernatorial Race" (1980, coauthor).

Laurence W. Moreland, Professor of Political Science, The Citadel; Codirector, Citadel Symposium on Southern Politics. Papers and publications include; Coauthor and contributor, *Party Politics in the South* (1980); *Contemporary Southern Political Attitudes and Behavior* (1982); *The 1984 Presidential Election in the South: Patterns in Southern Party Politics* (1985); "Group Affiliations and Party Activism" (1986).

T. Wayne Parent, Assistant Professor, Department of Political Science, Louisiana State University. Papers and publications include; "Voting Outcomes in the 1984 Democratic Presidential Primaries and Caucuses," (1987 with Calvin Jillson and Ronald E. Weber); "Critical Electoral Success and Black

Voter Registration: An Elaboration of the Voter Consent Model," (1985 with Wesley Shrum); and "The Declining Significance of Race? Political Consequences, Rhetoric and Ethnic Mobility" (1985 with with Paul Steckler).

Suzzanne Lee Parker, Director, Survey Research Center Policy Sciences Program, Florida State University; Member, Executive Committee, National Network of State Polls. Papers and publications include articles in *Legislative Studies Quarterly, Political Behavior,* and the *American Political Science Review.* Roundtable Participant, "Changing Party Identification in the American States," at the 1986 Annual Meeting of the American Association for Public Opinion Research.

Charles L. Prysby, Associate Professor of Political Science, University of North Carolina at Greensboro. Publications and papers include: *Political Choices* (1980, with James Clotfelter); articles in *Social Science Quarterly, Journal of Politics,* and *Public Opinion Quarterly;* and "The Structure and Dynamics of Southern Electoral Behavior" (1986) and "Southern Congressional Elections: Patterns of Partisan Competition" (1984).

Phillip W. Roeder, Associate Professor of Political Science and Public Administration, University of Kentucky; Director of UK Survey Research Center and Director, James W. Martin School of Public Administration. Publications include "Voting and Non-Voting: A Multi-Election Perspective" (1985), "Public Opinion in Kentucky" (1984), and numerous other articles in *American Journal of Political Science, American Politics Quarterly, American Political Science Review,* and *Social Science Quarterly.*

Robert L. Savage, Professor of Political Science, University of Arkansas. Member, Editorial Board, *American Journal of Political Science.* Publications and papers include "Recent Trends in Institutional Confidence among Arkansans: Updating Earlier Findings" (1985); "Regionalism and Political Opinion in Arkansas: An Exploratory Survey" (1984); and other articles published in *Publius, Arkansas Journal of Political Science, Polity, Southeastern Political Review* and *Western Political Quarterly.*

Stephen D. Shaffer, Associate Professor, Department of Political Science, Mississippi State University; Director, Mississippi Poll. Publications and papers include: "A Study of Mississippians' Political Attitudes" (1984); "Changing Partisan Patterns in a Deep South State" (1985); and other articles in *American Politics Quarterly, American Journal of Political Science, Western Political Quarterly,* and *Mississippi Government and Politics* (forthcoming).

Lee Sigelman, Professor, Department of Political Science and James Martin Center for Public Administration, University of Kentucky; Director of the Political Science Program, National Science Foundation; Deputy Editor, *Social Science Quarterly;* Publications include "Anti-Candidate Voting in the 1984 Presidential Election" (forthcoming); "Public Information on Public Issues: A Multivariate Analysis" (forthcoming); and other articles in *Public Opinion Quarterly, American Journal of Political Science, Social Science*

Quarterly, Journal of Politics, American Political Science Review, and *Political Methodology.*

Harold W. Stanley, Assistant Professor of Political Science, the University of Rochester; Papers and publications include: "The 1984 Presidential Election in the South; Race and Realignment," "Partisanship and Group Support over Time: A Multivariate Analysis" (with William T. Bianco and Richard G. Niemi), "Southern Partisan Changes: Dealignment or Realignment?"

Robert P. Steed, Professor of Political Science, The Citadel; Codirector, Citadel Symposium on Southern Politics. Publications include Coeditor and contributor to five volumes on southern politics issued by Praeger Publishers.

James Glenn Stovall, Associate Professor of Journalism, University of Alabama; Codirector, Capstone Poll; Director Communication Research and Service Center; Publications include "The Third Party Challenge of 1980: News Coverage of the presidential Candidates" (1985); "Incumbency and News Coverage of the 1980 Presidential Election Campaign" (1984); and other articles in *Western Political Quarterly* and *Public Opinion Quarterly.*

Arthur Vedlitz, Associate Professor, Department of Political Science and Associate Dean for Research, Development and Graduate Studies, Texas A&M University. Publications include "Turnout and Partisan Advantage in Presidential Elections" (forthcoming); "Voter Registration Drives and Black Voting in the South" (1985); and other articles in *American Political Science Review, Journal of Politics, Social Science Quarterly,* and *American Journal of Political Science.*